ournalists have been fascinated by the Middle East, but very few are
ʒ you just how it works. Having mastered both theory and practice,
found himself in the midst of an Arab media revival that has shocked
ɪts, has shaken social and religious taboos and has challenged the out-
significance of the change in the Arab media scene over the last fifteen
been fully understood. This book helps you understand – in an enjoy-
osri Fouda, former chief investigative correspondent, Al-Jazeera, editor/
ɪst Word*, ONTV

intak has written a superb book. As a professional journalist with decades of
nowledge of the Arab world, he writes well and provides sensitive insights into
ɔr of Arab journalists as they face constraints and opportunities in a changing
ironment. As a scholar, Dr Pintak's careful research puts contemporary practice
context of relevant journalistic theory and global practice. His many hundreds of
om Arab journalists and others provide valuable authenticity to his analysis. His
1 "portrait of the Arab journalist" adds to knowledge and theory. This book is a
e contribution and a must read for anyone interested in media and in Arab politics.' –
assador **William A. Rugh**, author of *Arab Mass Media*

ally, Arab journalists are given a chance to voice their views about their profes-
1 and their societal roles. Lawrence Pintak does a terrific job of cutting through the
yths that have distorted Western judgments about Arab news media. This book is
1 invaluable contribution to the long-needed reappraisal of the significance and stan-
ards of Arab news purveyors.' – **Philip Seib**, Professor and Director, Center on Public
Diplomacy, University of Southern California

A thoughtful, impassioned and well-informed look inside the challenges facing Arab
ɔurnalism today – and the new opportunities.' – **Marc Lynch**, Director, Institute of
Middle East Studies, George Washington University

Lawrence Pintak remains the foremost chronicler of the interaction between the Arab and
Western media worlds, which occasionally connect with empathy but more often clash in con-
emptuous disinterest and even disdain. Understanding how the media view themselves and
heir tasks is crucial today. Misreporting and disinformation help fuel one of the most dangerous
onfrontations in the world, with Arabs and Westerners often battling in the arenas of ideology,
ulture, identity and policy. There is no better starting point for defusing this clash of national-
ɪsms and worldviews than absorbing the kind of factual understanding that emanates from this
ook.' – **Rami Khouri**, Director, Issam Fares Institute for Public Policy and International Affairs,
American University of Beirut and Editor at Large, The Daily Star (Beirut)

The real story in Lawrence Pintak's *The New Arab Journalist* is its serious attempt to
rapple with one of the ma… abs alike: the intrac-
able overlap between A nd Arabness, as an
ncient and diverse ident world, Pintak takes
he reader on a hunt for li Western journalism
nd politics. Whether you will find something
ot only to satisfy your h book lays bare to
ɹe the fault-lines, shifts ɪne future successes
r failures of Arab journalism as it overlaps not just with Arab identity and daily life,
ut also with Western perception of, and policy towards, the Arabs and their world.' –
Abderrahim Fouk…

26 0165058 6

About the Author

Lawrence Pintak is a veteran journalist and scholar who has reporte[d] East since 1980, and now writes and lectures on America's relati[ons] Muslim world, the role of the media in shaping global perceptions a[nd] policy, the future of journalism in a digital/globalized world, and th[e] ties of reporters covering conflict and social injustice.

As CBS News Middle East correspondent in the 1980s, Pintak [covered the] Lebanon conflict, the Iran–Iraq War and the first suicide bombings of [the] age, which marked the birth of radical Islamist terrorism. *The Washingto[n Post]* his book on the US intervention in Beirut "one of the most perceptive [about] the nightmare in Lebanon," and *Middle East Journal* said his more rece[nt book on] post-9/11 US–Muslim relations, *Reflections in a Bloodshot Lens: America[, Islam and] the War of Ideas*, is "an example of the best of contemporary journalism."

Pintak won two Overseas Press Club awards for his Middle East cover[age and] was twice nominated for Emmys. In the 1990s, Pintak was based in Ind[onesia,] where he reported on the Asian economic collapse and the overthrow of Indo[nesian] President Suharto for *The San Francisco Chronicle* and ABC News.

He returned to the Middle East the following decade and spent four yea[rs as] director of the Kamal Adham Center for Journalism Training and Research at [the] American University in Cairo, where he led the only graduate journalism progra[m] in the Arab world, headed a variety of professional journalism training program[s] and created *Arab Media & Society* (a scholarly journal), *Mogtamana.org* (a port[al] for Egyptian civil society), *Intihabat2008.org* (a US election resource site for Ara[b] journalists), and the first "virtual newsroom" in Second Life.

In 2009, he was appointed founding dean of The Edward R. Murrow College [of] Communication at Washington State University, where he oversees undergraduat[e] and graduate programs in a variety of fields and Northwest Public Broadcasting, [a] network of PBS and NPR stations across the Pacific Northwest.

Other books by the author:

Reflections in a Bloodshot Lens: America, Islam and the War of Ideas. 2006

Seeds of Hate: How America's Flawed Middle East Policy Ignited the Jihad. 2003

Beirut Outtakes: A TV Correspondent's Portrait of America's Encounter with Terror. 1988

Portions of this book are adapted from the following and reprinted with the[ir] permission of the publishers:

Pintak, Lawrence. "Borderguards of the 'Imagined' *Watan*: Arab Journalists and the Ne[w] Arab Consciousness." *Middle East Journal* 63, no. 2 (2009).

——. "Satellite TV and Arab Democracy." *Journalism Practice* 2, no. 1 (2008): 15–26.

Pintak, Lawrence and Jeremy Ginges. "Inside the Arab Newsroom: Arab Journalists Evaluati[ng] Themselves and the Competition." *Journalism Studies* 10, no. 2 (2009).

——. "The Mission of Arab Journalism: Creating Change in a Time of Turmoil." *Th[e] International Journal of Press/Politics* 13, 3, no. 3 (2008): 193–227.

The New Arab Journalist

Mission and Identity in a Time of Turmoil

LAWRENCE PINTAK

I.B. TAURIS

LONDON · NEW YORK

Published in 2011 by I.B.Tauris & Co Ltd
6 Salem Road, London W2 4BU
175 Fifth Avenue, New York NY 10010
www.ibtauris.com

Distributed in the United States and Canada
Exclusively by Palgrave Macmillan
175 Fifth Avenue, New York NY 10010

Library of Modern Middle East Studies: 85

ISBN: 978 1 84885 098 9 (HB)
       978 1 84885 099 6 (PB)

A full CIP record for this book is available from the British Library
A full CIP record is available from the Library of Congress

Library of Congress Catalog Card Number: available

Printed and bound in Great Britain by TJ International Ltd, Padstow, Cornwall

MIX
Paper from
responsible sources
FSC
www.fsc.org   FSC® C013056

For my Dakini: No matter how often our paths diverge, we will inevitably be joined anew. And for our children, Annya, Shantara and Justin, always ready for the next adventure.

Contents

Illustrations

Figures

Images

Acknowledgments

It would be impossible for me to list – or remember – all the people who helped me get to know the Arab media over the last 30 years in newsrooms and bars, on airplanes and battlefields. Some were colleagues passing in the night; others became lifelong friends. *Al-Arabiya* Washington, DC bureau chief Hisham Melhem; Yosri Fouda, formerly *Al-Jazeera*'s Chief Investigative Correspondent; *An-Nahar* Publisher Ghassan Tueni; *Al-Masry al-Youm* founder Hisham Kassem; *Daily Star Beirut* Publisher Jamil Mroue; *Al-Jazeera* Chief Editor Ahmed Sheikh; *Arab News* Editor-in-Chief Khaled al-Maeena; Al-Arabiya Executive Editor Nabil Khatib; Hafez Mirazi, now at Egypt's Al-Hayat Television; *Al-Quds al-Arabi* Editor Adel Bari Atwan; and Abdul Wahab Badrakhan, longtime opinion editor at *Al-Hayat* newspaper are but a few.

Like many of those above, Osman Mirghani of *Asharq Al-Awsat* also deserves thanks for urging his staff to take part in the survey that is at the heart of this book, as does George Hishmeh of the Washington (DC) Arab Journalists Association. It was the tireless work of Usama Najeeb, the lead research assistant in the Middle East and a network of young journalist/researchers across the region who made the survey a success. Thanks also to my research partner on the survey, Jeremy Ginges of The New School.

This book was made possible by grants from the Rockefeller Brothers Foundation, the Carnegie Corporation of New York, the Marsh Foundation and the University of Michigan, and, at least indirectly, by USAID, which, during my tenure as director of the Kamal Adham Center for Journalism Training and Research at The American University in Cairo, provided close to $2 million in funding for Arab journalist training programs. Exposure to the scores of reporters and editors who took part in those projects enriched my understanding of their journalism. Bruce Abrams, then head of the Democracy & Governance program at USAID Egypt, deserves a special thanks for his commitment to fostering Arab journalism. Thanks also to Gary Bunt of the University of Wales, an expert on "virtual" Islam who guided a recovering journalist through the shoals of academia; and to Naomi Sakr of Westminster University, author of several important books on Arab media, whose detailed comments on an early iteration of this work greatly enhanced its depth.

A special thanks to William Rugh, the godfather/grandfather of Arab media studies, whose seminal work, *Arab Mass Media*, is the foundation for all that followed, and who has become a valued friend and colleague.

Introduction

A Matter of Perspective

[L]et not the scribe refuse to write: as Allah has taught him,
so let him write.

al-Qur'an (2:282)

In the years after the 2003 US invasion of Iraq, the Aspen Institute, a US-based think tank, periodically brought together a small group of elite American and Arab journalists to discuss their respective roles in the context of broader US–Arab/Muslim relations. Participants included top editors, White House and State Department correspondents, and columnists from news organizations such as The Washington Post, *The Wall Street Journal, USA Today*, and National Public Radio, along with their counterparts from Arab news organizations such as Al-Jazeera, Al-Arabiya, and *Al-Ahram*. Deep into the second day of one of these gatherings, discussion turned, once again, to the question of whether American and Arab journalists were doing their jobs. "Do we even agree on what that job is?" this writer asked. The organizer and moderator, himself not a journalist, quickly responded, "Of course," and moved the discussion in another direction. But the reality was that not one of the Arabs in the room believed that they and their American counterparts had the same view of the mission of journalism.

"I do not think we agree," Jamil Mroue, publisher and editor-in-chief of *The Daily Star* in Beirut, told me later in the hall outside. "And I do not think it is as simple as saying, 'you are a journalist in New York and I am a journalist in Lebanon or in the UAE, and that means the same thing.' It does *not* mean the same thing. And certainly when we go further and talk about your institutional role as a newspaper or my role in a newspaper, or the role of the media industry in your society and mine, we are comparing apples and oranges and not apples and apples. They are in the same orchard, in the sense that they are in the same profession, but they are not the same tree."[1]

Hussein Shobokshi, a Saudi columnist and television host who also participated in the Aspen session, was equally emphatic in his rejection of the idea that US and Arab journalists had the same view of their mission. "No, I do not buy that. I think it is part of the confusion," he told me. "In the West, media seeks to maintain what it has achieved, while in the developing country it seeks to achieve what it inspired."

"Two places and two cultures, and everything is different," said Al-Jazeera's Ahmed Mansour, summing up the vast divide. With a democracy almost two-and-a-half centuries old and a tradition of dissent, the US was a world away from the Middle East. So, too, was its media. Where America had hundreds of journalism schools that had been training generations of reporters, you could count on one hand the number of such programs in the Arab world. Where a free press was enshrined in the US constitution and the media served as the fourth estate, every Arab country had countless laws that could serve as an excuse to send journalists to jail on the flimsiest of pretexts. And where 9/11 had been the first foreign attack on US soil since Pearl Harbor, foreign armies had been using the Arab world as a shooting range since the dawn of history.

"Arabic TV does not do our country justice," President Bush complained in early 2006. "They put out some kind – sometimes put out propaganda that just is – just isn't right, it isn't fair, and it doesn't give people the impression of what we're about."[2] Since Al-Jazeera first aired a videotape of Osama bin Laden in the weeks after 9/11, the Arab media had been the target of a sustained campaign of criticism claiming an anti-American bias. The debate over the agenda of Arab journalists, carried out by Western policymakers, journalists, and academics, was largely predicated on the assumption that Arab journalists should ascribe to Western journalistic values and mores. Little attention has been given to a more fundamental question: How do Arab journalists perceive their mission and how do they define themselves?

When I was a young journalist covering Washington, DC in the mid-1970s, I proudly wore a belt buckle that an enterprising craftsman had sold to members of the White House press corps. Designed like the old Superman logo, it read, "Newsman: Truth, Justice and the American Way." Here, poured in lead, was the very essence of my self-perception as a journalist. It was my reason for entering the profession. It was, in short, my ideology and that of my colleagues.

Journalistically, I was a child of Watergate; part of a generation inspired by *Washington Post* reporters Woodward and Bernstein who helped bring down a president; and by television's role in ending the Vietnam War. If I had been asked at the time, I would have said my mission was to report the Truth, to bring evil to Justice and to defend the American Way. I was young and naive enough that there was no sense of contradiction in that mission; no soul-searching about whether I was qualified to determine Truth with a capital "T" or serve as final arbiter of good versus evil. Nor, in that Cold War era, was there any sense of irony in the notion that an "unbiased" reporter might wear patriotism on his sleeve.

That belt buckle carried the heart and soul of the journalistic mission articulated by New York editor James Gordon Bennett in the mid-nineteenth century: "I feel myself, in this land, to be engaged in a great cause – the cause of truth, public faith, and science, against falsehood, fraud, and ignorance."[3] A century and a half later, Arab journalists were translating those sentiments into their own language.

Like many Arab news organizations, the two major pan-Arab satellite television stations wear their Arab identity on their sleeve. Al-Jazeera's mission statement defines it as an "Arab media service with a global orientation."[4] Likewise, the mission statement of rival Al-Arabiya declares it to be "an Arabic station, from the Arabs to the Arabs, delivering content that is relevant to the Arabs." It further vows "to remain true to the voice of the Arab world, to the world, on a regional and international level."[5] In fact, this issue of Arab identity provoked a major controversy within Arab journalism circles as Al-Jazeera prepared for the 2006 launch of its English-language channel. The chairman of Al-Jazeera's board, Qatari Sheikh Hamad bin Thamer al-Thani, hired a British managing director, Nigel Parsons, who proceeded to largely fill the management ranks, as well as many of the on-air slots, with British, US, Australian, and New Zealand nationals, provoking accusations that

Arabs were actively being discriminating against. Attitudes were further polarized by Parsons' comments about the new channel's "global" perspective. "We might as well buy a new channel in the US," observed Mahmoud Shammam, the Washington, DC bureau chief for the Arabic edition of *Newsweek*, at a media gathering in Doha. The comment prompted a roar of angry agreement from staff members of the Arabic channel who were in the audience. "[Al-Jazeera English] will not have Arabic characteristics and that's a big challenge," he said.

The question of self-identity lies at the core of any discussion about Arab journalism. More than any other barometer, the way in which journalists see themselves speaks volumes about their view of their place in society and the role of their profession. Sitting in his London office, Osman Mirghani, deputy editor-in-chief of the pan-Arab daily *Asharq Al-Awsat*, touched on why identity was such an important question. "The culture we are trying to build in this newspaper is one in which people identify themselves as journalists," he told me. "We cannot deny that this is an Arabic daily newspaper but the perception we are trying to build is that this is an international newspaper. We have a good mix of people from all over the Arab world. They start from saying 'I have this position or these religious traits.' We say this is a newspaper and people should behave in that way that the news people do and hence, if we can build that culture and then to identify themselves as journalists, then to a great degree we free their minds of the bias."

But the absence of bias does not mean an absence of what media scholars like to call "framing," the particular angle from which a reporter approaches a story, which is, in turn, dictated by the reporter's unique "worldview" – the personal baggage we all carry, shaped by kindergarten, culture, and community. Nor does it mean universal agreement on what "objectivity" even means. That was underlined by two encounters I had in the space of a few months. During a visit to Qatar, I raised this issue of journalistic values with Ahmed Sheikh, Al-Jazeera's editor-in-chief. Seated at his desk just off the newsroom, he pointed to a TV monitor on the wall, which happened to be showing a report from the channel's Baghdad correspondent, and recalled that the whole question of objectivity had hit home to him when he was in Baghdad doing interviews for a documentary to mark the second anniversary of the US invasion of Iraq. He found that all his high-minded ideas about "objectivity," "balance," and "truth" evaporated in the face of the grim reality on the ground. "Because I was so horrified by the scene that I saw in the city – lawlessness, chaos, disorder, and the Americans were not capable of doing anything," he found himself asking leading questions that were unconsciously aimed at producing the answers he wanted. "Why did I fall into this trap unknowingly?" he asked rhetorically. He then volunteered the answer:

> We are human beings, we belong to this nation, the Arab nation, because this is our language, we speak in Arabic... If you are part of a society and you live in a society, this is going to affect objectivity. We belong to this Arab nation and we are there to cover from our own perspective. Sometimes it may prove to be very difficult to be impartial. You find yourself carried away with your sentiments, but you have got to work hard to keep that sort of essence.

Not long after that conversation, I was in the audience during a panel discussion at the Graduate School of Journalism at the University of California, Berkeley to mark the third anniversary of the Iraq invasion. On stage, *Washington Post* correspondent Jackie Spinner was asked how she had felt about the war before she went to Baghdad and how she felt about it after months spent covering the conflict. "I have a very platonic relationship to the war. I believe very fervently as a journalist that it's not appropriate for me to express my opinion about the war," she told the gathering. "I don't talk about it with my friends; I don't talk about it with my family. My family members don't know who I voted for or if I even voted. I'm an old school journalist. I don't believe it's appropriate at all. I'm an observer: I went to war, I saw what I saw, I wrote about what I saw, and that's the extent of it."

For Arab journalists, war – particularly a war in the Arab heartland – was not something with which they could have "a very platonic relationship." Beyond the issue of whether journalists like Spinner were being honest with themselves, much less their readers, the contrast raises the question: If, as some scholars argue, journalism is "a set of cultural practices,"[6] can they be expected to translate across borders? Few US reporters would go to the extreme of hiding their true feelings even from family members, but most do ascribe to at least an ideal of objectivity. And many US news organizations have rules against their journalists engaging in political activism. That often extends even to those who are not actually journalists. In the spring of 2007, for example, CBS News fired one of its military consultants, retired Army Major General John Batiste, after he appeared in an anti-Bush television commercial. According to the CBS News Vice President for Standards and Special Projects, Linda Mason, Batiste violated the network's regulations. "We ask that people not be involved in advocacy," she said.[7]

For many Arab journalists, rules like those at CBS or public posturing such as that of Spinner were all part of a smoke screen that artificially masked the real views of the reporter – or the news organization for which he or she worked. "I cannot be completely objective," says Al-Arabiya reporter Haitham Hussein. "Truth is the most important thing, but it depends on the media that you are working with. If you are working with BBC, Al-Arabiya, or Al-Jazeera, the truth is not the same. Maybe you can share the same information, but not the same truth."

"We don't *frame* news," Octavia Nasr, CNN's then-Middle East editor, snapped at me during an industry gathering when I told the group that a study conducted by one of my students found that CNN mainly used footage of an attack on the Danish embassy in Beirut to illustrate its coverage of the crisis over publication of cartoons depicting the Prophet Muhammad, while Al-Jazeera primarily depended on footage of peaceful protests in Southeast Asia, approaches that conveyed very different messages to their respective viewers. But of course "we" – all of us – *do* frame how we approach a story, consciously or not. One need only look at the dramatic difference between CNN's domestic US channel and CNN International, distributed around the world and staffed by many non-Americans, during stories like the 2006 Israel–Hezbollah war, to see how worldview shapes what appears on the screen.

"The way to select news and the way to select [quotes], the way to select the point of view, this still belongs to our cultural environment and background," argues Al-Jazeera's M'Hamed Krichen. "We cannot separate ourselves from this background. Like the American or French or British journalists cannot do the same." Journalists, he says, must still strive "to be professional, even if we are not 100% natural."

Who Cares?

Back when I first arrived in the Arab world in the summer of 1980, Arab journalists served as eyes and ears for foreign journalists like me, translating, arranging contacts, and occasionally negotiating us out of trouble. But with the exception of those who worked for Western news organizations, such as *Time*'s Abu Said Abu Rish, Nora Boustany, then a stringer for *The Washington Post*, David Zenian of UPI and a handful of others, we didn't take what they wrote very seriously. It was, from our perception, all suspect. In fact, many Arab journalists back then seemed just a little embarrassed around us. *They* knew *we* knew they were prisoners of whomever their news organization's paymaster happened to be. Today, many of those same reporters, now graybeards like me, are top editors at news organizations that are reinventing Arab journalism and running rings around the Western news organizations.

Why should readers in other parts of the world care what Arab reporters think or how they approach their jobs? The answer is simple: Arab news organizations are helping to shape global attitudes. Whereas the American TV networks, the BBC and a handful of Western newspapers and wire services once wrote the international news narrative, today Arab journalists are the eyes and ears for half the globe as news organizations across the developing world rebroadcast coverage from the Arab channels. That, in turn, has an impact on relations between governments, religions, and peoples.

The Middle East is one of the world's most intractable flash points. It is a place of constant conflict that consistently reaches out and embroils the West; a place where political and societal change can have dramatic implications around the world; and a region the industrialized world depends on to fuel its way of life. Thanks to the Arab media revolution, all that is being seen through an entirely new prism. The impact of television in the Arab world today is unrivaled. While newspaper readership is in the single digits, surveys consistently find that some 80 percent of viewers in places like Saudi Arabia and the Gulf get their news from television. In Egypt, with a population of 80 million, total newspaper circulation is only about one million copies a day. But everyone, from the richest real estate mogul to the poorest *fellahin* (peasant) watches TV. For the equivalent of $3 or $4, Egyptians can tap into a *wasla*, (shared satellite dish), that gives them access to hundreds of channels. How that *fellahin,* how white collar workers in the Gulf, how rich Saudi wives in their opulent palaces and shopkeepers in Morocco, Palestinians in the refugee camps of Jordan, and presidents, sheikhs, and kings all interact with their world is deeply influenced by the way in which the real-life dramas of the Middle East are depicted on their television screens. But the impact does not stop there. Satellites transmit Arab reporting around the globe. In places like Nigeria and Jakarta, it is translated, repackaged and retransmitted to a vast new audience. There is a new town crier in Marshall McLuhan's "global village" and he speaks with an Arabic accent.

PART I

The Media Landscape

1

Red Lines – The Boundaries of Journalistic Freedom

As long as you don't write about the king, the military, religion or sex you can cover anything you want.

Sameh al-Mahariq, Jordanian journalist

The Arab media is deep in the throes of change. It is a complex and often painful process, driven by regional rivalries, steeped in domestic political intrigue, and too often marred by physical violence.

"Anyone who tells you they are not scared silly is lying," retired *An-Nahar* publisher Ghassan Tueni, the living symbol of Lebanese media independence, said in the autumn of 2005 as we sat in his office overlooking Beirut's port and newly reborn downtown. Lebanon – and its media – had been experiencing a renaissance after decades of internecine violence during which most of the country's polarized media outlets were willing weapons of civil war. Now media was once more on the firing line, this time in a confrontation over Syrian influence in Lebanon.

As we spoke, a leading Lebanese television anchor, Mai Chidiac, lay fighting for her life after an assassination attempt, and in the *An-Nahar* newsroom down the hall was a silent memorial to one of the paper's columnists, Samir Kassir, blown up when he turned the ignition key of his car a few months before. "We built this glass tower as a symbol of the new Lebanon," Tueni said, motioning toward the floor-to-ceiling windows. "Now it has become a fortress under siege. I'm waiting for someone on one of those ships out there to fire a rocket through my window." Two months later, his son, *An-Nahar* publisher Gibran Tueni, was dead; his armored sports utility vehicle torn apart by a remote-controlled car bomb. The assassins struck less than 24 hours after the heir to the journalistic dynasty had returned from Paris, where he had been in self-exile after being warned he was at the top of a hit list. The Tueni assassination sent a chill through the Lebanese media, but for journalists there, fear was nothing new. "For years we had this paranoia," said Tania Mehanna, a reporter at the privately owned Lebanese Broadcasting Corporation (LBC). "Every time you get into your car before you turn the key you think it is the last time. Then you have another kind of pressure, which is the phone call which you get from the politician or from some kind of faction where they want to stop what you filmed during the day or they put pressure on the TV station not to run the story."

"I do not say anything related to politics, [I] hate politics," explained Hadia Sirrow, a reporter for the newspaper *Al-Mustaqbal*. "But you feel that you are involved too. So we're in this house and we are scared."

Media has always been a tool of power, nowhere more so than the Arab world, a region in which every country but three – Kuwait, Lebanon, and Egypt – were regularly ranked as "not free" on Freedom House's press freedom surveys, and none qualified as "free." "There's much to demonstrate in the last six or seven decades that media were accomplices in the general political cover-up of the truth," according to Lebanese Information Minister Michel Samaha.[1] And as Jamil Mroue, publisher of Beirut's *Daily Star* told a Dubai gathering in late 2005, the media continued to serve as "tools" of political structures in which "control is the name of the game." "The Arab media is still very much state-owned and state-controlled," agreed Anwar Gargash, a political science professor at United Arab Emirates University, during the same conversation. "The way forward is to break the chains of the media."

As the levers of media control, and thus the power to shape perceptions, slowly – very slowly – began to shift away from governments at the dawn of the twenty-first century, Arab journalists were being buffeted by an array of competing forces – some lethal – as they attempted to redefine themselves and their profession. *"Profession"* That word alone epitomized the sea-change underway in a region where reporters had too often served as apologists for dictators and autocrats or sold their souls for an envelope of cash. Most Arab journalists remained subject to pressures that ranged from subtle political "guidance" to threats of imprisonment and death, as the assassinations and attempted assassinations of journalists in Lebanon so vividly demonstrated. Yet in newsrooms across the Arab world, journalists were exhibiting a newfound sense of professional purpose.

This writer is part of a generation of American reporters who flocked to journalism schools in the early 1970s. Vietnam and Watergate had inspired us to believe we could change the world. That same sense of excitement could be found among aspiring young Arab reporters in the first decade of the new century – the journalistic children of the Al-Jazeera generation. "I can't criticize from *within* my country," wrote one of my journalism students at The American University in Cairo (AUC), explaining why she wanted to report for the Arab satellite channels, "but journalism allows me to criticize from *outside* and begin to make things different." Even many of the elders of Arab journalism had a new view of themselves and their mission. "We can't say the government changed the media, *we* changed the media," said Hassan Amr, a longtime reporter for Egypt's official press who helped found an independent newspaper, called *Al-Fajr* (*The Dawn*) to signify that a new day has arrived. "We face pressures but enjoy a lot of freedom now. Even in the [government-controlled] national newspapers, there is a lot of change taking place." It was "an exciting and disgusting" time to be a journalist, LBC anchor Tania Mehanna told me with an ironic grin.

Everywhere the rules were in flux; everywhere reporters struggled to maintain their equilibrium on the constantly shifting sands. In Egypt, where media regulations adopted in 1995 were referred to by journalists as the "Press Assassination Law," the 2005 election brought a slight loosening of the reins on media, but once the last vote was tallied scores of journalists – including women – were attacked, beaten, threatened, or jailed. "Egyptian journalism," said Osama al-Ghazli Harb, chief editor of *Al-Siyasah Al-Dawliyah*, "is developing on a tortured journey due to political manipulation." In Iraq, the deadliest place in the world for reporters and home to scores of newly created media outlets, journalists were being killed for being perceived as too close to the government, too close to the resistance, or too close to particular political parties. "Sometimes they target journalists just to scare journalists in general," according to Nabil Khatib, executive editor of the pan-Arab news channel Al-Arabiya. Militant groups ran their own pseudo-news agencies and one motive for the attacks was to make it impossible for actual news organizations to operate. "They are supplying the media [with information and footage] and they pressure you in a way to impose their agenda on you," Khatib explained. "Of course we refuse, because we do not want to be used by any party whoever it is – so we pay the price." The tactics were effective. By the spring of 2007, Al-Arabiya had lost 11 staffers to Iraq's violence, several in targeted assassinations, and was left relying largely on local freelancers. "You feel that you are covering the war as if through glass," Khatib told me sadly.

In less violent locales, the risks were different, but still very real. Saudi Arabia's *Al-Watan* went through four editors in three years as news executives tried to interpret conflicting signals from within the House of Saud, even as the number of journalists detained in the Kingdom continued to climb. That wasn't the only consequence of straying from the party line. For example, a religious court ordered journalist Mansour Nogaidan of the daily *Al-Riyadh* to receive 75 lashes for "calling for freedom of speech and criticizing Wahabism," Saudi Arabia's strict interpretation of Islam.[2] And across the region, many journalists were paying the *ultimate* price. In all, according to Reporters Without Borders, at least 88 Arab journalists were killed between 2001 and 2008, only some of them in the conflicts in Iraq and Palestine. Examples included Algerian newscaster Murad Belqasem, 43, stabbed in his apartment; Kuwaiti writer Hidaya Salem, 65, shot to death parking her car; Sudanese writer Mohammad Taha, 50, tortured and killed for writings that were considered offensive to the system and the community; and Palestinian Khalil Ziben, 59, known for his controversial writings over the Palestinian internal situation, who was killed as he was about to get into his car early one morning.[3]

In May 2007, I received the following email from Palestinian journalist Mohammed Omer, who was born and raised in a refugee camp outside the border town of Rafah in Gaza, from where he continued to report:

> I'm scared, I was almost killed or at least bleeding till death. three militants were closing all roads and they sudden, they said to me stop during the curfew, I stop and then the maskedmen open fire under my feet hitting the ground under my feet. I thought I'm killed, and I could not explain or scream as the shooting was louder than my scream, so I said: "No, don't do that, stop stop, please" oh, I was in tears, this is the first time I'm begging someone not to kill me, and then the other guy who's also militant was standing in my side and said, we don't want to kill him, lets shoot him in his legs and leave him bleed. I said, what? why? and then he said, your ID, I show it with the press card and then they let me go. I was scared that they would shoot at me once I turn my back, but alhamdllah this didn't happen, I was scared, scared, scared to death. This was not pleasant experience, and they were doing this, as I got stuck and could not find transport back home, so I went walking in the streets. I'm scared to death. Those are just evil and terrible people. I don't wish to be in that position again. I can't stand in my feet anymore, I feel pain and scared. Those [gunmen] are working for preventive security, which is working closely with Israelis. I was wearing my bullet proof vest, but this didn't protect me enough. Today, more than 10 were killed and tens were injured, many by Israelis, but still some by Palestinian clashes between Hamas and Fateh. They don't want this to be reported. I didn't tell about this to my mother, she will be scared again!
>
> sad greetings!
> Mohammed

In September 2008, this email arrived from Europe, where Omer was undergoing surgery:

> Dear Lawrence,
> sorry for not being able to keep in touch lately, but it's due to mistreatment and torture that I had to go through.
> Mohammed

"I am not exaggerating when I say the Arab press is witnessing one of the worst periods of its life," Salaheddine el-Hafez, vice editor-in-chief of Egypt's *Al-Ahram* newspaper and secretary general of the Arab Journalists Association, told a press freedom conference in late 2006. "The margins of freedom for the Arab press are severely limited and we have evidence of that in our daily lives."[4]

Journalism in the Levant

Lebanon has always been the region's media Tower of Babel; its highly ideological press representing – often bought-and-paid-for by – a range of Middle East governments and political movements. As the new century dawned, that was still true. What began to change in the spring of 2005 was the way reporters looked at themselves and each other. The media-led popular uprising against Syrian occupation that year produced a shared sense of mission. Journalism itself – briefly – began to emerge as a new ideology. "We feel we can no longer just represent some, we must represent all," I was told by a young reporter with the traditionally pro-Syrian newspaper *As-Safir*, which was reevaluating its own mission following Syria's withdrawal from Lebanon. But life at the hard edge of media independence could be dangerous. Journalist Mai Chidiac learned that in the fall of 2005 when her left arm and leg were blown off by a bomb placed under the seat of her car. An anchor and talk show host at the privately owned LBC, she had been an outspoken critic of Syrian involvement in Lebanon. The bombing was seen by journalists as a clear message to all those who dared use the media to attack the Damascus regime.

Driving down the coastal highway from Jounieh to Beirut after a televised media solidarity rally for Chidiac, anti-Syrian radio talk show host Rima Njeim fielded serial phone calls – one hand on the wheel of her BMW, the other on the phone – as her producer, Johnny el-Saddik, told me of the endless death threats Njeim received from what Lebanese reporters had come to call "the unseen hand." Warned one email: "We know where your children go to school." Unlike Njeim, many reporters in Lebanon no longer drove their own cars for fear of what might happen when they turned the ignition key. Some were also censoring themselves. "I think my life is more important than any other thing,"

Caroline Beaini, Beirut correspondent for Abu Dhabi TV, told me later that same day. "Even if I am a journalist that does not mean that I should die for the cause. The cause is not worth enough to die for."

In a twisted kind of way, the attacks on reporters in Lebanon were a compliment to the growing influence of Arab journalism. In the weeks before his assassination, former Prime Minister Rafiq Hariri had been called in by Syrian President Bashar al-Assad and ordered to either force Beirut-based *An-Nahar*, arguably the most respected mainstream daily in the Arab world, to end its criticism of the Damascus regime or to sell his 20 percent stake in the company. Hariri opted to sell. "Bashar al-Assad could not understand that Hariri could never make us stand with him [Assad]," Ghassan Tueni recalled of the incident. It was not the first time the Syrian leader had tried to force the paper to shift its stance. In one of the small glassed-in offices off the *An-Nahar* news-room, a Lebanese flag lay draped over the chair of Samir Kassir as a memorial to the outspoken, anti-Syrian columnist whose white Alpha Romeo had exploded in a ball of flames the previous spring. "I still can't believe it," whispered reporter Roula Mouawad as she paused before the glassed-in office. Kassir's likeness was etched on a plaque beside the door, along with the dates: 1960–2005. "We have to fight for them, and the next," Mouawad said later over coffee, referring to her fallen col-leagues, "because there *will* be a next." Subsequent events would bear her out.

The attacks also highlighted the degree to which journalism and politics overlapped on this new Arab media landscape. Gibran Tueni was a leader of the anti-Syrian bloc in parliament, Chidiac's program was a showcase for anti-Syrian politicians, just as her station, LBC, was a key media voice of the anti-Syrian opposition, and Kassir was a ral-lying figure within the *Kifaya* (Enough) movement, which targeted the Syrian presence. In him, fellow columnist Rami Khouri later said, "con-verged the job of a journalist and someone in the business of political and cultural mobilization." There was every reason to believe that this duality of roles – journalist and politician – would live on at *An-Nahar*. In a highly political speech marking the third anniversary of her father's murder, Nayla Tueni, heir-apparent to the newspaper dynasty, lashed out at Syria and its allies in Lebanon, appealed directly to fellow

Christians to support the anti-Syrian political block, and vowed that the "blood" of her father would brook no "treason," prompting one government minister to walk out of the hall. Over white wine in her late father's office later that evening, Nayla glanced at Gibran's desk, untouched since his death, and told me that the "Naharists" would not be silenced. *Naharists*: Newspaper as ideological movement. Not long after, she announced she was running for parliament. Meanwhile, across the border in Damascus, journalists like Michael Kilo, who would be jailed by the Assad regime in 2007 for "weakening national sentiment," openly campaigned for a radical overhaul of Syria's Lebanon policy.[5]

Climate of Violence

But Lebanon was just one front in a broader war between the press and power in the Middle East as the first decade of the twenty-first century neared its end. Other types of battles were being fought between journalists and the powers-that-be across the Arab world. "Arab rulers, regardless of their differences, agree on one thing – all of them consider the Arab press to be their sworn enemy," according to Jamal Amer, editor-in-chief of *Al-Wasat* in Yemen, where Reporters Without Borders (Reporters sans Frontières or RSF) warned of a "climate of violence" which "will inevitably encourage journalists to censor themselves."[6]

"Every authoritarian regime has agents everywhere so they can influence our reports. They control the television and the elections process by TV," Hassan Amr of Egypt's *Al-Fajr*, told me. They could also throw offenders in jail, or worse. Journalists who pushed the envelope in this atmosphere tried their best to protect each other. "I secure myself by my documents, my position," Amr explained, and, like others, he made sure government officials knew that "there are other people who will scandal them, attack them, if they attack you. You know this kind of blackmail." But, as countless jailed reporters could attest, such tactics provided only limited protection. Ultimately, Amr conceded of governments, "they can do anything." As Beirut's *Daily Star* observed in an editorial, "Many factors have contributed to the legion inadequacies of the so-called 'modern Arab state,' but perhaps none is so ubiquitous as the determination of ruling elites to silence their critics."[7]

Another example of the tug-of-war between government and media could be found in Jordan, where King Abdullah was trumpeting media reform as a harbinger of greater political openness. However, as elsewhere, media liberalization in Jordan was proving to be a matter of one step forward, one step back, with jailings, muzzlings, and "close monitoring" of journalists by the security services a fact of life.[8] A panel discussion about media reform organized by the Jordanian government at an international conference in Amman in the fall of 2005 turned into a free-for-all as Jordanian journalists mocked the government's decision to scrap the ministry of information and repeal a key press law. "You eliminated one law but there are 22 others on the books that can send us to prison," one reporter shouted at then Deputy Prime Minister Marwan Muasher. Eighteen months later, Jordan's parliament passed a new press and publications law that included jail terms for any journalist who "insult[s] religious sentiments and beliefs" or "slanders or libels" any individual.[9]

"Government and security interference have dwindled on the surface... but prior censorship remains like a phantom that controls the media scene," the Center for Defending Freedom of Journalists (CDFJ) said in its 2006 report on Jordan. "Despite government promises to support the freedom of media, [it] moved in the opposite direction."[10] At about the same time the report was published, Jordanian authorities seized all videotapes of an Al-Jazeera interview with the king's uncle, Prince Hassan bin Talal, who was once heir to the throne. An Arab journalist with close ties to the Jordanian palace told me state security had been monitoring the interview via bugs planted in Prince Hassan's office, then raced to the airport to intercept the Al-Jazeera team. The Al-Jazeera reporter, Ghassan Ben Jeddou, said Jordanian officials told him that the tapes were seized because the prince's comments "could affect Jordan's diplomatic relations with Saudi Arabia."[11]

Saudi Arabia was, after all, no fan of Al-Jazeera or a free media. Reporters Without Borders (RSF) named King Abdullah to its list of "Predators of Press Freedom," along with Libya's Muammar Gadaffi, Syria's Bashar al-Assad, and Tunisia's Zine el-Abdine Ben Ali. While most other Gulf countries were making slow progress on media reform, Saudi Arabia remained near the bottom of the list because of what RSF claimed was a total absence of free media. In place of independent news organizations were "only organs that spout government propaganda:"[12]

> The grip of the Saud family and its Wahabi ideology depends on rigid control of news. No laws protect freedom of expression so journalists dare not criticise the regime and self-censorship is the rule.[13]

In a 2007 interview, Shams Ahsan, national editor of *The Saudi Gazette*, told the Arab Press Network that, "Freedom of speech does exist and Saudi Arabia is beginning to offer a good environment for journalists" in which once-taboo subjects like human rights and women's rights could be discussed in the media. Ahsan insisted there was no censorship as such, but, he acknowledged, "There are certain issues we cannot write about. We do not write anything against Islam and we do not attack members of the royal family. We know our limits and in a way practice self-censorship. There have been troubles when red lines have been crossed."[14] One example: London-based *Al-Hayat*, the largest circulation daily in the Arab world, was temporarily banned in Saudi Arabia in September 2007 when it reported on links between certain Wahabi clerics and a Saudi extremist who was a key player in Al-Qaeda in Iraq. The paper was owned by Prince Khaled bin Sultan, the son of the Saudi crown prince, demonstrating that no news organization was immune.

For the Saudi press, the "red lines" around forbidden stories extended well beyond the country's borders. Criticism of Saudi and allied Arab leaders was *verboten*, but so too were stories that put other Islamic countries in a bad light. Former *Arab News* columnist Fawaz Turki claimed he was fired after writing about alleged massacres carried out by the Indonesian army in East Timor. "You don't write about atrocities committed by an Islamic government – even when they're already documented in the history books – and hope to get away with it," he said in an article in *The Washington Post*.[15] Journalist Mona Eltahawy had a similar experience. The US-based Egyptian was a regular columnist for the pan-Arab daily *Asharq Al-Awsat*, owned by the same Saudi publishing company as *Arab News*. Generally in the Arab

world, English-language newspapers were able to be much more critical than their Arabic counterparts because they are inaccessible to the
majority of the population. Eltahawy discovered that her criticisms of
the Egyptian regime were being published in full on the paper's English
language website, targeted to Western readers and Arab intelligentsia,
but softened considerably in the Arabic-language newspaper. This passage, for example, appeared in the English version of her article about
the Egyptian elections, but was cut from the Arabic version:

> When women huddle in a corner out of fear of these same
> security forces, we have to ask are we in Egypt or in Iraq,
> from where Arab media daily beam pictures of Iraqi women
> huddling in fear and anguish from American soldiers?

> When thugs (more often than not hired by the government)
> holding up swords and machetes stand between voters and
> polling booths, clearly challenging anyone who wants to vote
> to get past them and their weapons first, what else is there to
> conclude other than that the Egyptian government is at war
> with its own people?[16]

When Eltahawy complained about the editing, her column was sum-
marily dropped from the paper and the editors stopped returning her
calls and emails. "The major red lines at *Asharq Al-Awsat* could be quite
simple – in descending order they were the Saudi royal family, Saudi
Arabia's allies in the Gulf (Qatar, a rival, was considered fair game) and
then Saudi Arabia's other Arab allies," she wrote of the incident. "Within
such a hierarchy of red lines, the Egyptian regime can indeed pull rank
and demand that *Asharq Al-Awsat* silence a critic."[17] In a later conversation, she recalled receiving some advice from a friendly editor when
she started writing for *Asharq Al-Awsat*: "He said not to mention any
leader by name and do not say 'the president.' Say 'Arab government,'
[he told me] and that usually passes [the censor]." The paper was also
sensitive about stories touching on the ruling Assad family of Syria, due
to ties of marriage between the Assad family and the House of Saud.
As Yemeni editor Abdel Karim al-Khaiwani put it, "Our leaders have
become divine and their families sacred." So are their sex lives – and
those of their friends. Distribution of the Emirati magazine *As Sada*

was blocked in Tunisia in early 2009 because it contained a story that claimed that because the country banned polygamy, extramarital affairs were common among rich Tunisians.

Elsewhere in the Gulf, the media was operating under strictures less visceral, but equally real. "What kind of pressures do you face?" I asked the editor of one Gulf paper after chatting about the attacks on Lebanese journalists. "None," he replied. "We don't report about political issues." Complained another senior Gulf editor: "Our press is infected with the self-censorship virus."[18] An Egyptian journalist who had spent years working for newspapers in the Emirates told me he asked himself "two or three times what will be the reaction" before filing a story. "We have our own personal censorship." He had good reason to be cautious; he had repeatedly been dragged into court. "This is a way to try to make me more polite as a small child has to be a polite," said the reporter, who asked that his name not be used. "It was a very simple local news story. What if I wrote about some politics, or some political problems or what if I give some ideas about terrorism or about military or about security, the matters that really put journalists in serious cases?" One of my journalism students at AUC also worked as a presenter on an entertainment news show on one of the Egyptian satellite channels. Not only did she avoid any mention of politics, even during the elections, but "internal pressures" within the channel meant that she also had to tiptoe around Arab celebrities. "And if we do unintentionally say something they don't like, we must correct the information or apologize live on TV."

Othman Mahmoud al-Sini, editor-in-chief of the Saudi daily *Al-Watan*, said Saudi journalists were "in the cross-fire" as they tried to push the boundaries. "Our difficulties are not from the government," he told me. "The censorship is not like before. It is not strict, because if it were strict all audience will go to the TV or Internet websites. The margin is wider, but not that wide. It is like a pipe. Our difficulties are from the society. Some people, because they are against changes, they are very strict or conservative, so we must we fight the pressure, we fight sometimes the attacks from the society." Those pressures were evident in the comments of the top cleric at Egypt's al-Azhar University, a leading center of Islamic scholarship, who said journalists who published "incorrect reports" should receive 80 lashes.[19]

Journalists weren't the only ones in the crosshairs; their bosses were too. In late 2008, the chairman of Saudi Arabia's Supreme Judicial Council said it was permissible to kill the owners of TV channels that broadcast "immoral" content. Five months later, another leading cleric criticized by name Prince Alwaleed Bin Talal, a nephew of King Abdullah and one of the world's richest businessmen, who controlled the Rotana music and entertainment channels. The cleric said Alwaleed and Walid al-Ibrahim, another Saudi royal who was chairman of the MBC Group, which included various entertainment channels and Al-Arabiya, were responsible for "degenerate" content and should be taken to court because they were "no less dangerous to Muslims than drug dealers."[20]

There was contradiction wherever you turned. Kuwait's 2006 press and publication law marked the end of the government's monopoly on media since independence. Within two years, 15 newspapers, almost as many weeklies and dozens of privately owned television stations were operating. But a host of vaguely worded laws kept the media at heel. In the spring of 2008, the courts stripped the licenses of two weeklies, one for "besmirching the reputation of the prime minister," and the other for reporting about corruption. An Al-Arabiya television reporter found himself being sued for "insult" by a top cleric after a story about al-Qaeda's activities in Kuwait, while a reporter for Kuwait's *Al-Watan* was ordered to pay damages to the ruler of Qatar, one of the richest men in the world, for "harming his reputation" by reporting about Qatar's diplomatic ties with Israel.

In the United Arab Emirates, several new publications were licensed in 2008. That was a good sign. Yet the country slipped three places on the World Press Freedom Index because of increased restrictions on the press. The draft of a new UAE media law circulated early 2009 was greeted as "one step forward and ten steps backwards." It did away with jail terms for journalists, but, the *Gulf News* editorialized, "The right to publish, communicate and disseminate information has been minimised to being literally non-existent."[21] The drafting of new media laws became a cottage industry in the Arab world as governments sought to convey a *façade* of liberalization, but those surface reforms masked a legal sleight-of-hand that left a battery of other laws in place to keep reporters hamstrung. Bahraini columnist Lamees Dhaif was one of many who found that out the hard way after writing a series of articles calling for reform of the country's family law. She found herself facing three years in prison for violating regulations that stipulated that those who "publicly insult, in any form, the National Council, other statutory bodies, the army, the courts, the Authorities or the public interest" may be punished with "imprisonment or a fine." But she wasn't being charged as a journalist under Bahrain's 2002 press code. Instead, she was remanded as a private citizen under the 1976 penal code. "The Public Prosecutor's Office has opened another channel by which to prosecute journalists outside of the framework of the Press Code," she complained.[22]

Bahrain issued licenses for its first private television and radio stations, Egypt pointed to the media as evidence of political liberalization, and Tunisia hosted the 2005 World Summit on the Information Society, but despite those seemingly positive signs, the Arab Network for Human Rights Information accused all three of "implicating opposition, activists, and journalists in cases, detaining them and imprisoning them, and physically attacking them...framing criminal cases against those opposition forces, attempting to defame their reputations and spreading fear amongst citizens to prevent them from participating in public affairs."[23] As a sign of just how bad things were in the region, and how disconnected government rhetoric was from reality, the 2005 UNDP *Arab Human Development Report* listed Egypt and Tunisia among just five Arab states that "assure" the right of journalists "to obtain information and news legally." Yet, it continued, "in some Arab countries," including Egypt, "the state of emergency [which curtailed press freedoms] has become permanent and ongoing, with none of the dangers to warrant it."[24] That same year, RSF ranked Tunisia and Egypt in the bottom 20 on its World Press Freedom Index,[25] and Freedom House singled out Tunisia – along with Libya, Syria, and the Occupied Territories – as "of particular concern."[26] A year later, Egypt had clawed its way up to 133 of 168 countries on the RSF list as a result of a slight easing of controls during the 2005 elections, but a subsequent clampdown made that seeming progress illusory, leading the Committee to Protect Journalists to name the country to its 2007 "Backsliders" list of

10 countries where press freedom had most deteriorated.[27] "Freedom of the press in Egypt is only a field of landmines," said Ibrahim Eissa, the controversial editor of Cairo's *Al-Dustour* who, by early 2009, had been convicted on charges of insulting the president and undermining the national economy and faced two dozen more criminal lawsuits, all connected with his reports that the president might be ill. "You enter the minefield and when it goes 'boom' it takes away your eye or your limb, but you are free."

Meanwhile, RSF called Iraq the "graveyard of freedom" for journalists, with more than 175 reporters, camerapersons, and other media workers killed in the five years since the US invasion,[28] many in targeted assassinations, such as that of Atwar Bahjat, a courageous female correspondent for Al-Arabiya, who, along with her cameraman, was executed in cold blood on the side of a road as she tried to cover the aftermath of a massive bomb that destroyed one of the holiest Shi'ite shrines, killing 130 Iraqis. Violence was the greatest danger to reporters, but what George Bush called the country's "democratic" government posed another kind of threat, waging a systematic campaign against independent media. The government expelled Al-Jazeera; temporarily shut down the Baghdad bureau of the other main Arabic satellite news channel, Al-Arabiya, charging its correspondents with inciting "sectarianism" and "violence;"[29] shuttered numerous other media outlets; barred reporters from covering parliament; and even issued an order banning journalists from the scene of bombings.

The contradiction between the Iraqi government's professions of democracy and its approach to media freedom was the kind of incongruity apparent across the region. While some Arab heads of state spoke against the jailing of journalists, the Arab Press Freedom Watch said at the end of 2004, "Sadly none of their words have become deeds."[30] The situation was little different two years later, when the Cairo Institute for Human Rights reported that monitoring of news organizations during elections in Egypt, Tunisia, Lebanon, and Palestine found that, "Subordination of media to politicians more than to professional standards was a problem observed in all four countries."[31] Even where a modicum of progress was being made, there was no assurance it would last. Gamal Hasanain, a cartoonist for one of Egypt's aggressive opposition dailies, learned that when he published a cartoon mocking the involvement of one of Egypt's opposition political parties in the 2007 legislative elections. His bosses were not amused, since the party he had mocked happened to own the newspaper for which he worked. Hasanain was suspended for a month.[32] *Al-Shorouq*, an "independent" newspaper launched with much fanfare in the fall of 2008, marked World Press Freedom Day six months later by suspending one of its journalists after she married the most prominent blogger from the banned Muslim Brotherhood.

Over in Syria, which had long maintained draconian control over the media, the government allowed the establishment of the first private newspaper and the first private satellite TV station, Al-Sham. But the day the station was scheduled to air its first newscast, the Information Ministry ordered it shut down. The government said it was all a bureaucratic snafu; but others speculated it had something to do with the fact that another channel, run by a businessman close to the president, was also about to launch. Either way, Al-Sham's owners said the temporary closure cost them millions of dollars. "We [Sham TV] are the pioneer and the sacrificial lamb. It has been difficult but now everyone can follow our lead," the station's director, Mamoun Bouni, told reporters.[33] Similarly, the launch of Jordan's first private TV station, ATV, was suspended just before going to air in the summer of 2007 when the government-run Audio-Video Commission called a halt for what it termed "technical reasons," which observers suspected had more to do with the channel's potential to undercut government-owned Jordan TV than with technology.[34]

In Doha, home to Al-Jazeera, the Qatar Foundation, headed by the emir's wife, Sheikha Mozah Bint-Nasir al-Misned, launched the Doha Center for Media Freedom in the fall of 2008, hiring the founder of Reporters Without Borders, Robert Menard, as part of a high-profile PR campaign featuring the slogan, "Let Us Give Freedom of Information a Better Future." Six months later, as the center struggled to maintain its independence, the head of research was prevented from leaving the country, prompting Menard to charge that "certain Qatari government bodies" were "trying by all possible means to obstruct our work."[35] Not long after the outburst, Menard announced he was quitting his post – the center said he was fired – and left Qatar. Meanwhile, local newspapers in Qatar complained of the government's heavy hand in controlling their content.

It was not all gloom and doom. Licenses for new publications and television stations *were* being issued in places like Egypt, Morocco, Syria, and Yemen; journalists *were* openly criticizing repressive governments; and in Bahrain, where the three government newspapers all carried identical front pages until 2001, opposition papers were taking on their own voice. In Saudi Arabia, a February 2009 cabinet reshuffle praised by reformists brought the former ambassador to London, Abd-al-Aziz al-Khujah, into the job of minister of information. He quickly announced that a new era had begun. "We must not stand still and refuse to change. We live in a universal village … and we must be realistic and bold in addressing cultural diversity in our country," he said in an interview with Al-Jazeera. Not long after, he lifted a two-year ban on a London-based internet newspaper that had angered Saudi authorities.

But it was all, literally and figurative, built on sand. In its first Media Sustainability Index for the Arab world, The International Research and Exchanges Board (IREX), a media and civil society NGO, measured a market basket of factors that contribute to a sustainable free press and found that only six Arab countries had crossed the Rubicon into the realm of "near sustainability."[36] In its 2007 study, Freedom House reported that even the "modest improvements in press freedom in the Middle East and North Africa over the last several years" had "reversed," leaving the Middle East at the bottom of the world's ranking of press freedom. Said Freedom House Executive Director Jennifer Windsor:

> The Middle East and North Africa are home to some of the most repressive governments in the world, and these governments have found a way to limit citizens' natural craving for free expression and unfiltered information. While there have been some changes in the past few years, ultimately we've also seen some real pushback on the part of governments.[37]

By its 2008 report, RSF described the state of Arab journalism as "between repression and servility."[38] Even those who wanted to believe that elements within their governments were on the right track sometimes sounded forlorn. Praising steps by the reformist information minister, Saudi journalist Samar Fatany wrote, "The ministry so far has been instrumental in influencing a more responsible citizenry... However, the harsh restrictions imposed both on media and cultural activities have delayed efforts to advance the social environment."[39]

Adding to the challenge was the growing suspicion and animosity between religious sects. This was particularly pronounced in Iraq, where membership in the "wrong" branch of Islam could – and did – get reporters killed; but it also played out in increased Sunni–Shi'a tensions across the region, as well in more localized schisms, such as between Muslims and Coptic Christians in Egypt. An impromptu poll of Arab news executives at the 2007 Arab Broadcast Forum found that a majority felt that the prevailing sectarian divisions in the Arab world were making their job more difficult.

History of Control

After its early pioneering years, Arab journalism "lost its soul," according to Ghassan Tueni, and "journalists became civil servants." Since the end of World War II, government control had been the hallmark of media in Arab countries, where "muzzling and suppression... manipulation and co-option"[40] by regimes that "claimed a monopoly on truth"[41] became the norm, news organizations were mouthpieces for governments and political movements, and the media was traditionally viewed with suspicion and little respect. Looking at the Middle East in the 1970s, William Rugh, a former US ambassador in the region and expert on the Arab media, divided the Arab print media into three classifications: the "mobilization press," controlled by revolutionary governments like those in Libya, Syria, Iraq, and Sudan; the "loyalist press" of Saudi Arabia, the Gulf, and Palestine, which was largely privately owned but beholden to the government; and the "diverse press" of Lebanon, Kuwait, Morocco, and Yemen, which was relatively free and reflected a diversity of views, but was subject to more subtle pressures.[42] A fourth category of Arab print media was the offshore pan-Arab press. Up until the early 1970s, Beirut was the media capital of the Arab world. Its rough-and-tumble mix of politics and religion covered the entire spectrum of Arab opinion, from the Arab nationalism and socialism of the Nasserites, Ba'athists and Palestinians to the Saudi-backed monarchists and Islamist sympathizers of the Egyptian Muslim Brotherhood. All these views were represented in the pages of the country's lively media. But the same political crosscurrents that fed the debate also fueled the communal violence that would take hold in the early 1970s and tear the country asunder for the next two decades. As documented in this writer's account of that conflict,[43] the battles of the Middle East were fought out on the soil of Lebanon. Journalists were among the countless victims. Assassinations of editors, newsroom bombings, kidnappings and threats from the plethora of competing factions, and the governments that sponsored them silenced the voices of debate. Many newspapers shut down.

Beirut's loss was London's gain. The Arab world's most respected newspaper, *Al-Hayat*, stopped publishing in 1976 after 13 bomb attempts on its offices (its founder had been assassinated in 1966). Eleven years later, it reopened in London, joining the Saudi-owned *Asharq Al-Awsat*, which, since 1977, had been edited in Britain and printed in the Arab world. The Saudi royal family soon bought controlling interest in *Al-Hayat* via Prince Khaled bin Sultan, who would become known in the West as the Saudi military commander during the 1990–91 Gulf War. London was also base for the third of the leading pan-Arab dailies, *Al-Quds Al-Arabi* (*Arab Jerusalem*). Reflecting the Arab media's reliance on political sponsors, the Palestinian paper carried few advertisements and received funding directly from various Arab sources.[44]

While it maintained a broadly pro-Saudi line, the opinion pages of *Al-Hayat* were "among the most varied and open fora for debate in the Arab world."[45] And although the move from Beirut to London took *Al-Hayat* out of the direct line-of-fire of the Lebanese conflict, it did not shield its staff of some 300 journalists from other pressures faced by their colleagues at papers based in the Arab world. In early 1997, the paper's offices in New York, Washington, London, and Riyadh were the targets of letter bombs that the then-editor believed were ordered by Egyptian Islamist Ayman Zawahiri. The militant, who would later emerge as Osama bin Laden's right-hand man, was apparently upset that the paper had not run an interview with him, something that would have likely angered Egyptian authorities and could have had repercussions for the paper's distribution there. Militants weren't the only threat. Governments could also reach out and touch the off-shore papers. In the spring of 2004, the Beirut bureau chief of *Asharq Al-Awsat* was convicted in absentia (he had fled the country) and sentenced to a year in prison for "disturbing national security and harming the president's dignity" after the paper reported that there had been an assassination attempt on the life of then-President Emil Lahoud.[46] In a telling commentary on the state of the Arab media, *Al-Hayat* saw fit to note in its article about the conviction that, "Despite occasional pressure from authorities in recent years, the Lebanese press remains one of the Mideast region's freest."[47]

The offshore print media and their counterparts in a few Arab countries may have enjoyed some modicum of leeway, but radio and television remained firmly in government hands. According to Muhammed Ayish, chair of the College of Mass Communication at the University of Sharjah, "the concept of television journalism, as a set of distinctive professional values and practices, was virtually nonexistent in Arab world television."[48] As Rugh told a Senate panel in the spring of 2004,

> Most Arab broadcasting laws prohibited criticism of the head of state, defamation of religion, or undermining public order. Additional taboos were observed by broadcast editors based on local custom and political circumstances. Arab broadcast audiences therefore had access only to news and commentary officially approved by their respective governments, unless they could tune in to the Voice of America, BBC, Radio Monte Carlo or CNN.[49]

Whatever their classification, Rugh told the senators, "Arab information media have always been closely tied to politics." While the policy has been used to cloak a variety of other motives – not least, that of keeping authoritarian regimes in power by stifling dissent – the most oft-cited reason for muzzling the media was the Arab–Israeli conflict.

> Arab governments have been able to justify explicitly and implicitly their influence over the mass media as necessary either while the country is "at war" with Israel, or politically confronting Israel's policies. Because of the degree to which

the Arab–Israeli dispute has become the central issue in Arab
foreign policy and a matter of Arab patriotism, this justi-
fication is difficult to oppose.[50]

Steeped in a culture of perennial confrontation shaped by the conflict with Israel, the patriotic fervor so often seen among reporters
in countries at war became a permanent fixture of the Arab media.
"Whether the government controlled the media directly or influenced
them indirectly," Rugh reported in an earlier study, "editors were more
likely than usual to make an effort to support their government in
the national interest during the conflict."[51] Many journalists voluntar-
ily subscribed to the concept of "responsible freedom,"[52] in which the
interests of the state – and the Arab nation – superseded all other considerations. Those interests could be defined in many ways:

> They involve anything that can be considered a threat to the
> ruling institutions and their interests, including negative
> statements about religions or beliefs, Arab nationalism and
> its struggle, values, and national traditions.[53]

Thus, from an early point, Arab journalists were expected to toe
the party line, often in a quite literal sense. "The press is an authority
whose function is to guide people and actively participate in building
their society exactly as does the People's Assembly," Egypt's Mohamed
Hassanein Heikal, the then-editor of *Al-Ahram*, wrote in 1960 to justify
Nasser's nationalization of five major publishing houses.[54]

It had not always been thus. In fact, just a few years earlier the political neutrality for which *Al-Ahram* was then known was perceived by
one researcher as "an extremely hopeful sign for the future of Arab
journalism."[55] That observation was made by Thomas McFadden, a
former US diplomat in Beirut who carried out a survey of journalists
in Lebanon, Syria, Jordan, Iraq, and Egypt in 1951 and 1952. It was a
time of optimism in the profession, a brief period of media liberalization between the end of colonial-era restrictions and the advent of draconian government controls that would arrive with Ba'athism in Syria
and Iraq, Nasserism in Egypt, and the ascension to the throne of King
Hussein in Jordan. McFadden was swept up in the sense of the possible
then pervading Arab newsrooms. In the Arab media's coverage of the

region's governments he found "more criticism and it is more vehement than is the case normally in most advanced democracies."[56]

Based on responses to questionnaires he distributed in newsrooms, McFadden concluded that "Arab editors believe the role of the press in society should be to fight for political causes. This is much more important, they think, than objectively to inform the Arab public." He identified five priorities of Arab journalists: (1) To fight against imperialism; (2) to fight against Zionism; (3) to fight for Arab nationalism and Arab unity; (4) to fight against government corruption and weakness; and (5) to fight for the reform, modernization, and democratization of Arab society.[57]

While suffering from a preponderance of opinion over fact and a shortage of resources, McFadden observed that the Arab media business had evolved to a point where many newspapers were no longer dependent on political subsidies and he noted that such a development had marked the rise of objectivity in the US media. "It can be predicted confidently that similar developments will occur in Arab journalism," McFadden wrote. "This day appears to be approaching on the Arab scene much more rapidly than anyone would have a right to expect."[58]

But that era of relative freedom would end with the wave of revolutions that swept the region a few years later. *Al-Ahram*, in which McFadden had so much hope, would emerge as the ultimate government mouthpiece. Soon, Morocco to Yemen, the press was regarded as a tool of nationalism and politics. To stray was unpatriotic; firing was the least of the penalties. Dissenting journalists were fined, imprisoned, or, in some cases, executed. Publications were regularly shuttered. As Ibrahim Nawar, head of the Arab Press Freedom Watch (APFW), has observed, "Freedom of expression is not something on offer in the Arab world. It has to be fought for."[59] Hoda al-Mutawa, who worked for a time as a presenter on Bahrain television, recalls being summoned by the minister of information and ordered to stop discussing some of the issues she had raised on the air. When she tried to object, the minister waved his hand to silence her, sighed, and said, "Hoda, why do you want to make life difficult for yourself? Just say, 'OK' like everyone else." The conversation was over. "They speak to you as a father to a child," she later told me.

As *Al-Hayat* had discovered, the pressure came not only from governments. According to the London-based APFW's 2001 *State of the Arab Media* report, "Clans in Yemen and Kuwait, criminal gangs in Algeria and Egypt and Islamic fundamentalists in Algeria all took part in the offensive against the freedom of speech [which was] a common denominator in all Arab countries."[60] That was underlined by the report's list of more than 50 "free speech victims" the previous year, a litany of assassinations, attempted assassinations, imprisonments, interrogations, beatings, and fines. The list was accompanied by a compendium of 15 publications in Morocco, Egypt, Yemen, Jordan, and Sudan that had been forcibly closed, confiscated, or taken to court.[61] The resulting self-censorship that pervaded the Arab media was exacerbated by the fact that, according to Hussein Amin of AUC, "most Arab authorities do not publish a list of subjects that they do not want to be covered, leaving the reporter in a state of confusion."[62]

The Arab–Israeli conflict may have been the cover, but for many governments survival was the real issue in attempting to control what their populations saw, heard, and read. In May of 2004, as the Bush administration was unveiling its "blueprint for democracy" in the Middle East and Arab leaders were preparing to gather for a summit to discuss, among other things, political reform, the APFW held its third annual conference under the telling title, "Freeing the Arab Media from State Control." The final communiqué was stark reading for supporters of press freedom, highlighting "the strong linkage between the hostile attitude of the state towards the freedom of expression and the press, and its deep rooted tendencies to resist public pressure for change and democratic reform of Arab societies in response to the wide democratization in the whole world."[63]

Beyond the issue of government control was the existence of a cash culture in which reporters – particularly in the "diverse press" of Lebanon and a handful of other Arab countries – were paid to write certain stories by competing political or business interests. "One of the major problems here is that conflict of interest is not considered to be a problem," Magda Abu Fadil, the director of the Institute for Professional Journalists (IPJ), told an interviewer. "This is a major, major problem. Journalists cannot be credible if they accept money, free trips, gifts and favors."[64] This same phenomena existed elsewhere in the developing world and was seen in the common practice of companies handing out envelopes of cash at news conferences just to get reporters to show up. The king of Morocco annually hosted a television broadcast on which he ostentatiously handed over government subsidy checks to executives of the major newspapers.

Even after the launch of international satellite television in the 1980s, for those members of the economic elite who owned satellite dishes the only real alternatives to the local media were the news broadcasts of CNN International and the BBC; less-privileged citizens were left to rely on the shortwave broadcasts of the Arabic service of the BBC World Service, the Voice of America, and a few European broadcasters, thus ensuring that Arabs and Muslims saw not only the world, but their own region, through the dominant frame of the Western media. To a large extent, this was even true for those depending on domestic news sources. With few exceptions, the Arab and non-Arab Muslim media was completely dependent on Western news organizations when it came to covering the rest of the world – and their own region. Carefully vetted wire copy from news agencies like the Associated Press (AP), Reuters and Agence France Presse (AFP) provided stories from Washington, Moscow, and Beijing, as well as other Arab capitals, while television viewers saw the world through the prism of the major US networks, CNN, BBC, and a few other Western television news agencies, such as Reuters Television and Associated Press Television, that supplied the videotape for Arab broadcasts.

This was the situation when, in the 1990s, Saudi entrepreneurs close to the government set up the first private cross-border Arab satellite television operations. The goal was to counter the influence of the Western broadcasters then beaming signals into the Middle East, as well as smuggled videocassettes of Western programs and movies, which offered the only alternative to government-controlled television. While illegal in many countries, satellite dishes – which had been shrinking in size – began to sprout like desert mushrooms on rooftops across the region in the late 1980s, even as "state broadcasting monopolies and strict government censorship remained the norm in most Arab states and Iran."[65] Just how strict, was demonstrated with Iraq's invasion of Kuwait in 1991. Viewers relying on Saudi state television for their news would not even have known war had broken out. The state broad-caster failed to mention the invasion of the neighboring emirate for more than 48 hours. It was the equivalent of a French TV station ignoring a German occupation of Belgium. For those with satellite dishes, all eyes turned to CNN.

Egypt was the first to introduce Arab satellite broadcasting in order to convey its official position during the first Gulf War. But Nilesat was a government-controlled operation, little different from the fare on terrestrial state-run TV. Nine months later, two well-connected Saudi entrepreneurs flipped the switch on the Middle East Broadcasting Center (MBC), ushering in the era of private satellite broadcasting in the Arab world. While MBC was "very serious about Arab news," according to a consultant who worked with the owners at the time, and brought in a group of "first-class" British and Lebanese news people, coverage of Saudi affairs was handled with kid gloves. Middle East Broadcasting Center was soon joined by the Arab Radio and Television Network (ART) and Orbit, both originally based in Rome, and Lebanon's LBC International and Future Television. But when it came to news, these new channels were anything but independent operations. One of the two Saudi partners in MBC was King Fahd's brother-in-law; the other partner later joined with another member of the royal family to found ART. Orbit was controlled by the son of the Saudi crown prince; LBC was founded with the help of another Saudi sheikh; and Future Television was created by Lebanese businessman Rafiq Hariri, who made his fortune in Saudi Arabia and was related by marriage to the Saudi royals (he would later become the Saudi-backed prime minister of Lebanon, helping that nation recover from 15 years of civil war, before dying in a massive car bomb in 2005).

Critics of Saudi domination of the region's media denounced the "eunuch-like condition" of Arab journalists and other Arab intellectuals who had sold out to the high salaries. This "media control," observed Abdelwahab el-Affendi, a Sudanese scholar at the University of Westminster's Center for the Study of Democracy, was not confined to the Middle East, but rather

> it constitutes a malaise that is most acutely manifested in the
> Arab heartlands of Islam, but which has gripped the whole

> Ummah (the World Muslim Community) in its tentacles.
> The impact of this phenomenon reverberates all over the
> land of Islam...[66]

There was then, compelling evidence for el-Affendi's grim portrait
of the state of the Muslim media in 1993:

> They have managed to force independent voices from the
> Muslim world using market manipulation, bribery and
> sheer intimidation... The result is a blanket dark age extend-
> ing from Indonesia to the Atlantic with long shadows falling
> over London, Paris, New York and other centers of Muslim
> exile. Debate is stifled, publishing is stymied and free think-
> ing all but eliminated in the Muslim world.[67]

This dominance of the channels of communication by the political
and economic elite affected the ways in which information spread in
the Arab and non-Arab Muslim world and the very nature of the information itself. Since they worked for organizations seen as government
mouthpieces, journalists commanded little respect among the public
or within the governments they served. For the most part, investigative reporting was nonexistent; challenging official statements or policies was unheard-of. There were no awards for uncovering government
malfeasance and few Western-style journalism schools. As Amin of
AUC has written:

> The central purpose of mass communication programs in
> the Arab world is to prepare generation after generation of
> semi-educated journalists whose job it is to promote the
> "achievements" of the state.[68]

With media quality suspect, Arabs in particular turned to quantity.
It is difficult to convey to those who have not visited the Arab world –
especially places like Beirut, Damascus, Amman, and Cairo – the degree
to which a hunger for information pervades all discussion. Many Arabs
skimmed several newspapers a day as they tried to piece together a
coherent picture of the news; the radio was always on, switching
from one newscast to another. In past decades, the distinctive jingle
of Radio Monte Carlo's Arabic newscast quite literally echoed through

the streets. With the advent of satellite TV, television provided constant background noise in coffeehouses and grocery stores. To a degree seen in the US only during times of national crisis or catastrophe, Arabs were fixated on the events that constantly buffeted their turbulent region. While newspaper circulation was in the single digits, surveys consistently found that some 80 percent of viewers in places like Saudi Arabia and the Gulf received their news from television. That was more viewers than entertainment programs attracted, the exact reverse of the US, where less than 50 percent regularly tuned in to television news.

Quantity versus Quality

But more information did not necessarily mean better information. The manner in which the media reflected official thinking, along with the absence of formal training, meant there was little space for Western-style notions of journalistic accuracy and objectivity to take root. Thus even coverage of issues of no consequence to the government was frequently rife with inaccuracies, innuendo, and falsehoods – some of them bought-and-paid-for, some the result of sloppy or lazy journalism. Put simply, if a reporter was expected by the government to print articles he or she knew were not true, there was little impediment to adopting a similar approach on other stories. In the West, the journalists who were most respected were those considered paragons of objectivity. Conversely, in the Middle East and other parts of the Muslim world, the most respected journalists were known not for unbiased reporting, but for their opinions. This was based on the logic that while the news stories on the front page could not be trusted, the opinion columns offered insights garnered from the writer's access to the corridors of power. For example, the Arab world's best-known journalist, the former editor-in-chief of the Egyptian daily *Al-Ahram*, Mohamed Heikal, was a close friend of Gamal Abdel Nasser at a time when the Egyptian president was seen as the father of Arab nationalism. Heikal's columns thus offered a window on the thinking of the region's most powerful leader. "When all is said and done, Mohamed Hassanein Heikal remains a legacy of journalism at its best," *Al-Ahram* opined in 2007, illustrating the degree to which the distinction between opinion and fact continued to blur.[69]

Beyond that was the very basic issue of a woeful absence of training. "Many working journalists lack the basic skills that would enable them to identify the right story, develop story ideas and investigate interesting and informative stories within a complex environment," according to a report prepared for the British Council in Cairo. "Young journalists often lack direction in their places of work and the competitive nature of the job market pressures professionals into conforming as opposed to carving out the space for new skills and innovative coverage."[70] Nakhle El Hage, the chief editor at the Saudi-owned satellite channel Al-Arabiya, went so far as to say that "500 well-trained Arab journalists would be enough to change the standard of the Arab media."[71] It was not a new problem. "[W]riting is one of the crafts which help society to live...now perfection in the crafts is relative...hence imperfection in writing is due not to a lack of religion or morals but to economic and social causes," the Arab philosopher Ibn Khaldun had written six centuries before.[72]

Given the local media's lack of credibility and the general suspicion of Western sources, what el-Affendi and others have called "a counter-culture" of "unofficial news channels" emerged, in which rumors and conspiracy theories prevailed. As a result, countless unsubstantiated stories – some worthy of the *National Enquirer* – ricocheted through the Middle East every day. For example, riots once broke out in Khartoum after word circulated that foreigners were causing the penises of Sudanese men to disappear by shaking their hands. One victim "felt his penis melt into his body," *Al-Quds al-Arabi* reported.[73] Some of the conspiracy theories were, to a Western mind, equally bizarre. During a spate of bombings in Baghdad, *The New Yorker* quoted a local cleric who had heard "John Kerry is behind this so Bush will lose his Presidency and look bad in front of the world."[74] Other rumors were based on long-standing myths, such as the story that the Wahabi sect of Sunni Islam was an invention of the British as part of a divide-and-rule strategy, an idea first suggested during the colonial era in an apocryphal memoir of a British soldier entitled *Confessions of a British Spy* and repeated by Iraqi Shi'ites during the US occupation.[75] An American professor living in Saudi Arabia in the mid-1980s wrote that one was "likely to feel he lives amid a vast rumor, whose centre is nowhere and whose circumference is everywhere."[76] So all-pervasive were the rumors in Iraq during the first year of the US occupation, for example, that Coalition authorities began putting out a newsletter called the *Baghdad Mosquito* to swat away all the ill-founded stories.

Many of these rumors, frequently repeated and given new life in the press, reflected a set of stereotypes about the US that were, in many ways, the mirror image of those that Americans held about Muslims. As noted by American survey researcher Mark Tessler, "some citizens in Arab and Muslim countries embrace stereotypes every bit as disturbing as our own."[77] Central to these stereotypes was that of the "crusader-Zionist conspiracy" in which "the Western demon [is] bent on the eradication of Islam."[78] Though relatively little scholarly work has been done on portrayals of the US in the media of Arab and Muslim countries, there is substantial anecdotal evidence of bias for anyone who has ever picked up a newspaper in the Muslim world. Writing in an Israeli publication, journalist Adel Darwish argued that anti-Americanism in the Arab language media was "all-encompassing," and included selective showing of negative images of the US, selective language, exaggerated headlines, use of rumor and conspiracy theories in the place of facts, selective reporting, and the selective editing of translated articles from the Western media.[79]

In a study of Arab media coverage of the Arab–Israeli wars, William Rugh noted that while there was "less politically motivated distortion in the Arab media" in 1973 than in 1967, a key theme involved US support for "the Zionist entity."[80] Likewise, an examination of post-9/11 political cartoons from the Muslim world revealed a pattern of themes that included the US as "deceptive" and the moral equivalent of bin Laden.[81]

Arab Satellite Broadcasting

With the arrival of Al-Jazeera in 1996, the very nature of Arab journalism began to change. Based in the tiny Gulf emirate of Qatar, the news and information satellite channel was part of the liberalization effort launched by the new British-educated emir, Sheikh Hamad bin Khalifa al-Thani, who had ousted his father in a bloodless coup the previous year. Without Al-Jazeera, Osama bin Laden might never have achieved the mythic status he would come to enjoy. As the fireside radio chat was President Franklin Delano Roosevelt's "bully pulpit" – the means through which he reached the American people – during World War II, so too did the Qatar-based satellite channel serve as bin Laden's bully pulpit as he launched his military and propaganda assault on the US. Ironically, given later accusations of bias and unprofessionalism, Al-Jazeera's original news team were almost all veterans of the BBC's Arabic television service, which had just withdrawn from an ill-fated joint venture with Orbit TV when it became clear that the BBC and the Saudi royal family – not surprisingly – had different ideas about what constituted journalism. The Al-Jazeera team was given a $140 million subsidy by the emir and a mandate: launch an independent television station free from government scrutiny, control, and manipulation. The staff proceeded to do just that. The channel's journalists saw themselves as agents of democratic change in a region trapped in the grip of autocracies. One official in the Clinton White House called it a "beacon of light,"[82] and Israeli cabinet minister Gideon Ezra told the *Jerusalem Post*: "I wish all Arab media were like Al-Jazeera."[83]

Not everyone was enamored. "Using the Western style, we have broken many taboos," Ibrahim M. Helal, then Al-Jazeera's chief editor, told *The New York Times*. "Of course, we upset most other Arab countries."[84] To say the least. Arab rulers across the region were shocked by this new, largely unfettered approach that, as Mohammed el-Nawawy and Adel Iskandar noted in their book about the channel, was considered "nothing short of heresy."[85] Virtually every Arab government criticized Al-Jazeera. The Saudis were particularly incensed. Al-Jazeera not only impinged on their near-monopoly of satellite channels, but the station had the temerity to give voice to those who would question the House of Saud. As one Saudi newspaper wrote:

> The poisonous ideas that are conveyed via the Western satellite channels are easy to handle because the viewer knows the thought they are trying to convey in advance. However, when this poisonous thought is conveyed via an Arab satellite channel, it becomes all the more dangerous because it is concealing itself behind our culture.[86]

Morocco, Jordan, the Palestinian Authority, Bahrain, and Kuwait all closed Al-Jazeera offices, denied its reporters visas, or temporarily withdrew their ambassadors from Qatar. Al-Jazeera exhibited a "lack of professionalism and neutrality when dealing with Kuwaiti issues," a senior Kuwaiti official told reporters when that country expelled the channel's reporters for the second time.[87] Egypt boycotted an Arab summit in Qatar because of its anger at Al-Jazeera over interviews with Egyptian Islamists. Even at the height of the US invasion, Saddam Hussein expelled one Al-Jazeera correspondent from Baghdad and banned another from reporting, prompting the influential station to flex its muscles by ordering a complete work stoppage by its Baghdad team, thus denying the Iraqi leader direct access to its 35 million viewers. Across the region, governments and individuals alike were shocked when Al-Jazeera began to interview Israeli officials to hear their side of the Israel–Palestine conflict. Such an approach was in keeping with the station's motto: "Opinion and the other opinion."

The impact on the average viewer was profound. Where Arabs once patched together their view of current events through a plethora of news media, Al-Jazeera became the touchstone. As Nadia al-Saqqaf, editor-in-chief of the *Yemen Times* explained, "In Yemen, we hear about what is happening in our country through Al-Jazeera or CNN before it gets reported on the local TV. Sometimes it never does."[88]

The age of government monopoly of information and Western media imperialism was coming to an end. For the Arab public, the world would never look the same again. For Arab journalists, the impact was, if anything, even more dramatic.

2

Satellite TV and Arab Democracy

Al-sihafa [journalism] is an essential tool of democracy....
Freedom is the source of light for *al-sihafa* and the objective
desired by writers and thinkers who know how to employ it
and defend it.

Rafiq al-Maqdisi, *Fann al-sihafa*
(The Craft of Journalism), 1946

The red and white banners of Lebanon's anti-Syrian protests in the
spring of 2005 were a testament to the transformational power of the
Arab media revolution. The color scheme was made-for-TV by a team
of Lebanese advertising executives who, like the tens of thousands who
poured into the streets, were inspired by Ukraine's telegenic Orange
Revolution, whose orange-clad protestors waving orange banners provided vivid television images that were beamed around the world.
Arab television coverage of Lebanon in turn helped propel embryonic
pro-democracy movements from Egypt to Bahrain, whose mantra
Kifaya (Enough) – which essentially meant they had "enough" of the
entrenched regimes – became a media catchphrase.

Without Al-Jazeera and the new constellation of Arab satellite
broadcasters, it is unlikely there would ever have been a "Cedar Revolution," as a Bush Administration official quickly dubbed the spontane-
ous protests that ended Syria's 29-year military presence in Lebanon.[1]

The assassination of popular former Prime Minister Rafiq Hariri was the spark that lit the fires of protest, but plenty of other Lebanese politicians had been murdered in the past, often at Syria's hands. Anyone protesting back then faced a similar fate. What was different this time was that the Arab world was watching. It was an unprecedented event: Arabs standing up to a dictatorial regime. Syria had once wiped out a significant portion of the population in its own rebellious city of Hama. But that massacre had taken place far from the probing eyes of the world back in the days when Arab reporters did what they were told. Al-Jazeera had changed the rules of the game. Eventually, Syrian President Bashar al-Assad – who forlornly demanded that TV cameras "zoom out" to show the Beirut crowds weren't as large as they appeared in close-up – recognized that the new media landscape had altered geopolitical realities and ordered his troops home.

On the surface, Lebanon would seem to bolster the notion that media is, as some have called it, the "arsenal for democracy."[2] Yet its impact can easily be overstated. Political scientists like to note that journalists – and those who study them – tend to have an inflated sense of the media's influence. That's particularly true when it comes to talk of television and emerging democracies. There is a strong case to be made that the unblinking 24/7 lens of the Arab media provided an electronic safety net to the crowds assembled in Martyr's Square to demand Syria's withdrawal; but so, too, did the political cover resulting from Bush administration pressure on Damascus that had – almost coincidentally – been building in preceding months.

Television did not drive out the Syrians, any more than it gave birth to some new form of Lebanese democracy. A complex confluence of events – accelerated by television – produced the withdrawal. And freed of the Syrian presence, Lebanon quickly settled back into political gridlock built on an outdated power-sharing arrangement that had not substantially changed in more than half a century, then once more descended into violence in the summer of 2006. As for a democratic "domino effect" among all those countries watching the Lebanon protests on television, by decade's end not one of the Middle East's entrenched regimes had changed. *Kifaya* (Enough) may have been the mantra of the masses, but "the son always rises" was an equally fitting catchphrase for Arab politics, where dynastic rule was the preferred form of politics, with the sons either ascending to power, as in Syria, Jordan, Morocco and the sheikhdoms of the Gulf, or waiting in the wings, as in Egypt and Libya.

TV cannot alone *create* change. It is an *agent* of change – more specifically, a tool used by the architects of change. There is a broad and deep literature documenting the fact that, even in the US, where journalists see their mission as that of defending democracy, the media rarely leads public opinion, but instead reflects it. "The error," wrote J. Herbert Altschull in his seminal work on the power of the media, "is to fail to recognize that *the news media are agencies of someone else's power*."[3] Political scientists maintain that this is particularly true in the period before democracy takes root. This argument can be found as far back as the now-dated *Four Theories of the Press*, which argued that media is *shaped by*, rather than *shapes*, social and political structures.[4] Those theories were developed in an age of Cold War confrontation; the authors were writing from a worldview that saw a geopolitical landscape in which democracy was pitted against totalitarianism. Perhaps most importantly, in the context of a discussion of media and democracy, the "footprint" of the television signal in those days largely followed national boundaries. The arrival of trans-border television, particularly in a part of the world where governments always controlled the airwaves, introduced a huge new variable into the equation. As Arab media scholar Naomi Sakr has pointed out, "people gain a different sense of their own potential when they can use electronic media to overcome restrictions on social interaction that are imposed by physical space."[5] Yet the core truth remained, the media both *shapes* and *mirrors* public attitudes. That was as true in the Middle East as in the West. "Arab writers and columnists have a tendency to affirm populist notions, whether they're good, bad, factual or false," according to Abdul Rahman al-Habib, a columnist with Saudi Arabia's *Al-Watan* newspaper. "They write what people want to hear. They write not to educate or challenge the readers' notions, but rather to affirm the readers' pre-conceived opinions and views."[6]

As the final communiqué of a 2005 conference on "Media and Good Governance" in the Arab world put it, "The role of the media in supporting good governance is conditional on the freedom and the independence of the media as well as its professionalism," and

> the lip service pledges made by the governments through various official declarations have not been translated into serious and effective acts. ... An arsenal of laws and regulations have remained that block any attempts for accountability and transparency, both in the areas of access to receive and impart information ... which make the attempts of the press to question corruption and abuse of power next to impossible.[7]

Most political scientists subscribe to the view that a free press that helps citizens to understand policy decisions is an essential element of democracy. But it does not, in and of itself, produce democracy. The actual political effects are "varied and highly conditional."[8] Shanto Iyengar has demonstrated that media can "prime" audiences by highlighting some issues and ignoring others, as well as "frame" stories in such a way as to contextualize an issue to bolster a particular viewpoint,[9] but, as one study of media in Eastern Europe concluded, these effects are less likely to *influence* public opinion and attitudes than to *reinforce* them.[10] Legal scholar Monroe Price is among those who emphasize the complex relationship between media and the emergence of democracy. He argues convincingly that while media liberalization can be a facilitating factor in the emergence of democracy, it is neither a requirement nor a sufficient cause by itself to bring about political transformation. The factors that form the relationship between media and democracy are many and varied. In short, "the conventional wisdom is most commonly found to be inadequate or simply wrong."[11]

Even when media does help to produce change, it does not necessarily produce the kind of change democracy advocates in the West might hope for. Witness Hamas' 2005 election victory in Palestine. "For every society in which a 'people's power' revolution is helped along by international cheering squads and satellite television, another is daily becoming more cosmopolitan while adhering to traditional (and often authoritarian) practices," according to Catharin Dalpino, a former US diplomat.[12]

That may have been true, but there were also signs that Arab television was emerging not only as the new battlefield of ideas, but even showed signs of supplanting at least some of the traditionally more bloody battlefields of the Middle East. Witness Beirut in the waning months of 2006. In an earlier era, the assassination of Christian leader Pierre Gemayel would likely have been the spark that ignited a new round of civil war. But instead, hundreds of thousands of Lebanese supporters of the so-called March 14 Movement took to the streets in a televised reprise of the rallies that forced Syria's withdrawal. Then, in answer days later, hundreds of thousands of Hezbollah supporters staged their own mass protests, likewise transmitted live, 24/7 across the region and around the world. For the moment, the power of the camera had trumped the power of the gun.

Restructuring the Arab Media Landscape

There has been a television revolution in the Arab world, of that there is no doubt. As noted earlier, Arab satellite television news was a riposte to CNN, the BBC and other Western channels flooding the airwaves of the Middle East. For Arab governments, satellite TV was an attempt to take back some control of the message, even if it meant that long-suppressed ideas might also seep in.

The arrival of Arab satellite television brought urban renewal to Marshall McLuhan's "global village." No longer did all the world view events through a Western lens. But neither could Arab governments any longer control the televised message. Most of the clichés that have been written about Al-Jazeera and its successors are true: The genie was out of the bottle; with their fingers in the electronic dike, Arab governments tried vainly to stem the flow of information, with only limited success. Al-Jazeera reframed – and in many cases *created* – the debate. By serving as a forum for diverse – and once rarely heard – views, the Qatar-based channel and its imitators provided an outlet where otherwise there was none, establishing "a common, core Arab narrative."[13] But that electronic revolution had yet to be matched by even the beginnings of a political revolution. Satellite TV's grand opening of the marketplace of ideas was an important first step in the process of democratization, but it was just that – a first step.

Hazem Saghieh, a columnist with the pan-Arab daily *Al-Hayat*, once told an international editors gathering that "Al-Jazeera is the most influential [political] party in the Arabic World"[14] It has also been suggested that Middle East reality shows like *Super Star* and *Star Academy*, on which viewers vote for their favorites, offered Arabs their first real taste of democracy.[15] Both these observations were vast oversimplifications. What arose on Al-Jazeera and its successors, like Al-Arabiya, Abu Dhabi TV, LBC, Future TV and the rest, was a forum for discussion, offering debates that were "a verbalization of Arab publics' critiques of government."[16] On some level, these broadcasts acted as a safety valve, releasing the pent-up anger within the Arab body politic without overtly threatening governments. News programs meanwhile, shined a spotlight on some of the worst excesses of the region's regimes. "For democratic institutions to survive and flourish, there has to be a source of trusted information," writes Philip Meyer.[17] But mass communication does not equal – or necessarily produce – mass democratization. As Rami Khouri, editor-at-large for Beirut's *Daily Star*, told me, "There remains a large gap between an informed citizenry and an empowered citizenry." For evidence, one need look no further than Iraq, with its plethora of media outlets and paucity of political stability.

"Democracy may be a political system, but it is also a social ethos," argues Fawaz Turki, a former *Arab News* columnist fired for criticizing governments in the Muslim world. "How responsive can a country be to such an ethos when its people have, for generations, existed with an ethic of fear – fear of originality, fear of innovation, fear of spontaneity, fear of life itself – and have had instilled in them the need to accept orthodoxy, dependence and submission?"[18]

The 2005 Egyptian elections demonstrated the gulf between the act of *reporting on* the democratic process and the *production of* a democratic result. The fact that Egyptians and other Arab viewers of satellite television were able to see bloody images of baton-wielding thugs driving opposition voters away from the polls, hear human rights officials denouncing the results, or watch as opposition presidential candidate Ayman Nour was taken away to prison, did nothing to halt the abuses or prevent the Mubarak regime from declaring the vote "completely fair."[19] The elections "helped to open up public debate in the country," Human Rights Watch concluded, "[b]ut the main features of decades-long authoritarian rule remain in place, making a truly free and fair election at this moment beyond reach."[20] Real democracy requires the infrastructure of civil society. In Egypt, that was embryonic at best. In many other parts of the Arab world, it was virtually nonexistent. By the 2007 local elections in Egypt, the media had been driven back into its corral through a campaign of intimidation, which a lawyer for the Press Syndicate estimated included more than one thousand summonses and five hundred court cases.[21]

Further hobbling the media's ability to contribute to an informed electorate was the fact that a culture of secrecy prevailed in the Arab world. "The sad fact is that journalists are left too often without the facts, and in the absence of reliable information the entire press, official, opposition, independent, call it what you will, is reduced to a single enormous rumour mill," according to Gamal Mkrumah of Egypt's government-owned *Al-Ahram weekly*.[22]

A study of media coverage of the 2006 Bahraini elections by a human rights group concluded that despite "the relative margin of liberty in Bahrain...the media played a role in hindering democracy instead of supporting it" through self-censorship, favoritism, and one-sided access. The report concluded:

> When radio and TV channels lack independence and refuse to take a campaigning role, and when the national newspapers lack impartiality and professionalism, and when candidates lack effective means to reach voters, that all reflects negatively on participation, the voter's right to access to information, and their ability to make the right choice, which would put under question the credibility of the entire democratic process.[23]

The report was issued by the Bahrain Center for Human Rights, whose own Internet site was blocked by the government prior to the election, one of several dozen websites shut down by the authorities in the tiny island nation. Subsequently, the government would detain dozens of journalists and ban publication of a controversial report that claimed the Sunni Muslim royal family had financed an effort to undermine the majority Shi'a during the elections through tactics that included handing out Bahraini citizenship to Sunnis from other countries. Elections in Yemen that same year saw broadcast outlets relegate opposition candidates to the late night hours and newspapers simply reprint identical accounts of President Ali Abdullah Saleh's rallies written by the official national news agency. Numerous websites were blocked, and in the run-up to the election, five new newspapers, suspected of being funded by the government, appeared on the street, reporting positively about the president and attacking journalists who took a less laudatory approach. Syria's government-controlled media took a somewhat modestly professional approach to that country's 2007 elections, yet journalists, bloggers, and human rights activists regularly found themselves being questioned or behind bars.

As one study of the media and political evolution in Eastern Europe concluded, "democratization through the media is highly improbable, if not outright impossible."[24] As for infotainment and other forms of pseudo-democratic participation, charges of vote-rigging and manipulation on Arab TV reality shows led some commentators to draw parallels with actual elections in the region, where regimes cook the results if they don't like them. Marc Lynch has noted, "Like Al-Jazeera's online polls, reality TV gives the illusion of participation and democracy, but it is easily manipulated and has no real impact on the world."[25]

Incremental Change

That is not to say the news broadcast and talk shows of the satellite television channels – and the journalists who staff them – were not having an impact. "There is no *Kifaya* if there is no TV," Abdulwahab Badrakhan, a former senior editor at *Al-Hayat*, told me. Television, insisted Al-Jazeera senior producer Samir Khader, was "part of the revolution." In places like Tunisia, where the government and its cronies controlled all mass circulation media, "people in different towns and villages in Tunis who can't know what happens in their country are able to know those things and this creates a new public opinion in our society. It is a very new situation that makes a pressure on the government," according to Rashid Khashana, editor of a free opposition newspaper. Giselle Khouri, host of a Beirut-based program on Al-Jazeera's rival, Al-Arabiya, believes a watershed for the Arab media came with the second Palestinian intifada (uprising). She points to the September 2000 coverage of the death of Mohammed al-Durra, a 12-year old

Palestinian boy whose final moments, shielded by his father as they were trapped under a hail of Israeli gunfire, were caught on videotape by a Palestinian cameraman and shown around the world. "I guess this is the point where the Arab media realized the importance of Arab media and Arab television," she told me later. "Because the opinion *mondiale* changed – their opinion about terrorism, about the Arab world, about being a victim."

Egypt is a place where torture is institutionalized. Human Rights Watch calls the abuse of prisoners in the country's jails "epidemic,"[26] Amnesty International says it is "common and systematic,"[27] and the US State Department's 2007 Country Report on Egypt concluded that "police, security personnel, and prison guards routinely tortured and abused prisoners and detainees."[28] The country was one of several to which the CIA, under the now-infamous rendition program, sent prisoners to be interrogated using techniques too harsh for the agency's own operatives to administer.[29]

So when two Egyptian policemen were convicted of torture in late 2007 and sent to prison, it was a landmark victory for human rights activists. It was also a seminal moment for the media. The case, in which Cairo police used a nightstick to sodomize a cab driver in their custody, came to light only when Egyptian blogger Wael Abbas posted cell phone video of the assault on YouTube, sparking a media feeding-frenzy that ultimately forced the government to prosecute the kind of conduct that had long been condoned. It was a reminder that while media had yet to create broad political change, its impact on policy was beginning to become evident – even if still nascent enough that one could easily cite most instances when it had been apparent.

The Lebanon conflict in the summer of 2006 was one of the most vivid examples of media driving Arab government policy. At the beginning of the conflict, Saudi Arabia and other Sunni-majority Gulf states criticized the Shi'ite militia Hezbollah for provoking the Israeli assault on Lebanon. In the early days of the war, Al-Jazeera's main competitor, Saudi-owned Al-Arabiya, downplayed the conflict. But it was not long before it joined Al-Jazeera, the privately owned Lebanon Broadcasting Corporation (LBC), and Hezbollah's own channel, Al-Manar, in providing wall-to-wall 24/7 coverage of the war. The Arab world was transfixed. Public opinion from Morocco to Yemen united firmly behind Hezbollah's defense of the Lebanese homeland. Tensions between Sunni and Shi'a, political differences between Arab nationalists and Islamists, were – for the moment – largely set aside. Crowds in Cairo held high, side-by-side, pictures of the late Arab nationalist leader Gamal Abdel Nasser and Hezbollah chief Hassan Nasrallah, an unheard-of juxtaposition. As the conflict dragged on, LBC producer Marwan Matni, a Christian, later told me, "I felt myself changing. Lebanon was under attack. We were all Lebanese. By the end, I, too, felt myself to be Hezbollah." The sentiment was shared by Arabs across the region to a degree governments could not ignore. Soon after hostilities ended, Nasrallah was welcomed in the Gulf as a conquering hero. "The Lebanese people and their resistance have achieved the first Arab victory, something we had longed for," said Qatar's emir, Hamad bin Khalifa al-Thani.[30] In a matter of a few weeks, Gulf policy had come 180 degrees.

The impact of media was also seen on what were once purely internal issues, long ignored or hidden by the tame domestic media. A case in point was that of an 18-year old Saudi girl who was gang raped by seven men when they discovered her sitting in a car with a male schoolmate, who was also gang raped. Under Saudi law, it is illegal for an unrelated man and woman to be alone. When the woman reported the assault, she was arrested and eventually sentenced to six months in prison and 90 lashes for violating the separation of sexes law. But when she went public to protest the sentence, a rare move in that controlled society, the court increased the punishment to 200 lashes, because of "her attempt to aggravate and influence the judiciary through the media." Her plight set off a bitter debate in the Saudi media, which dubbed her "Qatif girl," for the town where the attack occurred. "Qatif girl's dream of redeeming any of her self-respect through the judicial system was crushed in front of her own eyes," the *Saudi Gazette* reported.[31]

The story was quickly picked up by pan-Arab satellite channels, with talk show hosts like LBC's Shatha Omar pitting government officials, the girl's lawyer, and her husband in live debates. The ministry of justice reacted to the media fracas by, as one Saudi blogger put it, "slandering the girl and portray[ing] her like a slut who deserved to be raped."[32] Adding fuel to the fire, an appeals court judge told the Saudi daily *Okaz* that the controversy was all a conspiracy on the part of the foreign media and said everyone involved in the incident – including the girl – should receive the death penalty.[33] By that point, the story was making headlines around the world and the Saudi government was firmly on the defensive, with the White House calling the situation "outrageous," Canada decrying the sentence as "barbaric" and Saudi commentators on both ends of the political spectrum expressing concern about the damage to the country's reputation. In the face of the domestic and international uproar, King Abdullah finally stepped in and overruled the court with a pardon read live on Saudi television by the justice minister. The crime, said the King, was "brutal," and a pardon was justified because "the woman and the man who was with her were subject to torture and stubbornness that is considered in itself sufficient in disciplining both of them and to learn from the lesson."[34] It was a ruling designed to placate both the critics and those on the right who felt the girl deserved punishment, but it also represented an undeniable, and unprecedented, response to media-driven pressure by a man labeled by Reporters Without Borders as one of the Arab world's "predators of press freedom."[35]

Along with violence against women in places like Saudi Arabia and Jordan, many other once-forbidden issues were being reported in the Arab media. In 2005, UNICEF, the UN children's agency, noted a sharp spike in the number of inquiries from journalists on topics such as HIV-AIDS and female genital mutilation (FGM). One reason was that the rise of Arab satellite television brought a growing acceptance of discussion about human sexuality. That had filtered down to national print media as well. Front-page reporting of the deaths of two young Egyptian girls who died after botched circumcisions sparked an unprecedented debate that led to a national campaign against the practice, led by Suzanne Mubarak, wife of Egypt's president. Much the same was happening with other sensitive topics. Governments like those of Egypt, Saudi Arabia, and the United Arab Emirates were still jailing on homosexuality charges men who were diagnosed as HIV-positive, but fact-based stories on the disease, its methods of transmission, and treatment were beginning to appear in media across the region.

Electronic Towers of Political Babble

Arab satellite channels represent an array of interests that span the ideological divide; from Hezbollah's Al-Manar to the LBC, founded by Lebanon's right-wing Christian Phalangist Party and later financed by a group of Lebanese and Saudi investors. "Arabs [have] proved that they have different voices," said Giselle Khouri. The strength was that channel-surfers in the Middle East could get a taste of a diverse range of opinion. The weakness was that everyone had an ideological axe to grind.

Lebanon itself was a microcosm of this discontinuity. A cacophony of opinions had always characterized the Lebanese media landscape, where news organizations were largely bought and paid for by paymasters representing the entire spectrum of Arab political thought. Recent years had witnessed an ebb and flow of that politicization. The lead-up to the Hariri assassination saw what Nabil Dajani, chairman of the Department of Mass Communication at the American University in Beirut, called a "re-feudalization of the public sphere" in which the media in general, and television in particular, "reflect and in turn reinforce the characteristics and contradictions of Lebanon's political and tribal confessional society."[36] That gave way to the aforementioned emergent sense of unity following the assassination campaign against reporters, which then collapsed in the face of the Israeli–Hezbollah conflict in the summer of 2006 as various media outlets initially took up positions for and against the Shi'ite militia, then coalesced in opposition to the mounting Israeli attacks that would claim more than 1,000 lives, and eventually splintered once more, assuming positions reflecting the heightened tensions the war produced among the country's various political and feudal factions. "Lebanon does not have a free press," argued Dajani. "Wealth, power and sectarianism are intimately intertwined in the Lebanese media, and knowledge plays no mediating role." Instead:

> What we find today in Lebanese television is a distinct imbalance between public interest and the interest of the political, financial and economic forces in the country [and] [t]elevision's new divisions advance the larger agenda of the tribal/sectarian authorities of which they are a small part.[37]

That was brought home when, not long after Dajani wrote those words, Hezbollah briefly took over West Beirut and immediately stormed Future TV and its sister newspaper, *Al-Mustaqbal*, both controlled by the rival Hariri family. Despite such communal tendencies, Hanna Ziadeh credited Lebanon's domestic television channels with "creating a democratic space, of establishing a greater relationship of trust and identification with the fractured Lebanese public than any pan-Arab TV is able to establish with the national subdivisions of their pan-Arab public."[38] However, that credit may have been premature. The Lebanese media might have been free of overt government controls and focused on local, rather than regional issues, but as Dajani pointed out, "[f]reedom of expression by the media does not bring about democracy except when access to all media channels is made possible to all Lebanese groups. True democracy cannot be achieved when the media serve as advocates, limiting access to some factions and denying this access to others." Television helped the masses in Martyr's Square achieve with the Syrians what militia fighters achieved against the Israelis in the South in 2000 and Hezbollah repeated in the summer of 2006: they drove out an invader. Changes to the political structures that would make Lebanon a more representative democracy were likely to be equally hard-won. That became evident in the postwar power struggle between Hezbollah and the Lebanese government.

In the previous three decades, such confrontations quickly resulted in armed conflict. An argument can be made that 24/7 pan-Arab television coverage of Hezbollah's mass rally and subsequent sit-in encampment outside the prime minister's office provided the Shi'ite group with a form of political leverage previously available only through the barrel of a gun. But the limits of this new virtual political sphere quickly became apparent. As regional TV channels grew bored with the interminable (and largely sedentary) sit-in, the eye of the camera shifted away to other, more "interesting" stories. It was not long after that the first armed clashes took place, quickly followed – on the eve of the anniversary of Hariri's assassination – by the bombing of two busloads of civilians, an act which – amplified by television – sent a shudder through Lebanese society and the Arab world as a whole. The old ways still had their place. Yet the following day, tens of thousands of Lebanese were back in Martyr's Square to mark Hariri's death, as pro-government politicians played to the live television cameras that they knew were once more carrying their message across the region and around the world.

Impact of Local and Regional Media

Ironically, the source of satellite television's influence was also its Achilles Heel. Pan-Arab TV functions as a political change agent on a regional, rather than national, level. Al-Jazeera and the others focused on pan-Arab issues, such as Iraq, Palestine, and major stories like the Lebanon crisis. Purely domestic topics were largely outside the purview of these channels. "The local issues are the primary issues that touch the human directly, just like life: education, poverty, unemployment, and corruption. And these issues are not dealt with closely on satellite channels for many reasons," Jaber Obeid, a presenter at Abu Dhabi TV, told an industry gathering. "Unfortunately some of the satellite channels run after broad headlines like Palestine and Iraq. But when it comes to dealing with political participation and plurality in a certain country, they do not deal with issues like that – like corruption and unemployment – that concerns the citizen directly." Yet the terrestrial channels did not tackle them either.

"There is huge amount of information that is missing because the local stations will not provide it to the viewer and we do not provide it to the viewer because it is local," Al-Arabiya news chief Nabil Khatib explained one day, as we sat in his glass office off the bustling studio/ newsroom. "Things that would make the Arabs better citizens by knowing more about their own realities they are not getting it from anywhere. So there is a huge portion of important data that is missing from their consciousness and this is negatively affecting any democratization process."

"On the local level we ignore the local aspects of interest to the people, such as raising children and educating them and leave these national issues for larger issues such as Iraq and Palestine," Abd el-Latif el-Menawy, head of news at Egypt TV, said in the same session with Obeid. "This is one way that some of the state owned channels use to escape, because of their inability to tackle local topics. Most of

[my] colleagues working in the local media lack the concept of local news." Aside from Lebanon, those local stations were controlled by the very governments that had so much to lose in the event of change. "We cannot afford to be objective," Hussein Jamal, the head of political programming in Kuwait television, candidly told the same group. "Redlines are drawn around political issues" that are both regional and local:

> The issue of the Sahara, the issue of relations between one country and the other, a local internal issue between the opposition and the government, the issue of the elections. Look at the television channels; if you allow a candidate in the elections to appear for 30 seconds, then you should also show the other candidate. And this is why we gave up the candidates. We tried not to deal with these political issues.

As a result, audiences largely abandoned the state-run channels for the more vibrant landscape of satellite. "Most Saudis respect the international press more, and they neither watch their TV channels nor listen to the local radio because of those outlets' inability to compete with their global and regional counterparts, which provide better content and more entertaining programs," said Saudi radio reporter Samar Fatany.[39] Scrambling to recover from what industry analyst Jihad Fakhreddine called "the clinical death of most local TV markets,"[40] government channels were trying to reinvent themselves by introducing slick new sets, flashy graphics, and waving bags of money at reporters and anchors who made their reputation at the regional channels, but there was little change in the actual content of the newscasts.

When the pan-Arab broadcasters did tackle big "domestic" stories, the contrast between regional and local media was often stark. That was vividly played out during the April 2008 bread riots in Egypt, centered on a textile mill in the Delta town of Mahalla. There, thousands of protesters clashed with government troops in violence that left several dead, including a 15-year old bystander, hundreds injured and resulted in scores of arrests. Al-Jazeera and other pan-Arab channels featured graphic footage of the violence; still photos of protesters stomping on posters of Egyptian President Hosni Mubarak and bleeding victims of the violence appeared on the websites of Egyptian bloggers and foreign news organizations, until the government banned journalists from the area. But such images were harder to find in the domestic media. Even Egypt-based pan-Arab broadcasters like Orbit, Dream, and Al-Mehwar, which were supposed to have significantly more freedom than the "domestic" media, largely avoided showing the more dramatic scenes. Editors of current affairs shows at those channels – they were not allowed to air traditional newscasts – privately told me that they had been warned by the Mubarak regime to tone down their coverage and to make sure their talk shows included a heavy representation of the government's viewpoint. The implicit "or else" did not need to be stated: just days before, Egypt had pulled the plug on Al-Hiwar, a London-based channel highly critical of the regime, which had been distributed on the Egyptian-owned satellite. And when Al-Jazeera tried to become more "local" by starting a daily news program broadcast from a studio in Morocco, the Rabat government quickly pulled the plug and charged the bureau chief with airing "false news."

Both moves were facilitated by the 2008 approval of an Arab League Satellite Charter, authored by the Egyptians and Saudis, who controlled the two main satellites in the region, Nilesat and Arabsat. The charter contained vague language warning against jeopardizing "social peace, national unity, public order and general propriety" and ordering that channels must protect "the supreme interests of the Arab countries."[41] Other sections warned against offending "moral, social and cultural values"[42] and "threatening national unity, spreading propaganda and harming the overarching interests of the country."[43] Similar catchall phrases had long been used to shut down newspapers, block Internet sites and jail journalists. "We are living in a very hostile legislative environment," observed Yemeni editor Samir Raheb, editor of an independent paper in Yemen that was closed two days after its launch.

Arab League Charter supporters insisted the document, and similar domestic legal regulations under consideration in Egypt and elsewhere, was aimed at hard-line Islamist channels that were allegedly radicalizing the youth; but the silencing of Al-Hiwar, a secular anti-regime channel, just weeks after the charter was adopted appeared to put lie to that claim. So too, did subsequent raids in Cairo to confiscate satellite transmission equipment used by Al-Jazeera and other international broadcasters, the closure of the Cairo offices of several foreign satellite channels, a campaign against satellite channels in the state-run Egyptian media, and the introduction of a draft law in the Egyptian parliament that would prohibit journalists from undermining "social peace," "national unity," "pubic order," and "public values."[44]

As the Mahalla riots dragged on, dozens of activists were arrested in security sweeps in Cairo. Bloggers were among the targets, including "Facebook Girl," a 27-year old woman who created a group on the social networking site that became the focal point for a one-day national strike in support of the Mahalla workers.[45] The government's attitude was summed up by Prime Minister Ahmed Nazif when, during a speech at Cairo University, he told a student in the audience who defended Facebook Girl, "There is a thin line between expressing your opinion and encouraging destruction, striking and rioting."[46] The fact that the student who asked the question was arrested and briefly detained a few days later underlined just how thin that line was in the eyes of the government.

Amid the Egyptian riots and roundups, which coincided with local elections widely condemned as rigged, the reporting in government-owned *Al-Ahram* seemed to hark back to an earlier era. As the paper framed it, the government's response to the riots was magnanimous: "President Hosni Mubarak agreed yesterday to give a one-month bonus to the workers in the Mahalla textile factory, in addition to a 15-day bonus granted to textile workers throughout the republic in appreciation of their noble positions." *Al-Ahram*'s "framing" of the story was an example of the problem so succinctly described by Tarek Abdel-Gaber, director of www.masrelyoum.com and a former correspondent for Egypt TV: "[When covering stories] [d]omestically, there are instructions about things." It was something faced by reporters on "domestic" media across the region. For Palestine TV, according to director general Bassim Abu Samaya, "The politician is the one who decides if the media will follow up on the political issues or the economic and social issues." Rashid Khashana, editor of a free opposition weekly in Tunisia, where the government maintained an iron grip over the media, reporters, and editors, said his colleagues were "embarrassed" because a country that once had a free press now required reporters "to bring news from the official agency and they can't change any word in this press releases."

Samir Khader of Al-Jazeera recalled that when he worked at Jordan TV, so pervasive was the notion that they were working as an extension of the government that staffers were not allowed to call themselves journalists. "It was forbidden," he told me. That same psychology exists at some government-owned newspapers. "If you look at media locally within the state, the journalists look upon themselves as officials paid by somebody, mainly by the state, and not as journalists, free people, holding their heads up and doing a profession," according to Aref Hiijawi, director of programs at Al-Jazeera and former head of the Media Institute at Birzeit University on the West Bank. Kuwaiti editor Mohammad al-Rumaihi agreed. "In general, Arab journalists are good politicians and lousy journalists."

For Palestinian journalists, the challenges of breaking out of that mold could be particularly complicated. "First, there are the families and the society," Al-Jazeera's Hijawi told me in 2007, "because the authority has been broken down by the Israeli occupation so the families are masters of the society. You cannot criticize a minister, not because he is a minister and the authority is behind him or any of the security apparatuses; no, it is because his family is big. Number two, I would say is the militias, and they are in abundance now. Number three is our heritage. You have also other countries you can feel their pressure. And then there are the religious people who have become very powerful."

That problem was not confined to Palestine. According to Othman al-Sini of *Al-Watan*, the greatest pressure on the media in Saudi Arabia came not from the government, but from reactionary elements of society. "If I write an article about the war in Iraq, about what the terrorists are doing there, I find a lot of people against me," he told me. "If I talk about reform or enlightening I find a lot of people they are against this. If I write one about women driving cars or cinemas, I do not find any problem from the government. But the conservatives are very deaf people, so they fight us."

"You [even] have to be careful about what you say about crowd control in the Hajj [the annual pilgrimage to Mecca]," according to Saudi journalist Abeer Mishkas.[47] Such pressure on nonconforming journalists ranged from overt attacks by religious militants in places like Iraq, Palestine, Yemen, and Algeria, to undercover "infiltration" of newsrooms by Islamists in the Sudan, to more subtle pressures akin to the lobbying the US media faced from religious organizations.

In one example of the problem, Salafist groups in Bahrain and the local branch of the Muslim Brotherhood "declared war" on the country's leading newspaper, *Al-Ayyam*, because of its alleged "liberal" leanings. "The Islamist groups have been calling in their speeches at the mosques to lead campaigns against any newspaper that clashes with their demands and direction in order to scar their image, their advertising market and annual subscription rates," the pan-Arab website elaph. com reported.[48]

Fear of backlash from religious conservatives, says Hassan Ibrahim, leads to self-censorship on issues of religion. "I believe there is still a very pervasive feeling in the Arab media that reporters need to pander to fundamentalists and to Islamic causes," he explained. "So, for example, if a reporter is to ask a Saudi Arabian about the role of the *Mutawa'* [religious police] in the Saudi life, they would have to start by saying, 'We all realize that it is good in Islam for all to observe the rules.' You have to first to explain to the audience your Islamic credentials. Even a reporter with a slightly more daring or secular agenda will make sure he is not offending their beliefs. To me, this is really sad."

The assassination of journalists in Lebanon; the jailing of journalists in Syria; the legal, physical, and psychological harassment of journalists in Egypt; the Middle East was still a place where journalists could, as in the case of one outspoken Saudi editor, be arrested for "harboring destructive thoughts."[49] When Libya's most prominent political prisoner, Fathi al-Jahmi, was jailed after he called Mu'ammar Qaddafi a dictator in an interview with the US government satellite channel Al-Hurra, a Libyan security official explained, "He's mentally disturbed and we're worried he will cause a problem for us."[50] A report by the Arab Network for Human Rights Information chronicled a campaign against journalists in Egypt, Tunisia, and Bahrain that included detentions, physical attacks, disappearances and "the most degrading violations, such as framing criminal cases against those opposition forces, attempting to defame their reputations and spreading fear amongst citizens to prevent them from participating in public affairs."[51] Women journalists were particularly at risk with threats of sexual assault and rumor campaigns designed to undermine their reputations. Tunisian police fabricated pornographic photos of *Kalima* editor Sihem Bensedrine and circulated them publicly. Plainclothes police even approached her children at school and showed them the pictures, another Tunisian journalist told me. To embarrass a Tunisian journalist popularly known as Om Ziad, who was in her sixties at the time, authorities Photoshopped pictures of her husband of having sex with another woman. To mark International Women's Day in 2009, the freedom of expression group Article 19 released a study that found women journalists in Yemen were "regularly subject to public slander" in publications owned by the government. The group noted that, "Yemen is a conservative society which has a rigid code of 'honor' and insinuations against an individual's morality can have a devastating impact."[52]

Criminal libel laws in many countries meant that journalists who tried to root out corruption and uncover malfeasance often found themselves being sent to jail as a result of lawsuits filed by the subjects of their stories. And truth was no defense. A reporter and editor for a newspaper in Alexandria, Egypt, for example, were given prison sentences after being convicted of libel, even though their corruption story was factually correct. That kind of through-the-looking-glass reality took many forms. Tunisia hijacked the websites of opposition publications, either replacing the publication with a fabrication or putting up a notice that the site no longer existed. Yemeni authorities did the same with whole newspapers. To discredit the paper or mislead its readers, the authorities "take a newspaper, they clone it and they publish it with exactly the same heading and they even use the same names of the journalists – they clone the journalists," Abdel Karim al-Khaiwani told a 2008 World Association of Newspapers (WAN) conference in Beirut. The former editor-in-chief of Yemen's *Al-Shoura* newspaper, al-Khaiwani had served a one year prison term in 2004 for "insulting the president," then was harassed for several years after being freed and was eventually arrested and detained for a month in 2007. After his release on bail, he was abducted by gunmen, beaten, and threatened with death if he kept criticizing the government. The following year, he was arrested and sentenced to six years in prison for allegedly conspiring with Yemeni rebels. The evidence consisted of notes of his interview with the rebel leader and photos of militia-men. Such terrorism-related charges were a common tactic of Arab governments after 9/11; conflating coverage with conspiracy was a handy tactic for hiding internal unrest as when the Yemeni security forces in 2009 seized and burned tens of thousands of copies of the *Al-Ayyam*, laid siege to the newspaper's office, confiscated copies of six other newspapers and ordered the government-controlled printer to completely stop producing another, *Al-Watani*, and individual news-paper employees received threats – such as having their throats slit – all because they had been covering clashes between armed protesters and government troops in the southern part of the country. But al-Khaiwani, who was eventually pardoned by the president, was ada-mant that Yemeni journalists would continue to speak truth to power, no matter the cost. "If we need a better future then we have to make it with our pens and with our dramas. Yes, the price is high, but the press is a tool for change. I am confident that any nation made by the ideas of its citizens would be much better than any nation forced by any ruler," he told colleagues at a WAN conference.

Such commitment could be heard from journalists coming from the length and breadth of the Arab world. "Maybe we are very far, maybe we are very small, maybe we are of a different nature, but freedom must be implemented everywhere," said Mohamed Rabeh, executive director of Mauritania's *Al-Rai Al-Am*. Jamil Mroue, publisher of Beirut's *Daily Star* agreed. "Democracy is the ability of a community to wash its dirty linen peacefully and we have got to find a procedure for a political pro-cess in which the media is a cornerstone," he said.

Partners in Change

There is a symbiotic aspect to the relationship between Arab satellite television channels – particularly Al-Jazeera – and democratization movements in the Arab world. But it was not necessarily built on altru-ism and political commitment alone. Television news audiences rise and fall with the shifting tides of world events. Arab satellite channels covered the anti-Syrian demonstrations in Lebanon and subsequent mass rallies because they were good – telegenic – stories. Not inciden-tally, they were also good for ratings. Put simply, big news is good news for 24-hour television channels. CNN's reputation was made with the 1990–91 Gulf War, when its reporters were among the only Western journalists in Baghdad during the US bombardment. The fledgling channel saw its ratings skyrocket during the conflict, only to drop down to prewar levels after the conflict ended.[53] Similarly, Al-Jazeera's reputation was cemented after 9/11, with its exclusive access to tapes from bin Laden and high-profile coverage of the US invasions of Afghanistan and Iraq, just as Fox News in the US seized huge market share with its unabashed flag-waving in the months and years after 9/11,[54] while its alter ego, Al-Jazeera English, made its mark with coverage of the 2008–09 Gaza war.

Critics have accused Fox and other US channels of sensationalism and fear-mongering in order to keep news interest – hence ratings – high. The democratization movement in the Arab world provided Arab satellite channels with a story of continuing interest for their pan-Arab audiences at a time when the daily drumbeat of bad news from Iraq was producing conflict overdose in Arab viewers. The *Kifaya* story, like Hezbollah's 2006 battle with Israel, also reinforced the self-view of the television journalists. As scholar Marc Lynch has written, "The powerful images from the streets resonated with the core Al-Jazeera identity and narrative: the Arab people fighting against the repression and corruption of Arab regimes."[55]

3

Media Politics and Corporate Feudalism

> [T]he media serve, and propagandize on behalf of, the pow-
> erful societal interests that control and finance them.
>
> Edward S. Herman and Noam Chomsky,
> *Manufacturing Consent*

Media is power, nowhere more so than in the Middle East. By controlling the messenger while fostering some perception of media independence, Arab governments could at least attempt to control the nature
and pace of change. At a major Saudi-financed conference on the media
in Dubai in the fall of 2005, I asked the president of the Arab Thought
Foundation, Prince Bandar bin Khaled al-Faisal, why a nation that was,
after all, a feudal monarchy with no pretensions to representational
democracy, would finance a gathering on media freedom, itself a historic precursor to democracy. "Journalism is a part of change," said
Bandar, the owner of Saudi Arabia's *Al-Watan* newspaper and grand-
son of the late King Faisal. "And this conference is an effort to say, 'OK,
maybe we should expedite the process a little bit because we really do
have a lot to lose.'"

Note that choice of words: "Expedite it a *little* bit." On the free-
for-all television talk shows, Arabs could vent their political emotions without – necessarily – endangering the region's political status
quo. While, in theory, satellite television can mobilize publics, this

presumes a unified agenda around which the channels are seeking mobilization. Al-Jazeera's "vision and mission statement" declares that the channel "aspires to ... support the right of the individual to acquire information and strengthen the values of tolerance, democracy and the respect of liberties and human rights." Even if one accepted the notion that Al-Jazeera's *raison d'être* was democratic change, some found it much harder to argue that the region's other satellite news and talk powerhouse, Saudi-owned Al-Arabiya, shared that goal, much less their many and varied competitors among the 400 or so channels on the Arab satellite spectrum. However, Al-Arabiya's Giselle Khouri rejected doubts that the channel was advocating for change. She argued that the seeming contradiction between the Saudi ownership and an agenda of change was just part of the inherent "schizophrenia" of the Arab world. Some of that schizophrenia came from government television stations, which had been forced to respond to the avalanche of new – sometimes unwelcome – ideas pouring into their countries via satellite. Mohammed al Gamsha of Saudi TV made a similar point: "If you do not talk [about these issues] on your local channels, another channel will talk about it with the wrong information. This is more difficult if the public knows about these issues the wrong way and it sticks to their minds. Then it is difficult to correct it."

But even in places where there seemed to be a commitment to media reform, the contradictions between words and actions abounded. At a gathering of American and Arab reporters at the Dead Sea in the spring of 2008, Princess Rym Ali, sister-in-law of Jordan's King Abdullah, made an impassioned speech in support of press freedom. There was no doubt of her sincerity. The former Rym Brahimi was herself a veteran CNN correspondent who had covered the Iraq war. Sitting beside me as we listened to the talk was Osama al-Sharif, former editor of Jordan's *Al-Dustour* newspaper, who, just days before, had been sentenced to three months in prison on charges of contempt of the judiciary for reporting – correctly – that a Jordanian had filed a lawsuit against a court that stripped him of his citizenship.[1] The disconnect between commitment to media reform in Jordan and its implementation, Al-Sharif and other Jordanian journalists said, lay in the gulf between the desires of the palace and the agenda of the bureaucracy that implemented the laws.

It was easy – and dangerous – for outsiders to romanticize the Arab media revolution. But all Arab satellite TV channels had red lines that surrounded their coverage. For Al-Arabiya, that involved "terrorism and anything to do with religion and religious politics" a senior news executive told me. For Al-Jazeera, the sensitivity involved Qatari foreign policy. In the complex evaluation that took place in the newsroom and at the upper reaches of Al-Jazeera's management before controversial stories were aired, the essential question became, 'Will this have a negative impact on Qatar's foreign policy?' Al-Jazeera had put Qatar on the global map and had given the Qatari royal family an important weapon in the regional geopolitical equation – as did the shift of the US military's central command from Saudi Arabia to Doha. But the Qataris walked a fine line between the desire to exercise that influence and the need to maintain stable relations with fellow Arab countries and the US. One Al-Jazeera staffer I spoke with quoted Sheik Hamad bin Thamer al-Thani, the Qatari royal who ran the growing Al-Jazeera empire, as telling the staff on at least one occasion, "Do you think the Emir likes getting angry calls from the President of the United States?" Another sign of the link between Al-Jazeera and Qatari foreign policy came in the late spring of 2007 when Wadah Khanfar, the Palestinian director general of the Al-Jazeera group of channels, was temporarily removed from the corporate board and demoted back to his earlier position as managing director of Al-Jazeera Arabic, reportedly for his pro-Hamas sympathies, which then conflicted with Qatar's support for the Fatah faction of Palestinian President Mahmoud Abbas.[2]

At the same time, the board was reorganized to include a former Qatari ambassador to the US, Hamad al-Kuwari, and Mahmoud Shammam, the editor of the Arabic edition of *Newsweek* and a critic of Al-Jazeera's coverage, leading to claims by Khanfar's defenders that the channel was about to be silenced. "The evidence is clear that the US government is using its influence in Qatar to try to neuter the station's independence, bring it to heel and shift its coverage in a pro-western direction. If it succeeds, it would be a disaster for the Arab world and its chance to shape an independent and democratic future," British MP George Galloway wrote in London's *Guardian* newspaper.[3] It is noteworthy, however, that Khanfar would later re-exert his authority and, by the 2009 Gaza war, not only was Al-Jazeera being accused of flag-waving for Hamas – even by former Al-Jazeera stars like former Washington, DC bureau chief Hafez Mirazi and chief investigative correspondent Yosri Fouda – but Qatari foreign policy had also shifted in favor of the Islamist group at the expense of the more secular Fatah-led Palestinian Authority.

Nowhere did the national agenda take a backseat to media reform. Even the much-vaunted "free zones"– such as the Media City complexes in Dubai, Abu Dhabi, and Cairo – that were supposed to allow news organizations to operate unhampered by local government control, proved to be something less than completely "free." Two private Pakistani channels based in Dubai's Media City, GEO TV and Ary One, discovered that when Pakistan declared martial law in 2007. After the channels refused a demand from the Musharraf government to sign a new media "code of conduct," Emirati authorities gave them two hours to stop broadcasting. Officials left little doubt that the principles of press freedom on which Media City was supposedly based had taken a back seat to Emirati foreign policy. "As an entity within the UAE, Dubai Media City would also observe the broadcast principles of the country's foreign policy and prevent the telecast of news and material that would undermine those principles," said Amina al-Rustamani, executive director of Dubai Media City.[4]

But it wasn't just foreign policy the sheikhs were worried about. With the global economic crisis, foreign business reporters for Media City-based business news organizations like CNBC, Bloomberg, and Dow Jones, who had been writing paeans to Dubai's economic "miracle," started chronicling the collapse of the economy. The government struck back, warning them to "be careful" in what they wrote and banning issues of overseas magazines that contained stories with titles like, "Dubai: End of the Dream."[5]

Arab media outlets that took an editorial line at odds with that of the UAE also found they were not welcome. Abdel Bari Atwan, the editor-in-chief of London-based *Al-Quds Al-Arabi*, a thorn in the side of the Saudi government, claimed he was refused permission to set up in Dubai's Media City. His paper was also suffering from an ongoing advertising boycott by the region's advertising agencies, which were largely owned by, or answerable to, the Saudis. It was the same boycott that prevented Al-Jazeera from reaching profitability, even though it had the highest news ratings in the Middle East and was regularly ranked as one of the best-known brands in the world. "Once we have advertisement in our newspaper, there is a phone call [to the advertiser] from the Saudi ministry of information. 'Why do you publish advertisement in a hostile newspaper?' [they ask the advertiser]. You have to watch yourself because we could cause problems for your business in our country.' Even on the internet they blocked our site in Saudi Arabia," explained Atwan, who claimed his paper was $200,000 in debt as a result. Over on the tiny island of Bahrain, efforts by three independent newspapers to turn a profit were hampered by the fact that the government was "providing ghost funds under the table" to allow three other supposedly independent papers to keep siphoning off readers and advertisers, *Al-Wasat* Editor Mansoor Jamri told a World Association of Newspapers conference in 2008.

What was true in the Arab heartland was also true out on the periphery of the Arab world. In Mauritania, where media "freedom" essentially dated to the 2005 *coup d'état*, when the previous press law was scrapped, advertising depended on the closeness of the owners to the regime and newspapers could only be distributed in the tiny capital. "This allows the government to control the pen of the journalists, because there is no newspaper that is viable," according to Mohamed Rabeh of *Al-Rai Al-Aam*. "We always have this juncture between economic and political power."

Tunisia's *Al-Mawqif* was one of the few newspapers in that tightly controlled country to report on civil society organizations. As a result, most newsstands refused to carry it and revenues were sparse. "We do not even have access to private advertising because companies know that buying ad space in our paper can lead to problems," said editor in chief Rachid Khechana. "Companies even remove their ads from newspapers if they write about sensitive issues." As a result the paper's reporters and editors practiced self-censorship when it came to issues like corruption and coverage of the president, which freed them to continue to focus on civil society. "We have to choose between carrying a part of the message or present ourselves as victims of repression. We have decided to pass the message," Khechana explained. But, as in many Arab countries, the "red lines" of self-censorship were constantly moving. "Even sunny weather can be censored if it is a bad news for agriculture. Taboo topics are updated by the government on a daily basis," said Sihem Bensedrine, the editor of the online magazine *Kalima*, who had been jailed, kept under constant surveillance, and roughed up by security police at Tunis airport on several occasions when she tried to leave the country. When the magazine tried to launch an internet-based radio station, security forces surrounded *Kalima*'s headquarters and the managing editor was threatened by a policeman wielding a knife. "All the journalists working with *Kalima* have been persecuted in their family life, in their job and so on. Every member of our team has faced a great many violations of their rights," she told me.

In Algeria, the government used a somewhat different tactic, flooding the market with newspapers directly or secretly funded by the government. With some 65 papers competing for readers, said *Al-Watan* Publisher Omar Belhouchet, "This gives a good international image. We think it is a country of freedom. We have the freedom to launch newspapers, but when we analyze the content we [see] the majority of private daily newspapers are only mouthpieces for the authorities." Yet even in places where there were a limited number of newspapers, low literacy rates and high levels of poverty meant reaching critical mass was a challenge. Morocco's population was 30 million but, according to Ahmed Nachatti, editor-in-chief of *Sada Al-Massaiya*, total paid circulation was just 350,000 copies. To break through that bubble, *Sada Al-Massaiya* was launched as a free newspaper with a commitment to professionalism and an aggressively grass-roots approach that focused on citizen concerns. It was distributed in train stations, at bus stops and in cafes, slowly building from 10,000 copies a day to 300,000 in the hope that the audience size would attract advertisers. The idea was that "if we work on the basis of profit and loss, then the state cannot expect much" influence on content.

Beyond the issue of advertising, most Arab governments also had the so-called independent media in a stranglehold because those papers depended on government-owned publishing houses for printing, distribution and, in some cases, advertising. The result can be seen in the images below. The first shows the front page of *The Daily Star Egypt* the day after an opposition rally in 2007. The second is a close-up of the anti-government message that was written on the protestor's placard before the paper was sent to the printing plant run by the government-controlled *Al-Ahram*, where the message was erased, leaving only the empty placard. From there, the paper was distributed by *Al-Ahram*'s delivery trucks to the nation's news stands, which were also owned by *Al-Ahram*. "We didn't know [about the censorship] until we saw the [printed] copies; what were we supposed to do, ask that they all be returned to us?" *Daily Star* publisher Mirette Mabrouk ruefully asked later.

Image 1   *The Daily Star*, Egypt, Dec. 19, 2006
Source: Courtesy, *The Daily Star*, Egypt

Image 2   Original photograph
Source: Courtesy, *The Daily Star*, Egypt

While it may have been true that, as Al-Jazeera anchor M'Hamed Krichen put it to me, "We no longer have presidents or leaders as prophets" and governments no longer had "the monopoly on truth," those governments – and the men who led them – still controlled most of the purse-strings, which meant to a large degree, they continued to control the message and the messengers.

Corporate Feudalism

What was emerging was a corporate feudal model of media ownership, with television shifting from government control to the control of power-ful business interests closely aligned with – or part of – existing authori-tarian regimes. "I'm competing against countries, not companies!" Mohammed Alayyan, publisher and chairman of the independent news-paper *Al-Gad* and CEO of ATV in Jordan, complained.[6] "Unfortunately," said Khatib of Al-Arabiya, "this is the game. This will continue until the public will have its own mechanisms to defend itself and to push us media to be set free and respect the ethics. This will take time." As Ali al-Ahmed, the then-director general of Abu Dhabi television told fellow Arab TV news executives at an industry gathering, "Many channels are there for profit; others are there because the owner wants a channel."

Industry analyst Jihad Fakhreddine reported that "financial malnutrition amongst an overpopulated pan-Arab satellite TV market" meant the sector was "far from achieving financial independence." Problems included the "irrationality" of politically driven advertising spends and the low cost of entry. "Any entrepreneur with funds from $1 million and above can contemplate setting up a TV channel. As much as this is good news, it is disturbing news as well," he explained. Then there was the over-hyping of the "pan-Arab" market's potential when, in reality, the prime consumer market in the region was "Saudi Arabia first, Saudi Arabia second and Saudi Arabia third." And even then, in television terms, the country's 20 million consumers really amounted to the half largely confined to their homes. "Simply imagine what will happen to TV consumption should the Saudi government allow women to drive a few years from now," he wrote in a study of the flawed economics of the industry.[7]

It was all a natural extension of a similar system of control in the pan-Arab print media. "*Al-Hayat* is not a commercial project," the paper's then number two, Abdulwahab Badrakhan, told me in 2005. "It is in the first place a political project, like *Asharq Al-Awsat* [another Saudi-owned newspaper]. *Asharq Al-Awsat* and *Al-Hayat* never [make] money, and you can understand that because you can consider us as public relations." Hussein Shobokshi, whose reporting appeared both in *Asharq Al-Awsat* and on Al-Arabiya, said these Saudi-dominated outlets all put out "a beautiful display, a strong progressive product," but ultimately media owned by this new generation of Arab media moguls "all wear the straight hats of the government or semi-government." Echoing the comments of Prince Bandar, Shobokshi said the reform agenda of Arab journalists had Arab leaders on the defensive. "That is why they want to own the media as well. They are so nervous because they see it as a catapult of change, but they want to control the catapult of change." The emir of Qatar didn't finance Al-Jazeera to get a membership card at Washington's National Press Club. He did it for the same reason he invited the US Central Command to set up shop outside Doha – to make himself a player in the region. That's also why the Saudis and Emiratis were building media empires in the Gulf, Jordan's King Abdullah was talking up media liberalization and Syrian intelligence and its Lebanese minions were – all evidence suggested – killing journalists.

The degree to which these pseudo-independent organizations were subject to the vagaries of regional power politics was evident in the evolution of Al-Jazeera's coverage of Saudi Arabia. As noted above, the channel was created to break Saudi Arabia's media hegemony in the region. It was one piece in the regional power struggle between Qatar and Saudi Arabia. On Al-Jazeera's airwaves, Saudi Arabia was fair game. Few negative stories about the kingdom were off limits. But in the face of the rising threat from Shi'ite Iran in late 2007, Sunni Arab governments began to close ranks. In Doha, the palace sent word to the Al-Jazeera newsroom: Back off on the Saudis. The channel's coverage wasn't the only victim. Plans for an Al-Jazeera newspaper to challenge Saudi Arabia's stranglehold on the pan-Arab print media were also put on hold. "We were sacrificed on the altar of regional politics," Abdulwahab Badrakhan, who had been hired as chief editor for the project, told me. When a London-based talk show host on a TV channel owned by Seif Qadaffi, son of the Libyan dictator, launched a verbal attack on the Egyptian regime, Egyptian President Hosni Mubarak called Qadaffi senior, who immediately arrested the station's program director and announced he was nationalizing his son's channel. Similarly, five Moroccan journalists were charged under their country's press law with "publicly harming" Qadaffi and "hurting his dignity" in various articles about North African politics and another that reported on the arrest in Geneva of Qadaffi's daughter-in-law for allegedly assaulting her Moroccan and Tunisian servants.

In their landmark study of American journalism, veteran editors Bill Kovach and Tom Rosenstiel warned that, "we are faced with the possibility that independent news will be replaced by self-interested commercialism posing as news."[8] In the Arab world, there was an additional danger: that independent news would be still-borne. Economic sustainability was one of the greatest challenges to media organizations in countries transitioning from an authoritarian model to a free press. The tendency was for a plethora of media organizations to spring up in the first heady days after deregulation, fragmenting the market and making it difficult for anyone to make money. As Russia exemplified, the survivors were frequently gobbled up by business tycoons – usually cronies of the government-of-the-day – and the rest were susceptible to economic coercion, becoming mouthpieces for political parties and special interests.

The Arab world in the first decade of the new century showed signs that it might be in the process of skipping that intermediate, free-for-all step. The development of Arab media stood in stark contrast to the pattern elsewhere, such as Hungary, where "[m]edia globalization favors highly concentrated Western interests in alliance with powerful domestic corporations."[9] In the Arab world, outside investment was generally not required. So a purely home-grown industry was emerging, but it was one that replaced the government-controlled media feudalism of old with a form of corporate feudalism, in which wealthy individuals closely aligned with – or part of – governments built vast media empires. Unlike in the Balkans or Africa, virtually unlimited capital in the Middle East meant that poor, scrappy journalistic entrepreneurs were few and far between. Idealistic startups like Jordan's first private FM station, Ammanet, a spin-off of an innovative Internet radio station based in the West Bank, were exceptions to the rule of corporate feudalism. The overwhelming number of pseudo-independent media outlets in the region were owned or heavily influenced by members of royal families, such as Al-Jazeera, Al-Arabiya and its cousin MBC; tools of mega-rich would-be politicos and influence peddlers, such as Hariri's Future TV and Gen. Michel Aoun's OTV in Lebanon; or bully pulpits for political parties and preachers of every stripe, from a channel run by interests linked to the Egyptian Wafd Party to the "moderate" Islamic entertainment channel Al-Resalah (The Message), owned by Saudi billionaire Walid bin Talal. One of my students, a part-time TV personality, perhaps put it best: "We Arabs have a lot of troublemakers who have access to the media and are not bothered by gatekeepers."

"Do private media and channels exist – and I mean by 'private' that they are independent from the authority of the audience or the ruling authority?" Bassim Abu Samaya, director general, Palestinian Radio & TV, asked rhetorically at a gathering of Arab broadcasters. "No. This does not exist. There are no private channels independent from the funding and the authority of the funding sides. And in many cases it is an economic corporation or institution that controls the sovereignty of this channel or that one, in one way or another." As IREX concluded in its *Media Sustainability Index*:

> Money available for media business investment has allowed outlets to better professionalize and access to new technologies ... [but] ... These oil-rich countries have demonstrated the ability to develop a media industry without loosening press freedoms beyond points the threaten the governing monarchies and regimes of the region.[10]

"All the media represent a political party or religious party," Michel Murr told me in the fall of 2005, referring to Lebanon. The Lebanese Christian tycoon was in a position to know. He was in the process of relaunching Murr TV, an anti-Syrian station closed down by Lebanon's pro-Syrian president several years before. It was the same story in the print media. "Making profit is not the main reason behind the flow of privately owned print media in Egypt," according to Sameh Abdullah, assistant editor-in-chief of government-controlled *Al-Ahram*. "Most of the newspaper owners are businessmen [who] aim to protect their businesses [or] increase their influence." Salah Diab, a founder of Egypt's leading independent newspaper, *Al-Masry Al-Youm*, framed it slightly differently. While he said "making profit wasn't our main goal" in founding the paper, "every businessman is aware that it's in his best interests to work in a stable political and social environment and having an independent media is one way of achieving that."[11]

This corporate feudalism particularly dominated the Gulf media. It was epitomized by Saudi Sheikh Walid al-Ibrahim, whose sister was a widow of the late King Fahd. His MBC group had launched the first "private" Arab satellite channel and controlled Al-Arabiya, the main rival to Al-Jazeera. "The private sector in the Arab world still considers itself in alliance with monarchies and with regimes; it will not confront them," according to Nabil Khatib, Al-Arabiya's news chief. While they were officially "independent," the way in which Sheikh Walid's channels were highly responsive to Saudi political interests was demonstrated with coverage of the 2006 Lebanon war. In the early stages of the conflict, when the Saudi government was criticizing Hezbollah for provoking the Israelis, Al-Arabiya's coverage was low-key, downplaying the story apparently in order to avoid stirring up Arab public opinion in support of the Shi'ite militia and, by extension, its Iranian sponsors. "In general, the rule of the game is that there is no black or white. There is always a grey area," said Khatib, referring to the restrictions within which the pan-Arab satellite channels worked.

> It would not be realistic to say that for our colleagues in the newsroom there are no redlines. There are redlines everywhere, sometimes for totally different reasons. There is no clear law. And there is no ethics that are accepted or agreed on. For example, it is known that nobody will go and investigate [issues like] where or how this fortune of money rewards of oil is being distributed. You will not see it on Al-Jazeera about Saudi Arabia, because if they say it about Saudi Arabia somebody will say it about Qatar. So they will not say and we will not say it. So it is a great step forward to have nongovernmental media, but it is still far from realizing its political role and social role.

Khatib told me that it was understood within Al-Arabiya that he would push the envelope until owner Sheikh Walid received a call from someone in a position of power telling them to back off. Then, he explained, he and senior management engaged in a carefully choreographed dance. Khatib gave the example of the channel's coverage of Egypt: "He would call us, saying 'What do you have on Egypt? I am getting phone calls from the [Egyptian] President's office,' and I would say, 'We have so and so,' and he says, 'That is OK.' 'OK' means for me that *is* OK [and the story stays on the air]. Then in 6 or 8 hours he [calls again and] says, 'I called and ordered you to stop it.'" Only then is the piece pulled off the air. "He needs to maintain some relationship with them."

Ghassan Tueni, patriarch of the dynasty that controlled Lebanon's *An-Nahar* newspaper, was contemptuous of such antics. "Today there is no Arab media," he told me in 2005. "[TV] is theatrical. These politics are theatrics. The premium media is either owned by governments or controlled by them," he said, adding that it was impossible to have serious news organizations "built on sand." He had no more respect for the many journalists working for government-owned or controlled media outlets. "Why do you want a civil servant in Egypt to risk his life for what he is going to write? He is going to get his salary anyway."

The reason for Tueni's cynicism was evident four years later when Israel launched its 2009 assault against Gaza. Saudi Arabia and Egypt sought to prevent the Islamist militia Hamas, target of Israel's wrath, from scoring political gains at the expense of the more secular Palestinian authority led by Fatah, while Qatar led a block that included other Gulf states and Syria, which equated support for Hamas with support for the Palestinian people. The fault lines produced a media war in the Arab world. "What journalism we have today!" a leading Saudi columnist declared in print, charging reporters and editors with "marketing the idea that any anger at the Israeli bombardment is unjustified and that any support for resistance is incitement for terrorism."[12] One of his Saudi colleagues issued a plea: "I call on all our brothers, whether they work in newspapers or Arab satellite channels ... to send out a clear and resonant message to the whole world and to Israel that there are no two camps when it comes to the Gaza massacre because all Arabs speak in a single voice."[13]

They spoke with anything but that. The rift was most evident on the broadcasts of the region's bitter television rivals. During the three week conflict, Al-Jazeera, owned by the government of Qatar, focused on vivid images of bloodshed accompanied by commentary thick with moral outrage. Al-Arabiya, owned by Saudi interests close to the royal family, chose to avoid the most graphic footage and take a more measured tone. The contrasting approaches reflected both the very different perceptions of the role of Arab journalism in the two newsrooms and the political rift between their respective patrons.

"Our coverage was closer to the people," Al-Jazeera's news chief Ahmed Sheikh told me when I called him as the ceasefire took hold. While he said the channel was "impartial" in that it gave airtime to Israeli officials, "we are not neutral when it comes to innocent people being killed like this. The camera picks up what happens in reality and reality cannot be neutral," he said, adding that, as with US network coverage of Vietnam, Al-Jazeera showed graphic images to turn public opinion against the war. "The goal of covering any war is to reveal the atrocities that are carried out."

"We belong to two different schools of news television in the Arab world," countered Al-Arabiya news chief Nabil Khatib, the target of death threats on Islamist websites for refusing to allow the word *shaheen* (martyr) to be used on the air to describe Palestinian dead. "There is the school that believes that news media should have an agenda and should work on that agenda for ideological and political reasons, which is Al-Jazeera's. We are in the school that believes you need to guarantee knowledge with the flow of news without being biased and by being as much as possible balanced."

Just days into the conflict, in a linguistic play on the name of Al-Arabiya, Hezbollah leader Hassan Nasrallah called the channel "Al-Ibryia," which roughly means "The Hebrew One." The resulting campaign against Al-Arabiya, which Khatib believed was fed by Al-Jazeera, brought into the open long-simmering resentments between the two channels. Al-Jazeera was "satisfying the mob" and "led a campaign for Hamas," Khatib told me. "They chose to highlight the dead bodies and bloody scenes in close-up, thinking this will create shock. We were cautious with this out of respecting our viewers and our code of ethics."

A few days later, I sat in the newsroom at Abu Dhabi TV and listened to its director of news, Abdulraheem al-Bateeh, explain that his counterparts were full of, shall we say, nonsense. "*Come on*," he exclaimed, hitting his desk for emphasis. "It's *obvious*. Al-Jazeera is showing that it is pro-Hamas and Al-Arabiya shows that it is pro-Fatah." His channel, he insisted, stood firmly in the middle in keeping with Emirati government policy. "We are with Hamas on the humanitarian side, but politically we are with Fatah."

Those same conflicting political prisms could be seen in the print media, reflecting the political rift made most evident by the convening of a series of rival summits as the conflict ended. Then both sides met at yet another summit held in Kuwait, where Saudi Arabia flexed its political and economic muscles to impose a temporary inter-Arab truce. Newspapers aligned with Saudi Arabia and Egypt quickly went to work papering over the divisions. "It is indeed heartening to see the Arab leaders finally close their ranks at the Kuwait summit," said Abu Dhabi's *Khaleej Times* in an editorial. A writer in Lebanon's *Al-Akhbar*, which supported the so-called "rejectionist" front, responded with a column dripping sarcasm: "Thus a new Arab era dawned on us all. What joke is this? The blood of one Palestinian child, killed by the attacks of the occupation to which some of you gave cover, is purer and more noble than you and all your thrones."

The reality was that Arab leaders remained so divided they couldn't even agree to whom the more than $1 billion in pledges for Gaza reconstruction should be given, Hamas or the Fatah-controlled Palestinian Authority. "Gaza's curse will haunt many, especially the eminences, the highnesses and the excellencies" who gathered in Kuwait, predicted Adel Bari Atwan, editor of the London-based Palestinian newspaper *Al-Quds al-Arabi*. And so it went across the region; verbal mud was thrown, accusations were made, frustrations were vented. There was, to steal Al-Jazeera's slogan, the opinion and the other opinion. But rarely were both heard from the same news organization. Though divisions ruled the day, one Gulf paper expressed a sentiment that most journalists in the region could agree on: "The Arabs can never prevent another Gaza if they do not speak in one voice and act as one bloc, if not as one nation." Judging from the region's media, that was not likely to happen soon.

Backdoor Control

It all came back to power and how it was leveraged. Arab satellite television might have been helping to fuel political reform but it also remained a prisoner of those reforms. The Egyptian elections provided an example of how this corporate feudalism affected would-be democratization efforts. In an attempt to maintain what many observers called the façade of democracy, the Mubarak regime imposed an equal time rule on the influential news broadcasts at Egyptian state television, requiring that Mubarak's main challengers for the presidency receive the same amount of on-air exposure as the president. But the media-savvy consultants brought in by Mubarak's son, campaign manager, and heir-apparent, Gamal Mubarak, quickly arranged an end-run on the rules. They approached Ahmed Bahgat, the owner of Dream TV, a four-year-old Egyptian satellite station, with a deal that gave Dream the exclusive rights to broadcast Mubarak's rallies. As a result, the Mubarak campaign gained access to one of the largest television audiences in Egypt without the need to offer equal time. At the same time, just months before the campaign began, an advertising agency owned by another businessman with close ties to the ruling National Democratic Party (NDP) purchased the rights to Dream's advertising time, then refused to sell commercials to opposition candidates. As journalist Charles Levinson wrote of the incident, "The experience with private satellite channels such as Dream, operating in the shadow of authoritarian regimes, cannot replace a truly independent media."[14] Still, the picture was not all dark. Mahmoud Abdulhadi, who headed Al-Jazeera's training arm, believed the media moguls were ultimately in for a surprise. "You cannot say that if you have money and you have this tool [Arab media outlets], you can control journalism," he said. Now that the free press genie was emerging from the bottle, he believed, it would be impossible to force it back in.

On one level, national leaders wanted the power and prestige of high-profile media outlets; the Saudis, Qataris, and Emiratis, in particular, were in a cycle of media one-upmanship. They pointed to their supposedly "independent" media as evidence of political and social reform. But the façade was often far prettier than what was going on behind the scenes. No project was more emblematic of this contradiction than *The National*, an English-language daily with a staff of some 200, including high-priced reporters and editors from *The New York Times*, the *Daily Telegraph*, the *Wall Street Journal* and a variety of other Western news organizations.

Hyped by its British editor as "the last great newspaper launch in history,"[15] the inaugural issue was modern and flashy in design but its content was vacuous; in all, the new paper was strikingly similar to that of Singapore's well-designed but toothless government-owned *Straits-Times*. The *National*'s front page in its first week highlighted cheer-leading stories about UAE government reform, "five-star food" in the country's prisons, and the first Emirati kidney transplant. Not exactly crusading journalism, but not surprising for a newspaper owned by the government and backed by Abu Dhabi's $850 billion investment fund. Within days, foreign reporters on the paper were grumbling about a "go easy" mandate from the top and a virtual ban on controversial stories like the plight of foreign laborers in the Emirates. A media executive who had considered taking a post at the paper told me the editorial approach was described to him this way by his would-be bosses: "It's not Arab censorship; it's Arab *sensitivity*."

But the paper's deputy editor, former *New York Times* correspondent Hassan Fattah, said that if they were going to help set the agenda, Arab media could not afford to emulate the attack-dog approach of some of their Western counterparts. "We're not screaming. We're trying to influence and convince," he told me by phone one week after the first issue hit the street. The lead story that day was a highly promoted "investigation" into the private trade in rare animals, which was actually based on the work of a government agency, not the paper's own reporters. "We are part of a broader reform initiative. By definition, we will push boundaries and try to make change, but in the Arab world change does come slowly."

Media alone cannot make revolutions. It takes people. While "an important learning process is underway" as Arab audiences watched political events unfold on their television screens, journalist Rami Khouri argued that there remained a "massive center of largely apathetic ordinary citizens who watch all this on television, concerned mainly by taking care of their families."[16] A year after Lebanon's "Cedar Revolution," which so energized proponents of political change, the death knell of Arab democratic change was already being sounded. Writing in the spring of 2006 of US efforts to counter the influence of Iran through democratization elsewhere in the region, Michael Young, the Lebanese opinion editor of *The Daily Star*, observed that, "The bulwarks of US policy in the region, the regimes in Egypt and Saudi Arabia, are moribund, and their ability to be flexible, democratic, legitimate, is negligible."[17]

But one thing *had* changed: The way Arab journalists viewed their own role in the process and the possibilities for the future.

4

Islam, Nationalism
and the Media

Muhammad was the epitome of all the Arabs. So let all the
Arabs today be Muhammad.

Michel Aflaq, Cofounder of the Arab
nationalist Ba'ath Party

To understand modern Arab journalism, it is necessary to have some
sense of the historical forces that shape Arab politics and society.
Conventional wisdom in many scholarly, journalistic, and policy circles
in the West posits that Arab nationalism and Islamism – the dominant
political influences in the Arab world in the past century – are war-
ring ideologies. Some observers of the Middle East have argued that
the belief systems of the two are fundamentally incompatible. However,
such views are too often based on black-and-white perceptions that
fail to take into account the complex realpolitik of the modern Arab
world, the shifting crosscurrents of Arab history, and, more recently,
the impact of Arab satellite television.

There is no dispute that the ultimate goals of Arab nationalism and
political Islam are fundamentally different. Arab nationalists seek to
erase the lines written in the sand by European colonialists and reunite
the Arab nation; Islamists ultimately want to restore the glory of the
Muslim Caliphate, an empire that grouped Europeans, Africans, Asians,
and Arabs alike. But for each, those goals are part of the long-term

game plan that can only be achieved through tactical victories. Arab nationalism and Islamism are two sides of the "Janus-faced" Arab cultural and political identity, and as David Laitin noted in his study of political culture, "shared cultural identities facilitate collective action."[1]

Islam is a religion, but it is also a form of religious nationalism; described by Islamic revivalist Maulana Maududi (1903–79) as a "revolutionary concept and ideology which seeks to change and revolutionize the world social order and reshape it according to its own concept and ideals."[2] Islamists are those who, in Graham Fuller's definition, believe that "Islam as a body of faith has something important to say about how politics and society should be ordered in the contemporary Muslim world."[3] And, like followers of many other political movements, they have demonstrated a willingness to make accommodations and alliances on the road to achieving the ultimate objective. The result is a collective political identity among Arab nationalists and proponents of political Islam that has produced short-term political alliances and a long-term synergy of interests that belies the notion of ideological movements eternally at loggerheads. Said the late Ayatollah Hussein Fadlallah, spiritual leader of Lebanese Shi'ites: "Islam is a source of strength for the Arabs and Arab nationalism, just as Arabism is a source of strength to Islam."[4]

Stripped of their ultimate goals, the immediate political aims of the two philosophies are strikingly similar. Some have gone so far as to call Arabism and Islam "unseparated Siamese twins."[5] The political program of "pan-Islamism" (*ittihad-i islam*) outlined by Islamist Modernist Jamal ad-Din al-Afghani (1838–97), a Persian, in the late nineteenth century sought to mobilize Muslim nations to fight against Western imperialism. That sounds much like the Arab nationalist agenda of the twentieth century and the broad Arab discourse of today. The artificial boundaries imposed by Western colonizers, the creation of the state of Israel, the pattern of Western aggression since the Crusades, the hypocritical contradictions of Western expressions of morality and political/military actions, Western support for authoritarian rulers, and the corrupting influence of Western culture, all these complaints and more fill the speeches of political Islamist and Arab nationalist leaders alike. Intellectuals representing each political philosophy feed and nurture the other. Journalists have usually been in the thick of it. The writings of Salafist journalist Abd al-Rahman al-Kawakibi (1842–1902), for example, are considered "a milestone in the emergence of Arab nationalism and the concept of Arabism within the Ottoman Empire."[6] His manifestos against Ottoman tyranny, the need for social justice and Arabism (in particular, the role of Arabs and Arabic as the cornerstone of Islam), the first by a Muslim Arab, struck a chord with Muslim *and* Christian Arabs.[7]

Similarly today, Osama bin Laden's influence stems in large part from his ability to give voice to fundamental issues of identity that resonate with the Arab mainstream: Palestine, Western support for autocratic Arab leaders, and the absence of political freedom across the region. Modern US policy, he said in his 1996 declaration of war, was part of a long history of humiliation. To bin Laden, the "Zionist-Crusader" aggression in Israel, Lebanon, Iraq, and elsewhere was of a piece with the heroic battles of a millennium ago. These are the same hot-button issues, save the more recent imposition of Western media culture, which formed the backbone of the Arab nationalist message. Each strain of thinking strives to overcome the "psychology of subjugation,"[8] occupation, and exploitation that has characterized modern Arab history.

The Push and Pull of History

"The history of the Arabs [shows] they have followed the admonition, 'religion is to God and the nation is to the people,'" said *Halab*, an Aleppo newspaper that, on behalf of the British, propagandized for Arab nationalism in the northern Syrian city, which had a strong orientation toward the defeated Ottoman Empire in the years after the Arab Revolt of the first world war.[9] It was all part of the European plan to use the imperial ambitions of the Hashemite sharif of Mecca, Hussein ibn Ali (1852–1931), and his sons Abdullah and Faisal, leaders of the Arab Revolt, to slice up the defeated Turkish-controlled Muslim Ottoman Empire and replace it with a new Arab identity and a new Arab ideology.

> The paper and its masters needed to obscure the religious bond between Arabic- and Turkish-speaking Muslims and thereby disengage the newly imagined ethnicities from a

dependence on Islam ... [which] presages the entire postco-
lonial ambivalence with Islam itself in Kemalist Turkey and
Ba'athist Syria and Iraq, where Islam both is (or was) a defin-
itive component of identity.[10]

Islam was thus subsumed *into*, rather than separated *from*, the
"Arab" identity that emerged in the interwar Middle East. The transformation was possible because Islam is a "discursive tradition" that
includes aspects of secularism and religion side-by-side.[11] All Muslims
consider themselves part of the greater *umma* but there is no "*Homo
Islamicus*,"[12] no clearly defined *species* of Muslim that is separated from
the ethnicities from which its adherents are drawn. "We ... made you
into nations and tribes," says the *Qur'an* (49:13) and, as cultural psy-
chologist Geert Hofstede observes: "We all think according to our own
local software."[13]

Shifting Definitions

To understand the politics of Arab journalism it is important to understand precisely what we mean when we use terms related to the development of political thought in the Arab world. For the most part, Arab
nationalism, Arabism, and pan-Arab(ism, ist), have been used inter-
changeably by scholars of the Middle East.[14] The terms all broadly refer
to the various iterations – Ba'athism, Nasserism, Arab Socialism, etc. –
in which a linguistic and cultural commonality among Arabs manifests itself in the aspiration for political unity in an Arab nation that
transcends existing nation-states. More recently, some scholars, such as
Shibley Telhami, have argued that a "new" Arabism was emerging, in
which Arabs rallied around certain regional causes, such as Palestine.[15]

In his history of the rise of the Arab middle class, Watenpaugh notes
that Islamism emerged in the interwar years in part as a reaction to
the division of the Muslim Ottoman Empire into separate states and
against "the nonsectarian, emancipatory, and bourgeois dimensions"
of the liberal/Socialist orientation of Arab nationalism.[16] However, that
did not preclude a simultaneous synergetic cooperation as Arabs of the
two philosophies sought to crystallize their own identities in the new
political environment. "On the level of practical politics, then, not only

was there no opposition between Islam and Arabism, there was actual co-operation," according to historian Elie Kedourie. "One can even go further and say that Islam actually gave great strength to Arab nationalism ... [and] ... produced a new theoretical amalgam in which Islam and Arabism became inseparable."[17]

Peter Mandaville argues that the world has entered a period of "post-Islamism," in which "Muslim political identities are oriented primarily toward national or even local concerns," the Islamist "project" is increasingly secular, and Muslim politics are being reconstituted "in forms more suited to a globalized world."[18] The agenda of these "new Islamists," he tells us, focuses on "progress and social justice," themes in synch with those of many other Arabs who seek political change and social justice – including Arabs of the media.

The principle of *ijtihad*, which literally means "endeavor" or "self-exertion," dictates that reason and independent judgment are used to articulate the applicable truths of the *Qur'an* that are relevant at any given time and place. This fundamental concept is subject to multiple interpretations and has for centuries been at the heart of Islamic theological debate over whether, and to what degree, interpretation is allowed.[19] The argument for the continuing validity of *ijtihad* underpins the demands of those seeking political reform in Saudi Arabia and it can also be seen in the broader context of legal reforms across the Muslim world. "Reading and understanding the *Qur'an* implies the interpretation of it and the interpretation in its turn includes the application of it which must be in the light of the existing circumstances and the changing needs of the world," Pakistani Judge Mohammed Shafi wrote in a 1995 legal ruling.[20] For many Muslims, this viewpoint leaves open significant maneuvering room when it comes to the application of Islam to the political environment of the day – and when assessing the nature of his/her own political identity. Technology has only amplified that maneuvering room as traditional mosque-based communication networks have been supplanted by cacophony of conflicting religious opinion on the internet and satellite television. Where *ijtihad* was once the purview of *ulema* (religious scholars, from the root '*ilm*), miriam cooke and Bruce B. Lawrence have written, "migrant engineer theologians changed all that by distributing authority among

Muslim cybernauts."[21] Tech-savvy clerics, militant Islamist groups, and democracy-hungry political movements across the Muslim world can all be counted among those "cybernauts."

But journalists, too, play a critical role in redistributing authority. At some overtly Islamist news organizations, like Islam Online, an information portal that offers everything from news to *fatwas*, and the Hezbollah TV channel Al-Manar, news is closely tied to religion. That is not overtly true of Arab journalists working for "mainstream" news organizations. However, the majority of Arab journalists are Muslims, whether or not they attend mosque, and no discussion of "mainstream" Arab journalism can be complete without an understanding of the intimate relationship between information and religion in the Islamic context.

Communication and the *Qur'an*

"Read!" So commanded the angel Gabriel in the first word of the first revelation, which, Islam teaches, was communicated to the Prophet Muhammad in a cave outside Mecca in 610 CE. The instruction is recorded in the 96th chapter of the *Qur'an*:

> Read (or Proclaim!) in the name of your Lord and Cherisher who created – Created man out of a (mere) clot of congealed blood: Proclaim! And your Lord is Most Bountiful, – He Who taught (the use of) the Pen, – Taught the human that which he did not know. (96: 1–5)[22]

Thus were laid the foundations of Islam's intimate connection with the written word. The Arabic terms for knowledge, understanding, writing, and reading are mentioned in almost 20 percent of the verses of the *Qur'an*, a mass medium known to the world long before Gutenberg (1398–1468) invented his printing press.[23] "Islam realized the religious, political and economic importance of information fourteen centuries ago and organized its means, stated its goals and exhorted Muslims to make good use of it for the sake of their religion and their commonweal," Abdelhadi Boutaleb, director general of the Islamic Educational Scientific and Cultural Organization (ISESCO), wrote in advance of the first Islamic Information Ministers' Conference in 1986.[24] '*Ilm*, a derivation of the Arabic root 'to know', is "a defining concept of the worldview of Islam."[25] It is generally translated to mean 'knowledge (of God)' and, implicitly, the communication of knowledge. "'*Ilm* was literally born in the first breath of Islam," according to Dagmar Glass, a scholar of Arab-Islamic information concepts, referring to *Surah* 96, al-Alaq, considered by most scholars to be the first Revelation.[26]

While the *Qur'an* does not contain a single reference to the sword, the pen is mentioned four times. The Muslim holy book and *hadith*, the collected accounts of the teachings and activities of the Prophet, include numerous references to *ra'y* (opinion, view), *haqq* (reality, fact, truth), *khabar* and its plural, *akhbar* (news), and *hikma*, generally translated as "divine wisdom" but a word also associated with the Western concept of objectivity.[27] In Islamic society, information has historically been considered not just a commodity, but a moral and ethical imperative.[28] Muhyi al-Din Abd al-Halim, the leading information theorist at Egypt's al-Azhar University and former head of Cairo University's faculty of Communications and Journalism, wrote in 1984 that information "provides the people ... with the truths of the Islamic religion on the basis of the book of God and the *Sunna* of his Messenger."[29] From the very beginning, the Prophet's own mosque in Medina was more than just a center of Islamic learning, but also

> ... a spiritual centre for worship, the political and military headquarters of the new state where internal and external affairs were conducted, an institute of learning where discussions and seminars were held, and a social institution where Muslims learnt and practiced discipline, equality, unity and brotherhood.[30]

In short, it was the communications hub of the new community. In the mosque's courtyard, followers gathered to exchange news and debate political affairs.[31] From there, the Prophet carried out an active flow of communications with the outside world,[32] dispatching missives to neighboring tribes and conducting diplomatic correspondence with the rulers of distant empires.[33] There, too, he received emissaries, meeting them at a place today still marked by the Pillar of Embassies.[34]

Lebanese scholar Adub Muruwwa believes "the seeds of [Arab] journalism" were planted in Islam's first century.[35] A case can be made that it was within the confines of the Medina mosque that the first Muslim journalists began to practice their craft, as a bevy of scribes, directed by the Prophet's secretary, Zaid ibn Thabit (610–56), copied down these dispatches and, more importantly in the context of the religion, transcribed portions of the revelations as dictated by the Prophet Muhammad.[36] They were soon joined by the first Muslim broadcasters, for with the growth of that first small community, "transmitters" – individuals with powerful voices – were called upon to repeat the Prophet's words for the crowds.[37] In 632 CE, two months before his death, Prophet Muhammad led what would be his last annual pilgrimage to Mecca, which would become known as the "Farewell Pilgrimage." He was accompanied by more than 100,000 of his followers. As he gave his final sermon in the valley of Uranah in front of Mount Arafat,

> The Prophet (peace be upon him) appointed a man called Rabi'ah bin Umaiah bin Khalaf al-Jumahi, who had a loud voice, to repeat after the Prophet (peace be upon him) so as to convey his words to the people.[38]

These were then relayed by others across the crowd. In a modern-day commentary, Ziauddin Sardar gave this account of the scene:

> [H]undreds of transmitters were positioned at key spots in the valley of Arafat near Makkah. As the Prophet spoke, the transmitters repeated his words sentence by sentence so that the whole valley resounded with the words of the Prophet and everyone present was able to hear what he was saying.[39]

After the Prophet's death, the various disparate sections of the revelations were collected "from palm-branches, flat stones and the memories of men."[40] Traditions disagree on which of the Prophet's first four successors – Abu Bakr (632–34), Umar (634–44), Uthman (644–56) or Ali (599–661) – ordered that the revelations be assembled in one place and bound in leather. "The revelations were transcribed onto sheets (*suhuf*) of equal size, presumably made of parchment, which were then gathered in codices (*mushaf*)," according to Bloom.[41] However, the result was a series of differing codices – which produced variant traditions, though Uthman is credited with canonizing one version and ordering the destruction of the others.[42] Meanwhile, the compilation of the *hadith*, the accounts of the sayings and deeds of the Prophet as reported by his companions, raised an even more complex problem: assessing the legitimacy of the accounts as handed down orally through a chain of transmitters. Here issues of reportorial credibility, the cross-checking of sources and questions of political and ideological bias first enter the Islamic lexicon through a process known as *Rijal al-Hadith* (the study of the reporters of *hadith*).[43]

As Islam spread along the ancient trading routes that linked Arabia with Mesopotamia, Damascus, and beyond, early forms of Islamic media – or sources of information – emerged, including public speeches, councils, poetry readings, and word-of-mouth in the market square. They were soon supplemented by more formal communications, such as sermons in mosques and, eventually, handwritten books and contracts, as a culture of writing emerged in the years following the Prophet's death in 632 CE, producing a "momentous change" in which "[w]riting came to play a crucial and pervasive role in virtually every aspect of life."[44] There emerged a new profession, the *warraqeen*, which combined the functions of scribe, publisher, bookseller, and writer. "The end result," according to Sardar, "was a cultural revolution based on the production of books on an unprecedented scale: the concept of *'ilm* was transformed into a truly distributive practice."[45]

By the fourteenth century AD on the Gregorian calendar, these "men of the pen" were among the most respected members of Muslim society.[46] However, concerned that the spread of the written word was opening the way to misinterpretation and distortion, and, some scholars argue, to safeguard their own authority, toward the end of that century the *ulema* effectively transformed the meaning of *'ilm* from *all* knowledge to *religious* knowledge and set in place stringent criteria for who could transmit such knowledge. This is one of several moments in history at which "the gates of *ijtihad*" – reason and independent judgment – are said to have closed. As part of this move, the *ulema* blocked the introduction of the printing press for hundreds of years, an action many scholars blame for the "stagnation" of Muslim culture, but others think it may also have been connected with the entrenched interests of the scribes themselves, who felt threatened by the new technology, and the complexity of Arabic script.

With the arrival of the first printed Arabic books via European colonizers in the seventeenth century and then the first Arabic newspapers in nineteenth century, Islamic – and Arab – discourse began to take on a new dimension,[47] which was then revolutionized in the late twentieth century with the advent of broadcasting, audio cassettes, fax and ultimately satellite television and the avalanche of new media that have transformed communication, redefined Muslim identity politics and put control of '*ilm* into the hands of anyone with a computer. "All of these media, whether they are traditional and of pre-Islamic and Islamic origin or modern and of Western origin, have one thing in common: They are all agents of social and intellectual change and have far-reaching effects on society and communication," according to Glass.[48]

Islamic Theories of News and Communication

The *Qur'an* may seem an unlikely journalistic primer, but its influence is felt in many Arab newsrooms, directly or indirectly. Islamic theorist Abd al-Latif Hamza defines *i'lam* (information) as:

> providing the people with proper news, correct pieces of information and firm truths, which help the people to form a correct opinion of an event of problem. Furthermore, information is an objective expression of the mentality of the people, their inclinations and ambitions.[49]

Social responsibility is a guiding principle of scholars who advocate an Islamic approach to journalism, but it is in the context of the journalist's duty to support the concept of *amar bi al-Maruf wa nahi an al-munkar* (commanding the right and prohibiting the wrong).[50] Scholar Mohammad Siddiqi notes:

> Throughout Islamic history many institutions as well as channels of mass communications such as mosques, *azan*, and Friday *khutba* have used this concept of social responsibility to mobilize public opinion and persuade individuals to work for the collective good of society in general and for their own individual pursuit of good in this world and the hereafter.[51]

Siddiqi defines news as "the reporting of events in a way which fulfils the needs of Muslim society" and leads to "peace and stability in conformity with the moral and ethical principles of Islam." He says Islam offers "a strong tradition" on which reporters can draw, including "critical evaluation of the sources of news," sound methods of verification and documentation, and a commitment to context and fairness.

"The Islamization of information" means giving precedence to *da'wa*, the straight path of Allah, while *khabar*, which usually translates as "news" (pl. *akhbar*, the name of many Arab newspapers), serves "as the basis of knowledge."[52] In other words, religion provides the framing and events fill in the details. Truth and objectivity, as defined in the Islamic context, occupy pride of place in this communication paradigm, since Islamic information means "clearly expressing the truth (*haqq*) in a way that attracts people" and objectivity is defined as "wisdom" (*hikma*), known as the "divine principle." In theory, news both informs and *reflects* society as a whole, thus implying that the media must not be out of step with the values and mores of such society. There are glimpses of this in Western journalism in terms of the reluctance to get too far ahead of the pack or stray into topics that are not politically correct. The Islamic approach takes that one step further, calling for the media to actively "form" or shape "a correct opinion" in the minds of the news consumers. That's not to say the media's agenda is always pure. The "straight path" – *da'wa* – can easily be twisted into nonreligious propaganda – *di'aya;* disinformation in pseudo-religious garb. Muslim thinkers have always been scathing about "false news" spread by governments via journalists who have neither "knowledge" (*'ilm*) nor authority (*sulta*).

The Muslim Brotherhood's leading theorist, Said Qutb, was dismissive of the Arab media, claiming it neither influenced, nor was influenced by public opinion, but was simply a mouthpiece for corrupt regimes,[53] thus failing the first test of *haqq* (truth). "Circulate knowledge and teach the ignorant, for knowledge does not vanish except when it is kept secretly," the Prophet Muhammad's successor, Umar ibn Abdul Aziz (682–720) wrote to Abu Bakr ibn Muhammad ibn Hazm (d. 737), the next in line, according to the *hadith* (1:3:98).[54] However, it can be argued that the banning of printing by the *ulema* (religious scholars) was itself an "illegitimate monopolization of knowledge,"[55] violating that precept and setting the precedent for state control of media in the Arab world. Indeed, the use of information as a tool of politics is enshrined in the Constitution of the Islamic Republic of Iran, the preface of which states:

> Mass media – radio and television – should be used for perfecting the Islamic revolution and in serving to propagate Islamic culture ... and strictly refrain from propagating and spreading harmful and anti-revolutionary notions.[56]

In principle, Islamic journalism is based as firmly on facts as any Western interpretation, since the *Qur'an* decrees that *'ilm* (knowledge) is the precise opposite of *zann* (guess-work, speculation, approximation).[57] "Conjecture [*zann*] avails nothing against truth [*haqq*]," according to the *Qur'an* (53:28). However, Sayeed al-Seini, who has written about the duties of Islamic journalists, says the ideas of Western objectivity and multiple sources are not enough:

> Almost any person or event in the news today is subject to numerous contradictory stories. Which should we believe, especially in light of the highly advanced techniques of deception used today? The situation becomes worse if deception is an organized political tool.[58]

He says journalists should look to the example of the reporters of the *hadith*, who used multiple sources to ensure the credibility of information, something with which most denizens of Western newsrooms would agree. But then Seini adds another dimension to the reporting process: "Islam offers a whole panoply of guidelines to restrain the publication of whatever can unjustly harm the innocent or falsify reality."[59] The criteria for judging the authenticity of spiritual instructions of Divine origin, such as the revelations to Moses, Muhammad, and other recognized prophets, include the truth (*haqq*) of the information itself, and the veracity of the *Rasool* (messenger) or *Nabiy* (news giver). Pasha says Islamic journalists must apply those same tests to news of earthly origin, finding support for his case in the *Qur'an*:

1. It must be based on truth unmixed with willful falsehood: "And cover not Truth [*haqq*] with falsehood [*baatil*], nor conceal the Truth when you know (what it is)." (*Qur'an* 2:42).

2. It must be conveyed by journalists of utmost character, competence and integrity and it is up to the public to ensure the story's veracity: "O you who believe, if a [*Faasiq*; person of questionable character] comes to you with any news, ascertain the truth..." (*Qur'an* 49:6). (This verse is, according to Sayeed al-Seini, of central relevance to Islamic concept of news. Pasha quotes a translation of the Surah that uses the term "verify").

3. Because "news has consequences," reporters must approach stories with "a strong sense of responsibility and accountability": "...lest you harm people unwittingly, and afterwards become full of repentance." (*Qur'an* 49:6).

4. "[M]ass media must not make mere suspicion the basis of their reporting." Journalists must avoid "gossip, rumor-mongering, muckraking, innuendo, backbiting and character assassination" and the news "must provide *nafa* (benefit) to the people."

That journalistic worldview is embodied in the two of the region's leading Islamist news organizations, Islam Online (IOL), a Muslim portal funded by Salafist interests in Qatar, and Al-Manar, the television station run by Lebanon's Shi'ite movement Hezbollah. The aim of Islam Online is to "present the unified and lively nature of Islam." Its goals are "To work for the good of humanity, as Islam teaches us," and "to uplift the Islamic nation specifically and humanity in general."[60] Al-Manar's website says the channel "assumes objective policy motivated by the ambitions of participation in building a better future for the Arab and Muslim generations by focusing on the tolerant values of Islam and promoting the culture of dialogue and cooperation among the followers of the Heavenly religions and human civilizations. It focuses on highlighting the value of the human being as the center of the Godly messages which endeavor to save his dignity and freedom and develop the spiritual and moral dimensions of his personality."[61]

In some ways, the precepts of Islamic journalism address many of the same "sources of error" as those about which Tunisian philosopher and historian Ibn Khaldun (1332–1406) warned scribes six centuries ago. These include "partisanship" and "bias;" "over-confidence in one's sources;" "failure to understand" the real meaning of the subject about which they were writing; "a mistaken belief in the truth" of what they were being told; the "inability rightly to place an event in its real context;" the "very common desire to gain the favour of those of high rank;" "ignorance of the laws" of nature, which could cause them to believe the improbable; and "exaggeration." On the latter, Ibn Khaldun advised writers to "check up" statements and claims and "weigh them up in a fair and critical spirit of inquiry."[62]

Other principles more modern reporters must keep in mind include the fact that "there are limits ordained by Allah" which must not be crossed (2:229); obscenity must be avoided; *ma'roof* (good community standards) must be maintained and *munkar* (that which violates community standards) opposed; journalists should reject partisanship and "recognize the limits of adversariality," thus balancing "the people's communication rights and freedoms with their communication duties, constraints and responsibilities;" and, finally, journalists must serve as "champions of justice and God's witness" and recognize their "sweeping global system service and social responsibility role involving not only the entire human race, but also the other species and the worlds beyond."[63] In short, Muslim cultural theory provides a complete handbook for "what the mass media should cover, when and how, and what, if anything, they should not cover and for how long." Of course, Pasha notes, in the modern Muslim world of monarchs, dictators, and Western hegemony, there exists "a fault line ... between Muslim cultural theory and Muslim reality with regard to political ideology and mass media."[64]

Hamid Mowlana identifies another fault line at work in the Islamic world today. This one pits two competing "cultural ecologies:" media globalization and the belief systems of the Muslim *umma*, which he describes as "a paradigm of revelation and not a paradigm of information." In the worldview of those who subscribe to the Islamic approach to communications, he writes, "secularism becomes alien to Islamic social and political thought when it attempts to separate religion from politics, ideas from matter and rationality from cosmic vision."[65]

One concrete manifestation of that can be seen in the Palestinian media. A study of *Al-Risalah*, the main newspaper aligned with Hamas, the Islamist party, found that while it largely avoided overt religious preaching, news events were covered through the distinct prism of an Islamic worldview driven by Islamist politics:

> This editorial policy reflects the view that Islam is not only a religion, but a social, economic, political, and cultural theory as well, and that no clear separation can be made between religion and other spheres of life just as there is no division between public and private.[66]

American Muslim convert Abdullah Schleifer, a longtime Cairo bureau chief for NBC News and journalism professor at The American University in Cairo, says Western norms of journalism – that the public has "the right to know" and that "nothing is sacred" – are "inherently anti-Islamic."

> What is news [to Western journalists]? Peace, stability and continuity is not news but conflict, contention and disorder is. Respectability and moral conformity (an Islamic virtue…) is not news, but erupting scandal is.

Schleifer, who later became Washington, DC bureau chief for the Arab satellite channel Al-Arabiya, says Islamic journalism offers an alternative that

> Encourage[s] good and discourage[s] evil by providing "news" written in a professionally acceptable, objective style that honors truth; that encourages the belief and practice of Islam and discourages practices and beliefs that deny Islam.[67]

Arab Nationalism and News

Opposing the proponents of Islamic journalism are those who argue for a more secular Arabization of the region's media. In place of religion, they emphasize the need to end both state media monopolies and the dominance of Western information channels in the Arab world, restructuring media systems to enhance Arab solidarity and bolster cultural mores.[68] Many Arab and Muslim journalists would likely object to the kind of overt linkage of news and religious politics advocated by Islamic journalism proponents; in fact, attacks on pro-Fatah Palestinian journalists in the aftermath of Hamas' 2007 takeover of Gaza were, in part, related to that distinction. But the degree to which variations on this theme form a backdrop to coverage of events in the Middle East and broader Muslim world cannot be discounted.

Which brings us to the fact that in Arab media and politics – as in life – there are no black-and-white absolutes. Identity can be a moving target. Cultural philosopher Walter Ong famously observed that all human beings are the product of their times, since we are shaped by our "sense of identity, if we take sense of identity to mean the sense of where one comes from and how one relates to those other than oneself, how one fits into what one knows of the universe."[69] Sheikh Yusuf Qaradawi, a conservative Muslim cleric who hosts a controversial program on Al-Jazeera and is one of the founders of Islam Online, says much the same:

> Culture is not a pure abstract knowledge; it is knowledge and cognitions mixed with values and beliefs, embodied in actions, and reflected in arts and literatures, which are learned and experienced. It is influenced by religion, language environment and cultural and civilizational legacies, as well as by interaction, positive and negative, with others.[70]

In its purest form, Islamism may reject nationalism as an artificial source of identity, but few Muslims in the real world are able to so easily shed this layer of their being. If one were to ask a Muslim on any continent to describe him or herself, it is unlikely he or she would stop at "Muslim." Even if Islam ranks as the primary self-identity, any description would likely include reference to his/her country, ethnicity and possibly even region, village, family and, in the case of a woman, husband's family. Each constitutes a separate but interwoven layer of identity. For an Egyptian, an Algerian, a Yemeni, or a Lebanese Muslim, the search for identity will, by definition, mean melding an ethnic and or nationalist identity into the Islamic whole. Middle East specialist Fred Halliday says that for an Arab, there are at least three separate "forms of identity:"

> ... 'religious' or confessional (Muslim or Christian or, till the 1940s not to be forgotten, Jewish); 'pan-Arab', defined in terms of the whole Arab *umma* or nation; and local, defined in terms of particular states...[71]

Even for political secularists, that Islamic layer is not easily shed. This is as true of journalists as the public. Arabs, said the late columnist Samir Kassir, have "a gift for synthesis," which meant that historically "Arab society was able to absorb the cultures of the Islamized peoples and not negate them in the process." Contrary to some nationalist teleology, he wrote, it is essential to recognize "how much more important Islam was than ethnicity as a unifying bond" in Arab history. This comment is striking, since it comes from a journalist who claimed that modern Islamism had "discredited" Arab culture by uniting its members "in a cult of misery and death."[72]

There has also been a more pragmatic aspect of this relationship between Islamism and nationalism. In recent years, Islam has become a cloak of convenience for those who have sought to benefit from the power and financial resources associated with its soaring influence. After the emergence of Hezbollah in the early 1980s, this writer encountered numerous "born-again" Islamists who had once been leaders of secular, leftist militias and had now joined the ranks of Sunni and Shi'ite Islamists, substituting Qur'anic quotations for Marxist dialectics. Likewise, after the fall of Saddam Hussein, many former Ba'athists too don the mantle of the Islamic resistance in Iraq, while Palestinian groups like the Hamas count among their commanders once decidedly secular leaders of the PLO. "Some of them have seen the light, but for many of them it's just political and financial expediency," Yosri Fouda, Al-Jazeera's chief investigative correspondent, who has reported extensively on Al-Qaeda and its offshoots, told me.

And what is true of the individual is equally true of the *Volksgeist* or collective identity of a people. Anthony Smith, a scholar of nationalism, maintains that Muhammad and Moses have become "national" leaders. He agrees that nations still lie at the core of political identity but argues that there is a duality between religion and nationalist politics, since while one taps the yearning for collective salvation beyond this world, the other feeds on a desire for political redemption for future generations.

> It is the achievement of nationalism to have given political expression to these twin appropriations by linking the memories of ethno-history and the older religious myths of

election to the striving for collective territorial recognition
and political autonomy in the historic 'homeland.'[73]

Though Smith was not specifically writing of the Middle East, his
comments perfectly sum up the "complex and mutually reinforcing"
relationship between transnational Islam and the modern Middle East
state,[74] exemplified by the way in which religion has, in recent years,
become a driving factor in Palestinian nationalism. A series of surveys
conducted in 2001 and 2003 found that while roughly three-quarters
of Saudis, Jordanians, and Egyptians considered religion to be the
most important aspect of their identity, nationality, rather than Arab
identity, was the second most common response, with just 9 percent
of Saudis and Jordanians and 1 percent of Egyptians responding positively to the statement, "Above all, I am an Arab." "It thus appears
that after religion, territorial nationalism is the distant second most
important component of identity for the publics of these countries,"
the study concluded.[75]

For many Islamists, the Arab world holds a special place in the
Muslim cosmology. "I want to say that the greatest glory in the Muslim
conquests goes to the Arabs, and that religion grew, and became great
through them; their foundation is the strongest, their light is the bright-
est, and they are indeed the best *umma*," wrote Rashid Rida (1865–
1935), an Islamist journalist and scholar who heavily influenced Muslim
Brotherhood founder Hassan al-Banna.[76] Arabic is the language of the
Qur'an, Arabia gave birth to Islam; the heritage of Islam and the Arabs
are bound as if by a spiritual umbilical cord.

The Politics of Manipulation

It was with the founding of the newspaper *Nafir Suria* by the Christian
publisher Boutros al-Boustani (1819–83), following sectarian clashes
in Mount Lebanon in 1860, that some of the early ideas of Arab nationalism were first elucidated, setting the stage for the intermingling of
journalism and Arab/Muslim politics still seen today. Al-Boustani
called for "non-sectarian patriotism" and the separation of state and
religion, drawing on and adapting the concept of *watan* (homeland)
that Rifaa al-Tahtawi (1801–73) had brought back from Europe three

decades before.[77] But like Kawakibi, a variety of *Islamist* journalists also helped to propagate the ideas of Arab nationalism. So, too, Islamist activists like Salafi Sheikh 'Izz al-Din al-Qassam (1882–1935), head of one of the most famous resistance units of the 1938 Palestine revolt, who was also closely associated with the pan-Arabist Istiqlal (Independence) Party.[78]

The best example of the symmetry of philosophies between Islamic nationalism and Arab nationalism involves the Muslim Brotherhood – the primary progenitor of twenty-first century political Islam – and the best-known proponents of Arab nationalism, the Syrian Ba'ath Party, the Iraqi Ba'ath, and Egypt's Gamal Abdel Nasser (1918–70). The aforementioned "conventional wisdom" would have it that the secular Ba'ath was the archenemy of Islam. The historical record indicates differently. In the view of the Ba'ath's Orthodox Christian cofounder, Michel Aflaq (1910–89), "Islam was not only a divine religious system, but also an expression of the genius of the Arab model." Ghada Hashem Talhami explains Aflaq's thinking:

> Since the Arab nation is eternal, renewing itself across human history, then Arab nationalism is one of its latest manifestations in the current historical stage. Thus, nationalism reaches its zenith only when it reunites with historical Islam, since both are no more than manifestations of the nation in two distinct times.[79]

It could be argued that crass politics was behind attempts by the Ba'ath and other Arab nationalist movements to present Arabism as a central tenet of Islam. "The beauty of Aflaq and [Ba'ath cofounder Zaki al-] Arsuzi [an Alawite] is that they just tweaked God a little to make him a source of nationalism and Ba'thi '*al-risala al-khalida*' or the 'eternal message,'" according to Syria scholar Joshua Landis.[80] But however opportunistic such tweaking might have been, evidence indicates that the Greek Orthodox Aflaq converted to Islam before his death, which would seem to indicate that, for him at least, the connection with Islam was more than just an expedient. Egypt, meanwhile, offered a vivid example of the complex and often opportunistic relationship between Islamic nationalism and Arab nationalism. There, the Muslim

Brotherhood, which was founded in Egypt in 1928, supported Gamal Abdel Nasser's overthrow of the monarchy. The Brotherhood's leading philosopher, Sayyid Qutb (1906–66), even became known as "the tribune of the Egyptian Revolution." "There is no conflict between Arab nationalism and Islamic patriotism if we understand Arab nationalism as a step on the road," he wrote at the time.[81] But there was no such understanding on the part of the Nasser's Free Officers, with whom the Brotherhood quickly came to blows after the coup. The confrontation ultimately led to the arrest of many officials of the Brotherhood and Qutb's execution (in the years immediately before his death, Qutb would sing a very different tune about the compatibility of Islam and nationalism than at the time of the revolution). In Syria, meanwhile, relations between political Islamists and successive nationalist regimes ultimately led to a bloody pogrom against Syrian Islamists in the early 1980s, which resulted in the virtual destruction of the city of Hamas. But just as Arab nationalism and Islamism have had their fallings-out, so have the various ideological strains *within* Arab nationalism. It was, after all, the Syrian nationalism of the Parti Populaire Syrien (PPS) that rejected Arab nationalism in favor of Syrian nationalism in the 1930s and the Syrian Arab Socialists who sent Aflaq and his compatriots into exile in Iraq in the 1960s.

The ideology of Arab nationalism, as embodied in Egypt, Syria, and the Iraqi Ba'ath regime, was dealt a body-blow with the Arab defeat in the 1967 war with Israel. For Nasser and Nasserism, it was, essentially, the end. A new phase in Arab politics would soon dawn, in which Egypt and other Arab regimes began courting the Islamists in an effort to find a new basis for legitimacy. The process was a continuation of the conscious readjustment in national worldview that Arab governments had long been engaged as they shifted emphasis between pan-Arabism (*quami*) and local identity (*qutri*) in the pursuit of changing domestic and regional agendas. Egypt was the best example of this. In the 1960s, Nasser became the symbol of pan-Arab aspirations. Broadcasting on the Voice of the Arabs, he galvanized Arab nationalists across the region. Yet he was, first and foremost, an Egyptian patriot who began his political career seeking ways to free his country from the yolk of British rule. That other Arab nations had similarly suffered was of little concern. In this, writes Dawisha, Nasser reflected the general view of his countrymen. Even after the Arab Revolt

> Egyptian, rather than Arab, nationalism continued to be the dominant ideology. Its roots dug so deep into the Egyptian soul that even by the end of the 1950s, the decade that witnessed the greatest triumphs of Arab nationalism under Egypt's own leadership, observers would note Egyptian indifference to the Arab identity.

Dawisha quotes Mohamed Hassanein Heikal, Nasser's journalistic confidant, as commenting that Egypt, the natural leader of the Arab world, "was unable to shift its attention from its own soil so that it can look across the Sinai and discover its Arab position."[82]

Media and Ideology

In the context of Arab journalism, it is important to note that, as in the shifting between pan-Arabism and local identity, the flirtation by nationalist Arab governments with political Islam beginning in the 1980s meant that the same state-dominated media outlets which had long been used to propagate the pan-Arab, Socialist, and nationalistic ideals of these secular regimes now shifted gears and beat the drum for what Nasser's successor as Egyptian president, Anwar Sadat, called the "corrective movement," which now brought Islam into the political fold. In Damascus, for example, the then-Syrian President Hafiz al-Assad (1930–2000) publicly adopted the symbols of Islam by, among other things, ordering that state-run television broadcast his weekly visits to the capital's largest mosques.

For Sadat, this flirtation with the Muslim Brotherhood, even as he made peace with Israel, would eventually backfire, forcing him to crack down on Islamist critics, a move that would cost him his life at the hands of a militant Islamist splinter group headed by Ayman Zawahiri, who would later emerge as Osama bin Laden's right-hand man and a principal architect of 9/11. Yet, a quarter of a century later, the complex, mutually reinforcing, yet ambivalent relationship between the regime and the Islamists would continue: the Brotherhood would control nearly 20 percent of the seats in the Egyptian parliament despite the fact that it was officially banned, while some 15,000 people, many of them Islamists, were held in prison without trial under the country's emergency laws.

A New Arabism?

"Their god had ... failed, spectacularly so. It had been called Arabism, or Arab nationalism, or pan-Arabism," Israeli academic Martin Kramer wrote in one of the many obituaries for Arab nationalism published in the wake of the 1990–91 Gulf War,[83] during which Saddam Hussein, one of the last of the Ba'athists, held high the banner of Arab nationalism. "The authoritarian state, the nihilistic opposition: the middle ground has been scorched," Fouad Ajami, who had been declaring the "end of pan-Arabism" since the 1970s, pronounced as if from on-high. It was all because, Ajami said, the "new classes, half-educated and bewildered, [had] sought to simplify the world around them."[84] But others saw a different future. In 1992, As'ad AbuKhalil wrote of the surfacing of an "emotional unity, *wihdat hal* (unity of situation)" among Arabs. He saw this unity as the kernel around which a new Arab ideology would coalesce, with three "organically linked components: Arab nationalism, Islam, and democratization."[85] Subsequent events – 9/11, the US invasion of Afghanistan, the Iraq war, and the conflict between Israel and Hezbollah – only underlined the commonality of interests and shared sense of identity among all Arabs. As Arab American leader James Zogby put it, reporting on a 2006 poll that showed a significant downturn in the mood in the Arab world, "The people of the Arab world are organically linked not only by geography, history and culture. They are tied by sentiment, as well."[86] Whether supporters of democratic change or the political status quo, secularists or devout Muslims, they were on the defensive, rallying in the face of the American and Israeli Other; off balance and adrift. "[T]he blurring of Palestine and Iraq has ... swamped the self-image of the Arabs of the Middle East – and the image the world has of them – in a tide of blood," the late Lebanese journalist Samir Kassir wrote.[87]

What had emerged was a duality of identity, overlapping and often deeply intertwined, in which Arab and Islam were inseparable. "Arab nationalism and fundamentalism, thanks to George Bush have become the same. The invasion of Iraq really galvanized the masses, made them feel that their identity as Arabs is being threatened," Hassan Ibrahim, an Al-Jazeera reporter, told me. This phenomenon was made more vivid by a heightened sense of Islamic identity in some quarters as the old ideas have been discredited and the promises of secular government have proven empty. "People have come to identify themselves more as Muslims during the last five years in response to the US-led 'war on terrorism,'" noted Diaa Rashwan, an Egyptian specialist on Islamic movements.[88] Unity in the face of adversity. It is always thus. "There is an implicit consciousness of common notions – an underlying framework of language, ideas, and values which, while not always self-evident or explicitly expressed, becomes apparent when the shared assumptions are violated or attacked," Dale Eickelman and James Piscatori have observed.[89]

It was a shared consciousness shaped, in part, by the television screen, as adherents of every *ism* take part in the electronically shared experience of siege by the Other. The result was what Khalil Rinnawi somewhat flippantly called McArabism – "a pan-Arab, regional expression of Arab identity conveyed through Arab transnational television" that invokes "Islamic symbols and religious elements."[90] – and Israeli researcher Barry Rubin more awkwardly termed "national Islamism."[91]

At the same time, many Arab intellectuals were engaged in a reassessment; a search for a new definition of the Arab-Islamic cultural heritage. Arabs were anything but united on the form that would take. "What constitutes the Arab-Islamic heritage and who is to define it remain the most pressing and controversial issue[s] facing the Arab-Muslim societies," according to Fauzi Najjar.[92] Make no mistake, deep chasms of belief still divided religious and secular Arab Muslims, paralleled by bitter resentments, rigidly held stereotypes, and nationalistic sentiments – sometimes bordering on xenophobia – among the Arabs themselves. Indeed, the chasms in the Arab world – between the haves and the have-nots, between the nationalists and the pan-Arabists, the secular elite and the Islamists, between each of the tribes with flags – ran deep. Egyptians used the word "Arab" disparagingly to describe the rich Gulf Arabs who crowded Cairo's hotels and nightclubs to escape the summer heat and/or cultural rigors of Ramadan – the so-called

"Saudi season" – each year, the resentment encapsulated in the lyrics of a popular Egyptian song: "Our daughters prostitute themselves in the Mercedes of filthy rich Saudis."[93]

"We need a reformulation of the idea of Arabism," Lebanese writer Elias Khouri told a crowd at a Beirut coffee house who had gathered to discuss the late Samir Kassir's book, *Being Arab*, in the spring of 2007, as Lebanon itself struggled to find a new national identity.[94] The "fragmentation" of the Arab identity was evident in both the nightly car bombs that sent the Beirut coffee house crowd scurrying home early and in the civil war between Sunnis and Shi'ites a thousand miles away in Iraq, with its regional reverberations. It all meant, journalist Rami Khouri, no direct relation to Elias, told the same audience, that while "the spirit of being an Arab is very real," the issues of identity, the norms of governance, and the values of society that are the foundations of a true sense of *being* remained elusive and ill-defined. "We face the question of how do we construct a new national myth that grabs people," Khouri said. "I don't think we have yet devised a language of how to address our description of ourselves; if we are despotic, free, united, Kurd, Christian, Shi'a, Berber," *Daily Star* Publisher Jamil Mroue observed on another occasion. "We in the Arab world have now a huge, very confusing, pile." For North African scholar Muhammad Abid al-Jabiri, the goal of any reassessment was

> to articulate the components of Arab-Islamic culture and to examine them critically, seeking to reconstruct the Arab self on new bases, free from the negative paradigms of the past...[95]

Many People, One Banner

In an earlier age, Sayyid Qutb wrote that "the idea of homeland (*watan*) [is] an idea in the consciousness (*fikrab fi al-shu'ur*), not a piece of land."[96] In the summer of 2006, the banner of that consciousness was seized by another Islamist leader, Hassan Nasrallah of Hezbollah, as the Arab world was galvanized by the Shi'ite militia's success in fighting Israel to a standstill in spite of the overwhelming firepower of the Jewish state. Nasrallah was hailed as the new pan-Arab leader. Hezbollah, an Islamist militia espousing an Arab nationalist cause – the defense of the Lebanese homeland and solidarity with their Palestinian brothers – galvanized Sunnis and Shi'a, the devout and the secular, alike. Abd al-Rahman al-Bazzaz (1913–73), a former Iraqi prime minister and Muslim theorist, once said that "the Muslim Arab, when he exalts his heroes, partakes of two emotions, that of the pious Muslims and that of the proud nationalist."[97] So it was with Nasrallah, who, at the height of the battle, said his militia fought on behalf of "every Arab, Muslim, Christian and honorable person in the world"[98] and that Hezbollah's "victory" belonged to all the "oppressed, wronged, wretched, and the people who love steadfastness, bravery, magnanimity, values and honor."[99]

"I feel Nasrallah lives within me," wrote Howeida Taha, a strongly secular Egyptian columnist, succinctly summing up a widely held sense of identification.[100] In Cairo, protestors carried Nasrallah's portraits alongside those of Nasser; newborns across the Arab world were named for the Hezbollah leader; in Damascus, a Hezbollah flag fluttered from the statue of Saladin (Salah al-Din ibn Ayyub, 1138–93), the great Kurdish general who led the Arab armies in victory over the Crusaders; and in the Occupied Territories, a paean written by an obscure Palestinian band became an instant hit:

> I hail thee, O Hawk of Lebanon/ Welcome Nasrallah/ Here you come, one who has become victorious with the help of God/ Nasrallah, you brave man/ You have responded to our call for revenge/ as the Arab blood became hotter and hotter.[101]

Hezbollah had previously led the Lebanese guerrilla war against Israel's 20-year occupation of south Lebanon. In 2000, it became the first Arab army to force Israel to withdraw from Arab land. After that "Arab victory," as Hezbollah called it, Shi'ite spiritual leader Hussein Fadlallah said his people "have always held fast to their Arabian nationalism and Islamism and to their homeland and Arab-Islamic identity."[102] Now, in the eyes of Arabs across the region, the Shi'ite Islamist militia had once more burnished its Arab credentials, proving it was equal to the mighty Israeli army, defending Arab honor and dignity and energizing the Arab world in the process. It all seemed to give new veracity to historian Elie Kedourie's observation a quarter century before: "Thus the ideology of Arab nationalism ... in one way or another affirms a fundamental unbreakable link between Islam and Arabism."[103]

Even Sunni Arab rulers in the Gulf, who had refused to endorse Hezbollah's war in its early stages, shifted direction in the face of public opinion, claiming the Shi'ite militia as their own. "The Lebanese people and their resistance have achieved the first Arab victory, something we had longed for," said Qatar's emir, Hamad bin Khalifa al-Thani, after the ceasefire was put in place.[104] Wrote Abdul Rahman al-Rashad, general manager of the Saudi-owned Al-Arabiya television channel, referring to Nasrallah, "If only Arab demagogues would stop falsifying facts, feelings and heroics, and follow the example of the war leader!"[105]

For the moment at least, Nasrallah seemed to fulfill what columnist Rami Khouri described as the "almost genetic need" of the Arab nation "for a strong political personality who emerges to lead its quest to regain its honor;"[106] as well as the periodic Islamic requirement for a *Mujaddid* (reviver), a powerful persona with the potential to transform politics and history. Yet Nasrallah was not alone in tapping – or attempting to tap – this new Arab consciousness. As if in answer to Nasrallah's growing popularity on the streets of his own capital, Gamal Mubarak, heir-apparent to his father the Egyptian president and bearer of the first name of the leader who symbolized Arab nationalism, sought to stake his own claim to regional leadership. "We do not accept visions from abroad that try to dissolve the Arab identity and the joint Arab efforts," he declared, in a carefully crafted speech in which he called for Egypt to develop nuclear capacity, in essence an *Arab* nuclear capacity.[107] *Arab* identity; joint *Arab* efforts. They were words calculated to both distance Mubarak from Washington at a time when anti-Americanism was again on the rise in Egypt and recall to the days when Cairo was the capital of the "Arab nation." The borders were still there, but so too was a revived regional consciousness that transcended the lines in the sand and the vagaries of skin tone. "Arab is not a race," says Abderrahim Foukara, Al-Jazeera's Washington bureau chief. "If it were, there would be very few Arabs in the world today. It is rather, a way of being."

By year's end, the sectarian spectacle of Saddam Hussein's execution, at which he was taunted and humiliated by his Shi'ite guards, once more frayed the tenuous bonds of unity between Sunni and Shi'a across the Arab world but, at the same time, charges that this humiliation of Iraq's Sunnis was orchestrated by the unseen hand of Iran brought to the fore a new "Other" against which Sunni Arab nationalists and Islamists alike could rally.

5

Covering Darfur – A Question of Identity

"I told the press not to attack other Arab states."

Anwar Sadat

There was no story that better demonstrated the limits of freedom of information in the Arab media, or the degree to which ethnic, national, and religious identity shaped coverage, than the conflict in the Sudanese province of Darfur. Nor was there an issue more controversial among Arab journalists themselves. Not Iraq, where, according to the Committee to Protect Journalists, by the end of 2008 about 120 Arab journalists, and another 51 Arab media support staff, had lost their lives since the US invasion; not Palestine, where journalists were caught between Israel and the Palestinians, and between Fatah and Hamas; not Lebanon, where reporters continued to be firmly in the crosshairs of rival factions and governments.

In Darfur, ethnic Arab militias were preying on ethnic African tribes in what President George Bush had labeled "genocide." The conflict was a hot-button issue in Arab newsrooms not because of the physical danger involved in reporting the story, but because the issue struck right to the heart of the mission of Arab journalism and the self-identity of those who practiced it. Two gatherings in the spring of 2007 provided a window on the internal debate among Arab journalists as they struggled to rationalize their coverage of the conflict.

The first took place in Cairo, when 50 journalists from across the Arab world came together for a gathering the center I ran organized with the International Crisis Group and Save Darfur to discuss the challenges and limitations to their reporting; the second, two weeks later, at the annual Arab Broadcast Forum convention of Arab broadcasters in Abu Dhabi. The central issue: "The Arabs see the victims are not Arabs, and we don't care," Khaled Ewais, Al-Arabiya's political producer, told the Cairo gathering. Fayez el-Sheikh Saleik, Khartoum correspondent of *Al-Hayat*, concurred: "Sudan is a marginal country when it comes to the Arab region." Some pointed to an even more insidious issue: In other regional conflicts, Arabs were the victims. In Darfur, Arab militias were the perpetrators. That was not a popular topic among governments or among Arab journalists. "The media are directly responsible for this crisis," an angry representative of the Liberation Front of Darfur told those assembled in Cairo. While few of the journalists were willing to go quite that far, there was widespread acknowledgment that Darfur was the biggest untold story of the Arab world.

"Arab journalists are working within non-democratic systems, so you can't expect them to talk about Darfur," said Saleik of *Al-Hayat*. The Arab media was "ultimately very interconnected with the ruling system" according to Ahmed Hissou, a Syrian journalist working for the Arabic service of Germany's Deutsche Welle radio, and Arab governments "do not accept any internal crises, whether religious or ethnic." As a result, said Kamal al-Gizouli of the Sudanese writer's union, when they did report on Darfur, Arab media "are talking only about sovereignty when the real issue is the rights of people to live in peace."

The numbers were grim. At that point, more than 250,000 dead; 2.5 million internally displaced; 4 million in need of relief assistance. "Why is there no debate in the Arab mass media?" asked Nadim Hasbani, Arab media officer for the International Crisis Group. Amani Tawil of the Al-Ahram Center for Strategic Studies offered one explanation: "Selective information." Television, she said, "reflects the special agenda of each government in the Arab region," while newspapers "have a tendency to marginalize stories about other Arab governments." Until the recent Saudi initiative on Darfur, Arab regimes – and thus most

Arab media – had a hands-off approach to Sudan. Non-journalists like Roland Marchal of the Centre d'Etudes et de Recherches Internationales in Paris and Khaled Mansour, spokesman for the World Food Program, praised some Western coverage – including that of the BBC and *New York Times* columnist Nicholas Kristof – for putting a human face on the Darfur conflict by focusing on the plight of individuals. *Al-Hayat* was also singled out as "indefatigable in its continuous coverage of the events in Darfur." But the overwhelming message was that when most Arab media bothered to report on the crisis, they focused on political machinations, not on human impact. "Arab media coverage is like a person on a plane looking down," said Sudanese Member of Parliament and political activist Salih Mahmoud Osman, while, he said, Western coverage portrayed the pain of the victims up close.

But it wasn't the "experts" alone who were critical. This writer had never heard a group of Arab journalists so brutally frank in public about the pressures and pitfalls of their own coverage. "We Arab journalists, sorry to say, deal with Darfur as governments do," said Tahir el-Mardi, Khartoum correspondent for Al-Jazeera. "We have 22 agendas on Darfur [for the 22 Arab countries] and the West has one. Arab journalists, to say the truth, are entangled in political issues." Mohamed Barakat, political editor at the Egyptian daily *Al-Akhbar,* said that in the Arab world, all politics truly were local: "There is an agenda which is local according to the country in which it takes place," which thus shaped how that nation's media reported the story. Others pointed to the constant talk of Zionist plots and Western conspiracies in Arab coverage of Darfur, the preoccupation with "strategic Arab interests," and what one political editor called the "fantasies" about a Western oil grab, all of which came at the cost of reporting on the human toll. Al-Gizouli of the Sudanese writer's union said the history of Arab journalism was to blame. An entire generation of journalists and intellectuals had been weaned on notions of Arab mobilization and confrontation in the face of the imperialist and colonialist aggressor. That legacy was heard loudly in the Darfur coverage. "There is no voice but the battle with Israel and the imperialists. That is what has been fed to the Arab intellectuals. If there is no role for Zionists, [the Arab reporter] creates it from his own imagination and Zionism means conspiracy, the main gallows on which hangs the conscience of the journalists," said one reporter.

"The Arab journalist is an offspring of his environment," agreed Hissou of Deutsche Welle "We had imperialism and Zionism with double-standards. Arab officials say Bush is jeopardizing Sudan, so Arab journalists must accept this conspiracy." He read a series of excerpts from Arab coverage that, he claimed, demonstrated that the reporting "is heavily freighted with ideological and political assumptions that...imperil our journalistic neutrality." Hissou quoted *Al-Hayat's* influential columnist Jihad Khazen as writing that the Bush administration and the Israel lobby were using Darfur "as a smokescreen to hide other crimes, from Palestine to Iraq," and Hissou claimed that while Al-Jazeera had given substantial coverage to Darfur, "it has invited Arab analysts, writers, and physicians to ridicule all reports transmitted by the global television networks on the various acts of murder, rape, and forced displacement." El-Mardi of Al-Jazeera's Khartoum bureau countered by saying that the channel covered the crisis "in an objective manner" and "any topic concerning policy in Sudan has the opinion, the facts and the counteropinion. If it does not, it does not go to air." However, he added, "Darfur is a political issue in the first instance" and "there is a very thin line between the professional journalist and the political person." Ewais of Al-Arabiya presented data showing that Arab media devoted a small fraction of the amount of time and space to Darfur that it did to crises like Iraq, Palestine. and Lebanon, while the Western media gave it significantly more attention. Salih, the Sudanese MP, said covering Darfur "doesn't prevent us from discussing the humanitarian suffering in Darfur as well." "If we say there are violations of human rights in Darfur, we are not denying violations by Israel and the U.S. in Iraq and Palestine," agreed Al-Gizouli. Still, he lamented, "It is very hard to put Darfur on a par with Arab stories."

"I know, sometimes the story is complex and difficult to communicate," Khaled Mansour of the World Food Program told those gathered, "but the Arab media's coverage of the humanitarian side of the conflict has been very weak" when compared to that of Western news organizations. For many newspapers, money was a big issue when it came to Darfur. Several Egyptian editors said their publications simply did not have the resources to cover the crisis properly. But others pointed out that the pan-Arab newspapers and satellite TV channels had plenty of money and a level of professionalism that had brought a human face to other regional tragedies. "Al-Jazeera focuses on the human side in Palestine," said al-Gizouli. "So you have to ask why they don't do the same in Darfur. There is a double-standard on human feelings. Al-Jazeera is operated by Arabs so they show sympathy for the Palestinian and Iraqi people and show the dead babies there, but when it comes to Darfur, they don't. They want to show Arabs always as victims."

At times the debate grew heated. Some journalists in the audience objected to the constant criticism. A divide began to arise between the foreign experts and black-skinned Sudanese journalists one side, and, on the other, print reporters from Egypt and other Arab countries. "We are here to participate in a discussion about developing better coverage, not to have scorn heaped on us," an Egyptian editor snapped at one speaker. "I have traveled to Darfur; I am not here to listen to criticism." Yet the comment opened a far-ranging discussion about the fact that many Arab news organizations saw – and reported – a distorted view of Darfur because they visited as part of tours arranged by the Sudanese government which, according to Sudanese columnist Alhaj Warrag, took the view that "everything in Darfur is a conspiracy of the Zionists" and imposed "redlines" on its own media that meant Sudanese reporters could not cover anything about violations of human rights, police or security. "I am an Arab and a Muslim and I was nearly ready to accept this," he said. Then he went to the camps "and I met someone who watched his sister being raped by the Janjaweed [Arab militia]." Barakat of *Al-Akhbar* said guided tours and journalist visits as part of official delegations "pave the way for getting to Darfur but you are besieged by the agenda of this particularly diplomatic mission, which means you cannot flee." The other problem was that such visits offered a skewed view. "Most of the journalists invited by the Sudanese government go to camps [that were] in good condition, that seem like the Hilton hotel, but Western journalists go in through Chad and see the real situation," said el-Mardi from Al-Jazeera.

As with the Western media, Arab journalists faced huge logistic hurdles in breaking out of the guided tour approach to covering Darfur.

Saleik, the *Al-Hayat* Khartoum correspondent, recalled that for a July 2004 visit to Darfur, he went on a cross-Africa odyssey from Khartoum to Nairobi, to Lagos, to Chad, and finally into Darfur. "The nature of the crisis is different from Iraq or Palestine," he told the gathering. "In Darfur, you can walk a long time in the desert to reach the news, but in Palestine it's easy." Then there was the issue every reporter ultimately confronted: How important was the story to the editor and the reader? "Palestine and Lebanon was the priority," Saleik recalled of his coverage in past years. "We sent many stories from Darfur, but they didn't get published." "What is news?" asked Hassan Satti of *Asharq Al-Awsat*. "That's a complicated question. There is the problem of who compiles the news; the psychological and mental structures and cultural and religious dimensions. Coverage is with the spirit of the editor and he can fall victim to his traditions. If it is news, you shouldn't take a point of view but if you are going to eat, some people will select the best food. Each editor or journalist has his internal censor." As one Egyptian journalist whispered to me in an aside, "You need to know who you are working for." He also said that when he tried to write stories about Darfur from Cairo, his editor would ask suspiciously, "Why are you writing this? What is your motive?"

The most emotional attack on Arab media coverage of Darfur came from Nabil Kassem, producer/director of *Jihad on Horseback*, the Darfur documentary commissioned by Al-Arabiya's parent company MBC three years before but killed after a phone call from Sudan's president to the then-Saudi crown prince, who in turn called the owner of Al-Arabiya, who also happened to be King Fahd's brother-in-law.

Kassem, who still worked for Al-Arabiya, was bitter about what he called "fantasy" reports in the Arab media that Arab tribes were forced to flee attacking Africans and media claims that the existence of refugee camps was just Zionist propaganda. "The Arab tribes fleeing from the Africans, where are they?" he asked rhetorically. "Then I went to the camps the Arab media said didn't exist." Kassem said he left his objectivity in the dust of the Darfur desert. "I am speaking as a humanitarian, not a journalist who is neutral," he told the gathering. "How can anyone go and see millions of displaced people and remain balanced?"

"Until now, I cannot forget what I saw. I left women and children lying there dying." With tears in his eyes, he confronted the Egyptian editor who had earlier bristled at criticism of Arab coverage and boasted that he, too, had visited Darfur. "Did you see that? Did you see them dying?" Kassem challenged the startled journalist. "Then why didn't you write it? I am in a rage. Arabs should be ashamed having one million Muslims begging for help. Shame!" Nadim Hasbani of the International Crisis Group said Al-Arabiya had largely abandoned Darfur coverage for several years after the documentary was pulled. Most of the channel's reporting was confined to pieces filed from New York by UN correspondent Talal Haj. There was "no information from the ground," which "left the audience thinking the UN controls the crisis" and thus, it was not an Arab issue. Al-Jazeera also largely ignored the crisis, he said, until its coverage "changed drastically" between 2004 and 2006. In the previous year or two, Al-Arabiya's coverage had likewise dramatically stepped up. "We run very critical coverage of Darfur now. We don't care who we offend," one executive of the channel told me. Why then, I asked, had *Jihad on Horseback* been killed and other Darfur reporting abandoned? "Back then," he said with a sardonic smile, "we cared [who was offended]." That Al-Arabiya's news executives shared the dais with producer Kassem said much about the change of viewpoint – and their willingness to press against the internal red lines (though Al-Arabiya itself had still not aired the documentary, they had sold it to an international NGO, which then made it available around the world).

Darfur was also on the agenda at the Arab Broadcast Forum in Abu Dhabi two weeks later. "I think we have less coverage from Darfur; I think sometimes we editorialize many issues in this part of the world, we feel that this is part of our pan-Arab world and we feel we should keep hands off this," a representative of Kuwait TV told his colleagues. Samir Sabbah, head of Middle East media for Reuters TV, concurred: "If you watch any Arab station any night you will have reporting on Iraq, on Palestine, but it is rare to see news about Darfur. So no, there isn't enough." The debate between NGOs and other policy experts who monitored the Darfur issue and those who covered it, which began in Cairo, continued in Abu Dhabi. And once more Al-Jazeera was in the crosshairs. "Al-Jazeera sees itself as voice of Muslims and Arabs in the world, but why don't they implement this policy in Darfur? Why don't they tell us it's Muslims killing Muslims?" asked Hasbani of ICG. There was a general acknowledgment from Arab broadcasters that Darfur suffered from the same subtle racist overtones that colored US coverage of sub-Saharan Africa; the perception that, in the brutal newsroom maxim, it's just "more flies on black faces;" just another interminable African conflict. In fact, James Zogby, president of the Arab American Institute, unveiled a survey that found that more than 80 percent of the Arab public in four Arab countries believed pan-Arab satellite channels should devote more coverage to Darfur. "The myth that Arabs don't care about Darfur is just that, a myth," Zogby told the broadcasters. But, Zogby revealed, Arab viewers only took that position after they learned that the victims in Darfur – like the perpetrators – were Muslims.

There may have been a public appetite for the story, but some Sudanese journalists were still skeptical that their Arab colleagues would give Darfur more than a glancing look. In Cairo, columnist Warrag used Auschwitz as an analogy for Arab media denial of the reality in Darfur. "Can you imagine having your village burned and people say nothing happened to you?" "We shouldn't kid ourselves," CNN's Nasser told the Abu Dhabi gathering. "Any coverage of the conflict is fraught with practical issues. It's often dangerous, it saps resources and access is difficult. But it's a story we must cover," Andrew Simmons of Al-Jazeera English said Western and Arab journalists alike – "regardless of your branding" – were obligated to devote resources to covering the conflict. "We have a responsibility to our viewers to analyze, explain, to further the political debate over Darfur."

For Simmons, a British journalist, and Nasser, an Arab working for a leading US network, such an approach was self-evident. But it was far more problematic for Arab news organizations that operated at the pleasure of their governmental and corporate masters. And for Arab journalists steeped in a culture in which Arabs were the victims – rarely the aggressors – it was an approach that challenged their very self-view, which underlined the ultimate question raised in Cairo by an angry and frustrated representative of the Darfur Liberation Front: "Arab mass media talk about journalists being killed in Iraq. But why don't you send journalists to be killed in Darfur?"

The debate over Darfur encapsulated in one story the many conflicting pressures that determine what makes it into the newspapers and onto the television broadcasts of the Arab world and what does not. Darfur did not fit the script and thus many Arab journalists felt they could not, or should not, cover the story. Ideology was the overarching factor shaping coverage. Here were the issues of "confrontation and mobilization" that had long defined the Arab media. Arabs were at war, according to this thinking, and a mobilization press had no business undermining the cause because, after all, there was "a thin line between a journalist and a political person." Extra-media influences were also clearly at work. The ability of the president of Sudan to pick up the phone and kill the story and the fact that the main shareholder in Al-Arabiya's parent company was willing to comply demonstrated both the power of politics and the power of politically wired owners in the Arab world. As the Egyptian journalist had whispered, "You need to know who you are working for." But at root of the lack of Darfur coverage was the self-view of the journalists themselves. There is an academic theory, self-evident like so many of them, that, "People who are similar to a journalist will be covered differently from people who are dissimilar."[1] If anyone doubted that, the lack of glaring headlines and absence of graphic video from Darfur, was, as the scholars say, "empirical evidence."

From the perspective of Arab journalists, the protagonists were "Us," and we rarely want to criticize our own. Those dark-skinned victims were, quite clearly, "Them." Us and Them. Self and Other. Darfur was emblematic of how that played out in Arab journalism, but in the big picture, the story was just a sideshow.

6

Arab Journalism in Context

It is too much to ask [reporters] to make impartial, quality
news if they are underpaid.

Ulin Ni'am Yusron, Independent
Journalists Alliance (Indonesia)

The Search for Objectivity

In the years after 9/11, officials in the Bush administration repeatedly
contrasted the "bias" of Arab journalists with that of the "balance" in
the US media. Such a dichotomy is thick with cultural assumptions.
From an Anglo-American point of view, the primary benchmark for
journalistic professionalism is the notion of objectivity, which is considered by some journalists in Europe and the US to be sacred. Media
historian Michael Schudson defines objectivity as "the view that one
can and should separate facts from values."[1] It is the polar opposite of
the Islamic view that "information and knowledge are not value-free,
but have normative, ethical and moral imperatives."[2]

One of the early elucidations of the mission and values of the modern
US news industry came in the "Canons of Journalism," a code of ethics
adopted by the American Society of Newspaper Editors (ASNE) at their
1923 convention. The code listed "Sincerity, Truthfulness, Accuracy" as
core journalistic principles. Under the principle of "Impartiality," the
Canon declared, "News reports should be free of opinion or bias of any

kind."[3] That approach exemplifies the "liberal" model of journalism, characterized by a commercial media – rather than one owned by political or governmental interests – limited state intervention, and a strong sense of professionalism, centered on the "'the objectivity norm' – the idea that journalists should be politically neutral and separated from attachments to political parties and organized social groups."[4]

The belief in the ideals of objectivity – or, if not pure objectivity, then at least, fairness and balance – lies at the heart of the self-view of US journalists, as well as that of many of their Western European counterparts. As veteran newspaper editors Bill Kovach and Tom Rosentiel wrote in their classic text, *The Elements of Journalism*, "Journalism's first obligation is to the truth."[5] "[E]xcellent journalists ... have core journalistic values running through them like a stick of rock: they report with impeccable accuracy [and] they know instinctively there are two sides to every story," according to Roger Mosey, head of BBC TV News.[6] Jack Fuller, former publisher of the *Chicago Tribune*, calls this commitment to objectivity "the truth discipline," which "requires news reports to withhold ultimate judgment on matters of value."[7] That aspiration is often far removed from the reality, as a host of studies of US coverage of the post-9/11 era have chronicled.

Mainstream American media literally and figuratively waved the flag following the attacks of 9/11 and the invasion of Iraq, as did elements of the British media. Western journalists – particularly those in the US and Britain – were also seen by many critics, this writer among them, to have framed their coverage of the 2006 Lebanon war in such a way that Hezbollah was cast as the aggressor, a framing disputed by many in Europe, much less the Arab world. This willingness of reporters to allow themselves to become weapons of war demonstrates that when covering routine news, journalists may approximate some semblance of balance, but, as a study of terrorism coverage found, when "society's core values are under threat – such as with physical or political violence or terrorist attacks – journalists switch to a cultural narrative that moves the public mind back toward the dominant cultural order."[8]

The search for objectivity can be traced back to Max Weber (1864–1920), who argued in *Science as a Vocation* that values are arbitrary and science cannot choose between them. Sociologists took up the cry with the rise of "value-free" social science, the goal of which was research independent of the researcher's values.[9] The concept of objectivity has its roots in Kant (1724–1804) who emphasized the distinction between "pure reason" and "practical reason," and separated the realm of nature from the realm of morals. In Kant's new world, "the distinction between facts and values, between what is – the natural, and what ought to be – and the moral, became fundamental."[10]

In journalistic terms, the idea was that the reporter must "stand outside oneself and so separate [the reporting] from one's own subjective preferences about what the world should be."[11] Walter Lippman (1889–1974), an outspoken proponent of journalistic objectivity, said it was essential for the reporter to "remain clear and free of his irrational, his unexamined, his or her unacknowledged prejudgments."[12] Yet, from the beginning, inherent in the concept of objectivity was a strong element of the subjective:

> [Objectivity] is not just a claim about what kind of knowledge is reliable. It is also a moral philosophy, a declaration of what kind of thinking one should engage in, in making moral decisions. It is, moreover, a political commitment, for the ideal of objectivity provides a guide to what groups one should acknowledge as relevant audiences for judging one's own thoughts and acts.[13]

This "declaration" of "*what kind of thinking*" one should engage in itself brings to bear the particular values of the declarer, and the decision on what is "relevant" can only be a subjective judgment. "Objectivity," says Fuller of the *Chicago Tribune*, "assumes an independence between the observer and the phenomenon observed that simply does not exist."[14] Indeed, objectivity is dependent on the shared worldview of those doing the perceiving. In other words, send an Israeli journalist and a Palestinian journalist out to cover the same story on the West Bank, and the result is likely to be very different, even if both set out to be meticulously balanced. The potential for distortion is also embedded in the sense of *noblesse oblige* with which some journalists approach their job, best summed up in the infamous comment by David Brinkley (1920–2003), then the anchor of *The NBC Nightly News*: "News is what I say it is. It's something worth knowing by *my* standards."[15]

Defining Objectivity

The quest to achieve objectivity – or Truth with a capital "T" – is a relatively new development in American and British journalism. As late as the 1920s, "objectivity" was not a term American journalists or critics of US journalism used and complaints about the lack of balance extend back as far as the industry itself. In the 1830s, author James Fenimore Cooper (1789–1851) engaged in a series of lawsuits against newspapers, which he considered "corrupt" and "vulgar":

> If newspapers are useful in overthrowing tyrants, it is only to establish tyranny of their own. … With loud professions of freedom of opinion, there is no tolerance; with a parade of patriotism, no sacrifice of interests; and with fulsome panegyrics on propriety, no decency.[16]

From the flag-waving Fleet Street journalists who filed paeans to British troops in the Crimea to the famous British correspondent Macdonald Hastings (1909–82), who said during World War II, "Objectivity can come back into fashion when the shooting is over,"[17] a commitment to truth was not historically the strong suit of English-speaking journalists on either side of the Atlantic.

Even though he once declared that he would prefer newspapers without government to government without newspapers, US President Thomas Jefferson (1743–1826) was also under no illusions about the credibility of newspapers of his day. "Truth itself becomes suspicious by being put into the polluted vehicle," he once wrote to an acquaintance.[18] The so-called "penny press" of 1830s America was largely bought and paid for by politicians and political parties, which not only provided investment capital, but also supported the papers through political advertisements. "Journalists," wrote the biographer of New York editor James Gordon Bennett (1795–1872), "were usually little more than secretaries dependent upon cliques of politicians, merchants, brokers, and office-seekers for their position and bread."[19]

That remained essentially true until Horace Greeley (1811–72) laid the groundwork for modern American journalism by founding the *New York Tribune* in 1841. But "objectivity" was still far removed from his mind. His goal, said Greeley, was "a journal removed alike from servile partisanship on the one hand and from gagged, mincing neutrality on the other."[20]

In his history of journalistic objectivity, Schudson chronicles the sudden and dramatic shift from opinion – and exaggeration – to strenuous adherence to what he quotes Julius Chambers (1850–1920), managing editor of the *New York Herald*, describing as, "Facts, facts; nothing but facts" and what H.L. Mencken complained was his paper's "craze for mathematical accuracy."[21] Lincoln Steffens (1866–1936), a reporter for the *Evening Post*, recalled that under the new regime, "Reporters were to report news as it happened, like machines, without prejudice, color, and without style; all alike. Humor or any sign of personality in our reports was caught, rebuked, and, in time, suppressed. As a writer, I was permanently hurt by my years on the *Post*."[22] But eventually, most American reporters "saluted an ethic in which nonbelief was their pride."[23]

Yet from the first time the mantra of journalistic objectivity was intoned, the contradictions inherent in the self-view of Western – and particularly American – journalism have been apparent. *The New York Times* has long been held up as the gold standard of US journalism. When Adolph Ochs (1858–1935), then publisher of the *Chattanooga Times*, bought the faltering New York paper in 1896, he set out to revolutionize the industry, laying out the *Times'* philosophy in a lengthy editorial. The paper's mission, he wrote, was to

> ... give the news, all the news, in concise and attractive form ... to give the new impartially, without fear or favor, regardless of any party, sect, or interest involved ... nor will there be a departure from the general tone and character and policies ... that have distinguished The New York Times as a nonpartisan paper – unless it be, if possible, to intensify its devotion to the cause of sound money and tariff reform, opposition to wastefulness and speculation in administering the public affairs and in its advocacy of

the lowest tax consistent with good government, maintain individual vested rights and assure the free exercise of a sound conscience.[24]

Thus, from the very beginning, protestations of impartiality notwithstanding, *The Times* emphatically had a mission, a "devotion" to a "cause," which meant it approached certain stories with a particular agenda. Today, it is generally recognized that there is no such thing as true objectivity. But with that recognition, come new concerns. Critics charge that the conventions of Western journalism are "used to contrive the illusion of objectivity,"[25] in a "strategic ritual"[26] designed to refute charges of bias or distortion,[27] thus allowing "journalists to maintain their pretence of dealing in facts and not values."[28] Former *New York Times* reporter John Hess called the quest for objectivity a "straight-jacket" that produces "bloodless journalism…no opinions, just the news, extruded in strings like sausage that could be cut to fit."[29] Thus, the critics say, are masked a host of underlying sins while audiences are provided with a distorted view of the world. There are many who argue that the best one can hope for is "functional truth,"[30] in which the journalist tries to put aside any conscious biases but acknowledges that he or she is reporting through a personal, cultural, nationalistic, or corporate frame. "This is what journalism is after – a practical, functional form of truth," according to Kovach and Rosenstiel. "It is not truth in the absolute or philosophical sense. It is not the truth of a chemical equation. But journalism can – and must – pursue truth in a sense by which we can operate day by day."[31]

However, an array of voices claim that even relative truth remains outside the grasp of the mainstream Anglo-American media. "The content of the news media inevitably reflects the interests of those who pay the bills," says former *New York Times* editor Herb Altschull.[32] That is not a new viewpoint. "[T]he Constitution does not guarantee objectivity of the press, nor is objectivity obtainable in a subjective world; and…the question…really raised is not whether the news shall be unprejudiced but rather whose prejudices shall color the news," wrote Morris Ernst in a "friend of the court" brief in the 1937 Supreme Court case *Associated Press* vs. *National Labor Relations Board*.[33]

In a scathing indictment of international coverage in the American media, Tom Fenton, former chief foreign correspondent for CBS News, charged that even if they are able to compartmentalize their own biases, reporters are subject to the institutional bias of their news organizations. "The news gets pre-selected to fit the political message. The home office rules over its correspondents, requiring them to acknowledge only the news that fits their vision of the world," Fenton wrote.[34] The British media has come in for much the same criticism. Even the vaunted BBC has not escaped, finding itself at the heart of a major controversy over reporting about British government policy toward Iraq, which eventually cost several of its top executives their jobs.[35]

The Vanity of Neutrality

There have been a number of movements in the US and Britain advocating that reporters shed their false "vanity of neutrality" and become change agents to drive policy and politics.[36] The "muckrakers" of the Gilded Age who attacked the privileged class "made no apologies for advocating change;"[37] the American journalist-participants of the Spanish Civil War, who believed in using their craft to stop the evils of fascism;[38] the "New Journalism" of the late nineteenth-century and early twentieth-century Europe;[39] and practitioners of American Tom Wolfe's brand of "New Journalism" in the 1960s, which blended fact and fiction in a search for a greater truth;[40] represented some of the best-known attempts to break out of the "straightjacket" of strict objectivity.

Even the patron-saint of American television journalists, Edward R. Murrow (1908–65) of CBS News, famously deviated from the ideal of neutrality when he took on the anti-Communist crusader Sen. Joseph McCarthy (1908–57) in the late 1950s. "The actions of the junior senator from Wisconsin have caused alarm and dismay amongst our allies abroad and given considerable comfort to our enemies," Murrow opined on his now legendary *See It Now* broadcast. "The fault, dear Brutus, lies not in our stars but in ourselves."[41] In an equally famous departure from that same network's strict commitment to objectivity, Murrow's spiritual heir, CBS News anchor Walter Cronkite, strayed into the realm of advocacy when, after a visit to Vietnam in the wake of the 1968 Tet offensive, he declared that negotiation was the only "rational way out" of the morass.[42]

In the latter part of the twentieth century, another wave of journalists also rebelled at the strictures of objectivity, arguing that they imposed a forced moral calculus when reporting war, under which each side must receive equal time and equal weight no matter the relative level of responsibility for the violence. Appalled by the slaughter of Bosnian Muslims at the hands of the Serbs, and of America's delayed intervention on their behalf, CNN correspondent Christine Amanpour and former BBC correspondent Martin Bell were among the leading voices calling for what Bell labeled a "journalism of attachment... which cares as well as knows."[43] Journalists, according to this approach, should help drive international policy, rather than simply report its effects. They aspired to emulate the noted Polish foreign correspondent Ryszard Kapuscinski, whose reporting was characterized by empathy for those he covered and who believed "truth still could remain hidden under an avalanche of facts."[44]

Meanwhile, in the US, the public journalism movement (also known as civic journalism), and the lesser-known communitarians,[45] sought to counter the "determined detachment" of the media that some critics claimed was destroying American democracy.[46] Proponents of public journalism, such as *Atlantic Magazine* editor James Fallows, argued that "many journalists are so wedded to the ideal of detachment that they fail to feel any loyalty toward their country, their community, their culture and religious institutions, and their fellow citizens. This idea of detachment leads these journalists to even abandon their own natural impulses as so much unnecessary human baggage getting in the way of capturing a good story."[47] A frequently cited example was that of an interview on the topic of journalistic ethics with Mike Wallace of CBS News and Peter Jennings of ABC News, in which the two were asked what they would do if they were with a group of enemy troops who had laid an ambush for US forces. Would they warn the Americans or film the action? Wallace said it was his job as a reporter to cover the event, not intervene; Jennings initially replied it was his duty as an American to warn them, then quickly backtracked and agreed with Wallace.[48]

Proponents of public journalism say such attitudes reflect detachment, elitism, negativity, and conflict orientation, which they denigrate as "the Four Horsemen of the journalistic apocalypse."[49] Conversely, on the international stage, meanwhile, they criticize what Edward Fouhy, a former news executive with all three major US networks, called the "bi-polar journalism" that has divided the world into "us" and "them."[50] Public journalists insist that "telling the news is not enough" and believe journalists should become "change agents" and "civil catalysts"[51] and should "remember that they are citizens as well as journalists"[52] and "transform their journalism into a mechanism for finding solutions to public problems."[53] Strict objectivity, wrote Johns Hopkins University professor and former *New York Times* reporter Herb Altschull, serves the interest of the powers-that-be, "for it safeguards the system against the explosive pressures for change. So long as 'both sides' are presented, neither side is glorified above the other, and the status quo remains unchallenged."[54] As *Washington Post* reporter Walter Pincus told Bill Moyers in a documentary about US media coverage of the lead-up to the Iraq war, balancing the Bush administration's statements with those of leading Democrats constituted objectivity "if you think there are only two sides" to the story "and if you're not interested in the facts."[55]

Paralleling the public journalism movement are the communitarians, who call for "a journalism of outrage" and insist that "reporting must be an instrument of social justice."[56] "Only a humane and just journalism has the capacity to affirm the newsworthiness of the oppressed," argued Leigh University professor Jack Lule in a study of US coverage of the killings of Brazilian street children.[57] The tiny "Peace Journalism" movement, meanwhile, insisted that conflict must be framed in terms of potential solutions rather than dwelling on body-counts.[58]

The idea of such social responsibility was a central theme in the Hutchins Commission report, which has been called "the most important statement on the media in the 20th century."[59] The US panel, officially called the Commission on the Freedom of the Press, was convened in 1947 by the president of the University of Chicago, Robert M. Hutchins (1899–1977), at the urging of *Time* founder Henry Luce (1898–1967) to examine the relationship between the media and government. The report, entitled *A Free and Responsible Press*, devoted considerable attention to concerns that American minority groups were not receiving adequate coverage in the media of the day. Among other things, it recommended that the press should (1) provide a "truthful and comprehensive account of the day's events in a context which gives them meaning;" (2) present and clarify "social goals and values of society;" (3) offer a "representative picture of the constituent groups of society;" and (4) serve as "a forum for the exchange of commitment and criticism."[60]

Cronkite of CBS News once said that American reporters tend to "side with humanity rather than authority,"[61] meaning they back the underdog, a perspective supported by a study that found a "majority of the journalists surveyed believe their work should be a force for social reform."[62] Put more simply, in the vernacular of the newsroom, the job of a journalist is to "comfort the afflicted and afflict the comfortable."[63] But many scholars argue that even if those ideals ever really took hold in the US media, they quickly became lost in the battle for audiences and ratings. Writing in a tone bordering on despair in the mid-1980s, Edward Lambeth of the University of Missouri School of Journalism surveyed a global landscape in which "news ... often brings pain, disappointment, and a frustrated feeling of individual impotence."[64]

In many ways, journalism in the US has come full circle. The dominance of "objective" reporting was challenged in the 1930s and 1940s with the rise of "interpretive reporting," which argued that facts alone cannot provide a fair and comprehensive understanding for the audience. "Show me a man who thinks he is objective and I'll show you a man who's deceiving himself," said *Time* publisher Henry Luce, whose magazine married news with a heavy dose of interpretation and opinion.[65] The proponents of public journalism and their allies are doing the same today, harking back to the days when a nineteenth century reporter approached the news not as an impartial observer, but "as a participant who spits on his hands, rolls up his sleeves, and jumps into the fight."[66]

That push and pull between impartiality and engagement is constantly at play in newsrooms. Indeed, partisan flag-waving in time of conflict has been the norm, from the American Revolution, during which the press played a major role in stoking the fires of rebellion; and the Spanish–American War, which featured William Randolph Hearst's famous telegram to photographer Frederick Remington, "You furnish the pictures. I will furnish the war;"[67] to the present day. Yet, public journalists and the like are the minority. In the idealized worldview of American newsgathering, as renowned White House correspondent Helen Thomas observed, "A journalist is detached, and the story is the thing" and "[t]he truth, rather than an agenda" is the goal.[68] Much the same is seen in the self-view of many British journalists, especially those at the BBC where, as BBC World Affairs Editor John Simpson put it, "First and foremost, there is a powerful tradition of objectivity and lack of bias."[69]

A certain sense of moral superiority is embedded in such an attitude. In his newspaper creed, E.W. Scripps, founder of the Scripps Howard media dynasty, wrote that the Bill of Rights was "a grant of freedom to the people; and we feel as journalists we are the trustees of this freedom."[70] "A newspaper is like a church," *Washington Post* columnist David Ignatius wrote in a novel about journalists. "It is built by ordinary sinners, people who in their individual lives are often petty and corrupt, but who collectively create an institution that transcends themselves."[71] A study of US journalism textbooks found them pervaded by a "belief in the morality and righteousness of journalism." So uniform was the message, journalism educator Bonnie S. Brennan reported, that the result was a prevailing "ideology that elevated the role of journalist to an almost sacred commitment and continued to reify a belief in the watchdog function of the press."[72] However, the "sacred" has often proven to be profane. In a historical study of investigative journalism, Mark Feldstein found that this "muckraking" model "has proved to be cyclical," waxing and waning with the political winds.[73]

Journalistic Soul-Searching

The prevailing view of the mission of journalism as articulated by many British and American reporters was summed up by Kovach and Rosentiel: "The primary purpose of journalism is to provide citizens with the information they need to be free and self-governing."[74] This definition is in line with the broader self-view of American and British journalists that they are serving the public good. Yet increasingly, reporters in the US and Britain are questioning whether the goal of serving society can be achieved by continuing to stand aloof from the world they cover. Writing in 1971, Johnstone found what he called two "pure" and competing ideologies of journalism: a "neutral" "nothing-but-the-truth" approach, in which journalists were messengers of information, and the "participant" "whole-truth" orientation, in which they played a more active role in covering the news. Most journalists, he reported, subscribed to elements of both.[75] A study of American journalists in the mid-1990s found them to be "less clinically detached than they were once expected to be."[76] As even the BBC's Simpson put it, objectivity does not mean journalists are required to be "moral eunuchs, blandly laying out different views as though they have equal value."[77]

Building on the studies cited above and others,[78] researchers David Weaver and G. Cleveland Wilhoit, both of Indiana University, surveyed 1,600 US journalists in 1982. They found that the reporters harbored "seemingly contradictory conceptions of their role (i.e. they were both 'objective' informers and 'subjective' interpreters)."[79] When they replicated their study a decade later, "a third of all journalists fully embraced both the interpretive and the disseminator roles."[80] Still, few were likely to subscribe to Henry Luce's defense of *Time* magazine's partisan coverage of the 1952 US presidential election that "it was *Time's* duty to explain why the country needs Ike. Any other form of journalism would have been unfair and uninvolved."[81]

Meanwhile, the rise of openly conservative news organizations, such as Fox News, *The Weekly Standard* and *The Washington Times*, the "Foxification" of some other cable channels with what some critics call "ideologues in seats that were once filled by real news reporters,"[82] and the appearance of avowedly liberal outlets such as Air America radio network and *Democracy Now*, signaled "a return of a partisan voice"[83] and a more polarized media. American journalists themselves were increasingly sensitive to the shift. While the majority still ranked fairness among their most important values, almost half expressed the concern that journalists too often let their own ideological views bleed into their coverage.[84]

7

Western Ethics, Western Arrogance

> If the code [of ethics] includes "tell the truth" and if we are to
> tell the truth, we will be put to death.
>
> Unnamed editor, *Gulf News*

In their quest to carve out their own brand of journalism, Arab news-
people have much in common with their counterparts in many other
parts of the world, who refuse to swallow whole the avowed mission
and values of Anglo-American journalists.

Europe is home to various journalistic approaches at odds with the
dominant US model. In southern Europe, opinion reigns supreme.
There, a survey in the early 1990s identified what researchers Thomas
Patterson and Wolfgang Donbach labeled the "polarized pluralist"
model, in which "journalistic professionalism ... is not as deeply rooted,"
writers and editors are "political actors above all," news organizations
are frequently "controlled by actors outside of journalism," and "a journalism of ideas" prevails in contrast to the "journalism of information."[1]
In northern Europe, meanwhile, the commitment to press freedom
is tempered by a strong sense of social responsibility. But if there are
differences in approach between American and British journalists on
the one hand and their continental counterparts on the other, the dis-
tinctions between how journalism is practiced in the West and in the
so-called "global south" are often even more profound.

Beyond the West

As in the US and Europe, the reality of journalism in other parts of the world has often fallen far short of the ideal. In the latter half of the twentieth century Western organizations such as the Ford Foundation funded institutions designed to establish a press based on Western-style notions of objectivity and independence. But those ideals did not always fit the local view that the media should *drive* development, not *question* it. In fact, this so-called development journalism has been identified as "one of the first major attempts to break away from Western concepts of news."[2] In its most idealistic form, Western-style journalism acts as tribune for the masses; a public sphere in which critical issues are debated and the body politic comes together to speak truth to power. In the development journalism model, media is closely aligned with the government. Ghanian leader Kwame Nkrumah saw the African newspaper as "a collective educator – a weapon, first and foremost, to overthrow colonialism and imperialism, and to assist total African independence and unity."[3] Many journalists themselves shared the view of Vivek Goenka, chairman of the powerful *Indian Express* newspaper, that the media should "don a steering mantle when the need may arise" in order to guide society and the nation in partnership with government.[4] To many journalists in the developing world, it is an approach self-evidently preferable, summed up by one Nigerian reporter who asked a Western researcher: "Why should we be like you? What have your ethics and morality brought the world beside injustice, cruelty, and war?"[5]

This cynicism about Western journalism contributed to UNESCO's efforts to create a "new world information order" that would reverse the north–south flow of information from the developed to the developing world. Its proponents mocked media theorist Marshall McLuhan's notion that television had created a "global village." In an examination of US and Indian coverage of Iran's Islamic revolution, John V. Vilanilam observed:

> If there were 100 residents of this global village, only one
> would get the opportunity for education beyond school
> level, 70 would be unable to read and write. Over 50 would
> be suffering from malnutrition, and over 80 would live in

sub-standard housing. Six of the 100 would hold off the entire income of the village. How would these six live in peace with their neighbors without arming themselves to the teeth and supplying arms to those willing to fight their side?[6]

In South and Southeast Asia, where development journalism was born, audiences gave state-run TV and radio channels high marks for trustworthiness.[7] But there were also contradictions. In the Philippines, reporters suffered severe repression under the regime of Ferdinand Marcos and under subsequent governments found themselves working in an environment that Reporters without Borders ranked as one of the most deadly in the world.

Development Journalism and the Muslim World

The *Pancasila* press under the three decades of Suharto's New Order regime in Indonesia, the world's most populous Muslim country, embodied many of the concepts of development journalism. *Pancasila* refers to the reigning ideology of the Suharto era, which consisted of five principles designed to unify the far-flung island nation of more than 300 ethnic groups. "The Indonesian press was supposed to be 'free and responsible,'" writes Janet Steele of George Washington University in her study of the country's leading independent magazine. "Yet unlike the Western concept of press freedom, which emphasizes freedom *from* government control, press freedom in the New Order was understood to mean freedom *to* assist the state in carrying out programs for social and economic development." Steele said it is likely the guidelines for the *Pancasila* press came from the American Hutchins Commission report, which stressed media responsibility:

> In the New Order, "responsible" meant adhering to a set of guidelines prohibiting the reporting of anything that was likely to inflame ethnic, religious, racial, or group (class) tensions.[8]

One of the problems of media scholarship is that it is largely produced from a Western-centric perspective. Even the most commonly used measures of press "freedom," such as the widely cited Freedom House report, view conditions through a decidedly Western prism. Contrast Steele's implied criticism of the Indonesian system with the description provided by an Indonesian academic, Onong Uchjana Effendi, who explained that the *Pancasila* press is not 'free *from*' or 'free *to*,' but rather 'free *and*' – because it is free *and* responsible. This "functional freedom," as journalist-scholar Jakob Oetama put it, means reporters have the freedom *not to* harm society.[9] Indonesia is a consensus-oriented culture in which the president is seen as the ultimate father-figure of the national family. In that spirit, the Indonesian Press Council's 1974 guidelines said it was the responsibility of the press to "hold high the national consensus" and to cooperate with community and government in a manner "inspired by the family principle."[10] Australian researcher Angela Romano's survey of 65 Indonesian journalists, conducted in the final years of the Suharto regime, found that the majority of them "were fired by a desire to improve their society." She identified five major roles emerging within the group:

> [W]atchdog who scrutinizes and critiques the powerful...
> agent of empowerment who seeks to enlighten and streng-
> then the masses...nation builder who aims to build unity
> and develop the nation's social and physical infrastruc-
> ture...defender of the truth...[and] entertainer.

The majority saw no contradiction between the role of a *Pancasila* journalist and the self-perception of "watchdog" expressed by half the sample. What they did object to was the aggressive way in which that watchdog role manifests in Western journalism. "I do not wish to be a fierce watchdog," one journalist told Romano. "I wish to be like [the Prophet] Muhammad and to spread a good agenda. Muhammad was not fierce." But they also objected to the reality of "freedom" under the New Order, with 80 percent complaining about restrictions on press freedoms, which included censorship, self-censorship, the closing of newspapers, and physical attacks. Still, some saw these restrictions as an unfortunate necessity. "I do not think the political system is developed enough to encompass the truth," said another reporter.[11]

A separate survey of 385 Indonesian journalists conducted three years after the collapse of the Suharto regime reported somewhat different findings.[12] By that point, many of the overt controls had been lifted from the Indonesian media sector, with a dramatic increase in the number of journalists and news outlets. Indonesia's media was by then rated "partly free" by Freedom House, though journalists continued to be subject to criminal prosecution, threats, and persecution at the hands of both business interests and individuals who objected to their reporting. Indonesian journalists, the survey found, "see themselves as neutral and objective disseminators of news, not as political actors and agents of development." The journalists rated highly the seemingly contradictory values of neutrality and the need to "support disadvantaged people." "[S]upporting national development" was considered "extremely important" by less than 25 percent of the sample. However, the findings were anything but clear-cut. Journalists at commercial media outlets – the vast majority of respondents – were both "more skeptical of the government [than those on government-owned outlets] and subscribe to the tradition of objectivity, [and] [a]t the same time, they are more willing to do good for society and its people."[13]

The survey also revealed that almost 57 percent of the Indonesian journalists accepted the so-called "envelopes" of cash that were a staple of the relationship between reporters and sources there, "because they do not see any evidence of being influenced or pressurized" by the bribe.[14] Such incentives are a common practice in many countries of the developing world, where journalist salaries are notoriously low[15] and, as in Indonesia, a sudden explosion of media outlets in the initial liberalization phase meant few were economically sustainable.[16]

Indonesian journalists, who have been called "educated but timid watchdogs,"[17] are not alone among journalists in Muslim-majority countries in pairing certain Western journalistic ideal-types with their own cultural values. Across the Strait in Malaysia, where a combination of draconian press laws and widespread ownership of media interests by state-owned holding companies led one US press group to rank the country among the ten worst places to practice journalism,[18] Mindy McAdams of the University of Florida found a wide discrepancy within Malaysia's news industry between the aspirations for

Western journalistic values and the reality of day-to-day life in the newsroom:

> The working journalists profess the same "missions" as Western journalists: They go on and on about truth, public accountability, objectivity, "afflict the comfortable, comfort the afflicted." They say "watchdog" and "gatekeeper." They share our language about values and use it in the same way we do ... [but] they all admit that they carefully self-censor to avoid retaliation.

McAdams, who spent a year in Malaysia on a Fulbright journalism fellowship, reported that as in Indonesia, bribes were *de rigueur*. She said Malaysian journalists justified the system of government controls because Malaysia was a "special case" with a special history, a reference to relations between the ethnic Malay majority and the Chinese minority.[19]

Malaysia was one of three countries where a content analysis by Brian L. Massey and Li-jing Arthur Chang detected the noticeable impact of "Asian values" and development journalism in news reporting. In examining articles from ten online newspapers, Massey and Chang reported that "harmony" and "supportiveness" were the dominant themes in domestic coverage. This was most noticeable in Singapore, Malaysia, and Brunei, the latter two Muslim-majority societies. "The press freedom limits in these three countries may be coincidental to journalists' role conceptions, or the restrictions could represent the codification of a close state–press relationship that has arisen naturally from a mutual sense of patriotism," they said. However, Massey and Chang found as much emphasis on conflict and confrontation in the foreign coverage carried in the news outlets of those three Asian countries as they detected in the Western media. The team speculated that this might be the government's way of both implying the superiority of "Asian values" and letting the journalists exercise their professional impulses in a way that doesn't threaten the domestic status quo:

> It could be that conflict and critical reporting are accepted under normative Asian-values journalism when they are directed at the "other." ... [T]he mark of professionalism on

the international stage for Asian journalists could be the similarity between their reporting of a foreign news event and that of their Western counterparts who are also covering it.[20]

International Media Values

Sitting, as I do, in that strange no-man's land between journalism and academia, I am frequently struck by the gap separating theory and reality. That's true when it comes to Middle East politics – it was, after all, neat theories of democratization disconnected from regional realities that led to Iraq's woes – and it's also true of media studies.

Journalism has been defined as "a set of cultural practices."[21] But the Western model does not always take into account the possibility of journalistic subcultures governed by varying values, norms, and mores influenced by the broader cultural practices of the society in which the journalist functions. Comparing the results of journalist surveys in 21 countries, Weaver concluded that "[t]here are strong national differences that override any universal professional norms or values of journalism around the world."[22] On specific journalistic ideal-types, the surveys found a general agreement on the need to get information to the public quickly (a top priority for American journalists), but there was "considerably less agreement" on the need to investigate government claims, with countries that did not have a long history of democratic governance giving the "watchdog" role a low priority. Journalists also expressed "considerable differences" on issues such as the analytical function of the media, the need to entertain the public, reporting practices and ethics, such as the use of confidential sources and paying for information, and the importance of reporting accurately and objectively.[23]

Even among those who did rate objectivity highly, there was a tendency in follow-up questions to express the belief that reporting facts alone was not enough. That was particularly true among those who have experienced a period of political change. Describing the differences in responses between younger Spanish journalists and those who grew up professionally under the Franco regime, Maria Jose Canel and Antonio Pique of the University of Navarra noted a pattern which may have implications for other emerging democracies:

> Journalists who have undergone the process to democracy fully established as professionals are more advocate than impartial, interpretive than factual, and more supportive than critical. They are more likely to identify with a party than young journalists and to be committed to certain beliefs. They regard as important influencing the public and championing ideas and values.[24]

The perspectives are many. Almost half of all Polish journalists surveyed did not see political or business activities as a threat to objectivity, though a majority espoused the ideal of objectivity;[25] Brazilian journalists "perceive themselves as emulating an American journalistic model" but in reality are just "imitating the appearance but not the substance of American journalism,"[26] and a study of Chilean journalists revealed "a wide breach or contradiction" between what they "understood as important values for journalists [and] their commitment to those values."[27] Mexican journalists conceive their profession as active and adversarial, their Ecuadorian colleagues exhibit a more "developmental journalism" orientation,[28] while, according to Columbian journalist Maria Cristina Caballero, journalism in her country is "about trying to help create an environment in which peace is possible."[29]

Based on surveys in Tanzania[30] and Nepal,[31] in which journalists were asked to rank a list of 31 functions, Jyotika Ramaprasad and James D. Kelly theorized that journalistic roles fell into two major categories, development journalism and democracy building/entertainment, not Western-style "objective" journalism."[32] Journalists in Bangladesh were asked to rate the importance of various functions and then to indicate how frequently they actually carried them out. As is so often the case, the researchers found "a gap between perceived importance and actual practice for most functions."[33] For example, "Examine government policies and decisions critically" was ranked high in importance by the journalists, but they indicated it was actually implemented only 65 percent of the time. The authors speculated as to the reason for the gap:

> In developing countries where control of the press by political leaders has been the norm, criticism of policies and practices

has not become common practice. ... Even journalists have some difficulty in directly criticizing leaders given the tradition in many of these societies of respect for or awe or fear of authority as well as indirect communication styles.

As for the readiness of journalists to accept development functions "as part of their jobs," the authors noted:

[D]evelopment is an important economic sector in developing countries and its vocabulary permeates discussion. ... Journalists cannot possibly escape this influence. ... Extending the expectation of communication of development messages to the news media is not as much of a stretch in local thinking as it might be in the West.[34]

In another small study, 34 journalists from 29 countries were asked to sort 50 opinion statements about journalistic functions. While all generally "agreed about the importance of the freedom of the press, journalistic autonomy and news media's public service role and watchdog function, they disagreed on government–press relations, press ownership and how to handle abuses of press freedom." The author concluded that although "the cultural distinction was not absolute in determining how journalists landed on the factors, it was the only significant variable in explaining the formation of the factors."[35]

In other words, culture matters.

Challenge of Professionalism

South African journalists faced a challenge to their journalism that had nothing to do with politics or violence. A survey there found that about half of the press corps "lacked the ability to develop a story or identify story ideas."[36] The South African media was still trying to emerge from the apartheid system, in which black journalists were given few opportunities. On the eve of independence, Nelson Mandela decried the state of the media. "It is clearly inequitable that in a country whose population is overwhelmingly Black ... the principal players in the media have no knowledge of the life experience of that majority," he told an international press gathering.[37] A decade later, the aforementioned study found a lack of analytical and critical skills, a lack of creativity, enterprise, and personal accountability. Though South Africa presents an extreme example, the struggle to build a foundation of professionalism is a common one in countries emerging from authoritarian rule.

In Eastern Europe after the collapse of Communism, "the explosive growth in the number of [media] outlets created a plethora of journalistic positions for which no new, trained, professional cadres and leaders were available." The new elite of journalism emerged from among the intellectuals of the anti-Communist underground press – journalist-polemicists carrying with them a tradition of advocacy and "doing their best to advance the cause of their own political and personal views."[38] A poll of Polish journalists conducted in 1990 found them espousing Western ideal-types such as impartiality, objectivity, enterprise, ingenuity, and courage, but, according to Karol Jakubowski of Polish Radio and TV, those ideals "were soon found to be lacking" as the old Communist press system was dismantled and Polish journalists embarked on a long search for identity in the free-for-all that followed.[39] Those same "malformed structures of public communication" existed in Hungary as it made a similar transition. An absence of training; bribery, due in part to poor pay; cronyism; and sensationalism all remained huge challenges a decade after the yoke of Soviet rule had been thrown off. Although a formal code of ethics was produced, in reality "ethical standards and the concept of the journalists' role in society [were] in disarray."[40]

Indeed, Peter Gross observes that across Eastern Europe, "the lack of a clear sense of the professional values underlying journalistic enterprise" led the region's journalists to exhibit a lack of respect for verifiable information, mislead themselves into believing they are "discoverers of truth" rather than "providers of accurate, verifiable, balanced, complete facts;" see themselves as "sociopolitical and cultural leaders;" and refuse to cooperate with fellow journalists. The perception among journalists was that of the media as a "counter-power" to the government, rather than an adversary or a watchdog, with an "absence both of a consensus on journalistic values, roles and standards" and of objective journalism.[41]

Models for a "Global Journalism Ethic"

So to what degree *do* journalists around the world share a basic set of norms and values? Writing of the evolution of Nigerian journalists

30 years ago, Peter Golding argued that "professionalism is induced in the form of an ideological convergence, a necessary emulation of the objectives and definitions of…foreign media."[42] But, as documented above, that convergence is not always a smooth one, given "the complicated cultural, political and socio-economic structure in which the journalist operates."[43] Some scholars, such as Alex Edelstein, believe that the very concept of professionalism "is a culture-laden concept that cannot be applied usefully to the Third World journalist" who faces "structural barriers to the attainment of this status."[44] Others go so far as to say that even American journalists cannot be considered to be part of a "profession" in its strictest sense, because "there is no system of abstract propositions to which new recruits are exposed and without which they cannot practice."[45] In short, anyone can call him or herself a journalist, and in this Internet age, anyone does.

Then there is the argument that journalism should, in fact, evolve in synch with the political and cultural milieu in which it operates. African media scholar Francis Nyamnjoh makes a strong case that there is an essential conflict of value frameworks between Western media norms – and those of the liberal democratic societies they represent – and the community consciousness of most African societies.

> Almost everywhere, liberal democratic assumptions have been made about the media and their role in democratization and society, with little regard to the histories, cultures and sociologies of African societies.[46]

In the context of Eastern Europe, Gross believes that while the Western ideal-values of journalism might be something which journalists in societies in transition will eventually adopt, in the meantime

> the media need to play still other roles: they need to serve as socializers, as champions of a democratic political culture, and, to that end, as teachers and mobilizers (in the larger sense of the word) and not simply guard dogs and disseminators of information.[47]

In comparing the results of surveys of journalists in 21 countries, predominantly from the West and *developed* world, Weaver ultimately concluded that the absence of agreement on the norms and values of journalism prevent the emergence of "universal occupational standards."[48] Similarly, in terms of the *developing* world, Romano observes that "it would appear not merely difficult, but in fact futile to attempt to devise a coherent, universal press model.[49] And when Kirat compared his own Algerian results to surveys of American, Nigerian, and Saudi journalists, he found that "each group of journalists conceives of the role of the press according to the peculiarities of its country."[50]

There has been much written about the emergence of a "global ethic" of journalism. Many of those articles are produced by Western academics safely ensconced in the ivory towers of North America and Europe and are peppered with unyielding dictates: Journalists "should" do this, they "must" do that, they are "required" to act in a certain way. Such prescriptions for a "new" journalism are thick with "paradigms," "hierarchies" and "models," often drenched in a sauce of cultural imperialism.[51] Sidney Callahan, for example, would seem to believe that journalists operate in a world of moral absolutes:

> The universality of ethical standards of journalism exists because ethics and morality are a universal human enterprise based on the discovery of universal moral truths by human beings with a common human nature always and everywhere. ... The human family is one. Evolutionary psychologists assure us of "the psychic unity" of human beings who share pan-species characteristics.[52]

A few go so far as to envision a media Utopia in which the borderless footprint of television is populated by a new breed of borderless journalists who report not through the prism of their own cultural worldview, but rather affect a "cosmopolitan attitude."[53] Stephen Ward sketched out a set of three "imperatives," to wit: "...to act as a global agent, to serve world citizens, and to enhance nonparochial understandings."[54] Roberto Herrscher would impose a Universal Code that includes a provision to "deal with the treatment of ethnic groups, sexes, minorities, religious and sexual persuasions, and other groups" because "[f]or the journalist, all people are equal." "The easiest experiment," he wrote, is to see if an article about a woman, an Indian, a gay man, or a Muslim would be written in the same way if it dealt with a White, Protestant, straight man."[55] "Easy," in the West perhaps, but not in a Muslim society where the story about the woman, by dint of culture and mores, would likely *not* take the same tone,[56] and the article about the gay would probably not be written at all.[57]

"A global ethics is a bulwark against undue influence of parochial values and social pressures on journalism," Ward insists.[58] But Saleh el-Saybehmi, political columnist of *Khaleej Times* in the United Arab Emirates told researchers Shakuntala Rao and Seow Ting Lee, "A discussion of media ethics is useless here where every bit of news is tightly controlled. The mere discussion of ethics implies the existence of some degree of freedom to make choices. We don't have that." Added an editor on the *Gulf News* who did not want his name used:

> And what use would such a code be to me? The broadcasting code we have says we cannot criticize even the seventh cousin of the Sheikh.

The reporters with whom Rao and Lee spoke expressed suspicion that there was some tie between the search for a global ethic and 9/11 and that they would be required to "sit and cry" about the dead Americans when "there is no one to cry" about Arabs who are killed, "especially in the American media." The pair reported:

> The postcolonial suspicion among journalists is a complicated mix of negative reactions toward Western interests who have historically "told us what to do" and governments of their own nations who have made frequent attempts to sabotage free exchange of information.[59]

It all came back to worldview. "American communication scholars of press–government relations begin most of their studies with a basic premise, that Western-style libertarian press theory is what the rest of the world should accept," according to Merrill. Such a viewpoint, he continues, is "not only an arrogant and ethnocentric one but also betrays a stultifying view of reality."

> Cultures are different. The values that shore up such cultures are different. Citizen expectations are different....

> [Yet] [t]he communication scholar or researcher is largely
> defined by ethnocentric forces that push away conflicting
> assumptions and articulate even basic hypotheses in the
> familiar and confining ethnocentric formulations.[60]

Much of Western media theory is based on the assumption that political "freedom" is a requirement for journalism to be practiced. Of course, to date that "freedom" and what constitutes "journalism" have largely been defined by the West. And as documented in earlier chapters, freedom can be a relative term. Most existing transnational codes of ethics, such as those of ASEAN, the Arab Federation of Journalists, the Islamic Media Charter, and the International Principles of Professional Ethics in Journalism do not even mention freedom of expression, "probably because it is hard to find a consensus on freedom issues among organizations with varying political backgrounds," according to Hafez.[61] The Kingdom of Jordan offers one example. In April 2007, the weekly newspaper *Al-Majd* was subject to prior censorship by the security services when it attempted to report about a multinational plan to strengthen the Palestinian Authority in the neighboring West Bank and Gaza and bolster its security services. The president of the Jordan Press Association, a group supposedly formed to represent the interests of news organizations, defended the ban on the basis that the article "contained material that violates its bylaws which prohibit the publication of any press material that the foundation believes would encroach upon the national security and defames a sisterly country."[62] The very issue of the corrupting influence of Western-style media "freedom" has helped alienate many living in the broad sweep of the Muslim world, producing what Pakistani scholar Akbar Ahmed calls "the restless generation" now coming of age in Muslim societies.[63]

Yet the assumption that American journalism trumps all other models remains at the foundation of much of the scholarship on international journalism. In response to Rao and Lee's questions about the efficacy of a global journalism ethic, the journalists they spoke with proposed their own set of "universal" ethics: Respect Others, Tolerance for Religious and Cultural Diversity, Freedom and Independence, and Tell the Truth with Restraint.[64] That last item alone, "truth *with restraint*," reflects the yawning gap in self-perception that exists between

US reporters and their colleagues in other parts of the world. Such a disconnect should be no great surprise. Cultural psychologists tell us that the "influence of values and of economic prosperity imply that a number of Western political axioms cannot be applied to non-Western countries and are not very helpful as global guidelines."[65]

Around the world, media scholars are grappling with new models that take economic, political, social, cultural, religious, and a variety of other factors into account when evaluating what Westerners often perceive as "imperfections" in the media, while responsible journalists, consciously or not, seek ways to integrate their own unique perspectives – and the realities of the world in which they live – into the normative values Western journalists have long held up as the Holy Grail. Reporting on developments in the former Soviet bloc, de Beer and Merrill observed that those countries have shaken off the trappings of the old system and "have edged toward a new but uncertain kind of journalism."[66] It is a comment that is equally applicable to the Arab world, a region in the midst of violent upheaval and systematic change.

PART II

Survey Findings

8

The Mission of Arab Journalism

> [We] declare our total adherence to the basic instruments
> which guide the struggle of the Egyptian people.
>
> Egyptian Charter of Work and
> Code of Ethics in the Press, 1972

Modern Arab news organizations and the modern Arab state were both born from the ashes of the Ottoman Empire. Historically, Arab media has been a vehicle for the spread of Arab nationalism, Arab culture and the Arabic language itself. But the chief allegiance of most Arab journalists has been to the individual nation-state, not the "Arab nation" as a whole, and their primary mission has been to support the status quo. That attitude is changing.

A survey I carried out with my colleague Jeremy Ginges of The New School for Social Research found that Arab journalists at the dawn of the twenty-first century see their mission as driving political and social change in the Middle East and North Africa.[1] They most closely identify with the pan-Arab region and the broader Muslim world, not with an individual nation-state; they see political reform, human rights, poverty, and education as the most important issues facing the region; and while protective of the Arab people, Arab culture and religion, they are not overtly anti-American.

Shattering the Myths

Arab politics: Central to any discussion of journalists and their profession is the question of how they perceive their mission. Othman al-Sini, editor of the Saudi newspaper *Al-Watan*, put his finger on the essential question being asked in many newsrooms: "I wonder if media should be change-makers or reporters of change?" The vast majority of his colleagues opted for change maker. "Encourage political reform" was the "most significant" job of a journalist, chosen by 75 percent of respondents to the survey [Figure 1];[2] and "political reform" was at the top of the list of "most important issues" facing the Arab world, followed closely by human rights, poverty, and education. "The role of journalist is to criticize people...who are [acting] against the national interest. And the first national interest for us now is to build democracy, to build pluralism and to protect the human rights in our country because," Tunisian editor Rashid Khashana told me, "the fundamental thing [is] to build a new society."

The failure to build that society, or "lack of political change," ran a close second to US policy (34% vs. 32%) as the greatest threats facing the Arab world (beyond the ever-looming presence of Israel),[3] followed by an array of regional issues such as human rights abuses (23%), the economy (20%), and political instability (18%) [Figure 2].[4]

"Democrat" was the primary political identity of almost half of all Arab journalists responding to the survey, eclipsing Arab nationalist (15%), Islamist (10%) and nationalist (8%) [Figure 3].[5] "We need democracy like you, we need freedom like you," Ahmed Mansour, host of the Al-Jazeera program *Bela Hodood* (*No Limits*), told me. When it

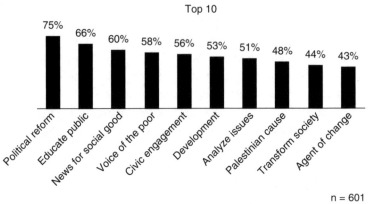

Figure 1   Job of a journalist

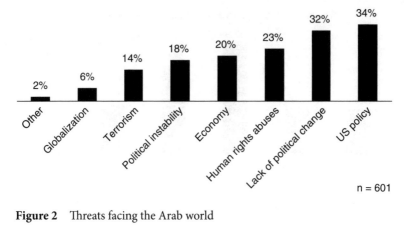

Figure 2 Threats facing the Arab world

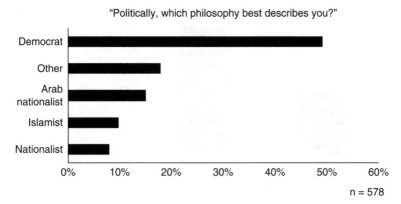

Figure 3 Political identity

came to geographic identity, twice as many respondents identified first with the Arab world (32%) than with their individual nation (15%), and a quarter indicated that they belonged first to the Muslim world (25%) [Figure 4].[6]

A regional Arab reform agenda: Arab journalists responding to the survey were almost unanimous in their belief in the need for systemic change in the Middle East. Asked to choose one answer that best describes their own opinion, 64 percent selected "Arab society must be gradually improved by reforms" and another 32 percent selected, "The way Arab society is organized must be radically changed" (70 percent

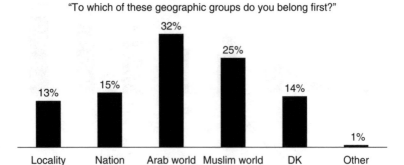

Figure 4   Geographic identity

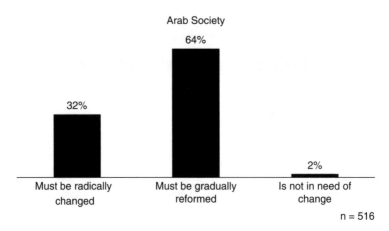

Figure 5   Reform

of Moroccan journalist supported radical change). Just 2 percent indicated that "Arab society is not in need of change" [Figure 5]. That desire for change permeates all levels of the Arab media.

Since Al-Jazeera went on the air in 1996, its staffers have seen themselves as agents of democratic change in a region trapped in the grip of autocracies. It is a key reason Al-Jazeera's reporters have been expelled, at one time or another, from most Arab countries. However, the other leading cross-border news organizations – Al-Arabiya television, the privately owned Lebanese Broadcasting Corporation (LBC), and the largest newspapers, *Al-Hayat* and *Asharq Al-Awsat* – are all controlled by individuals close to, or part of, the Saudi royal family, not known for its appetite for reform. It is therefore noteworthy that 58 percent of respondents working for pan-Arab news organizations identified "encouraging political reform" as their most important journalistic priority. But it is even more significant that 78 percent of journalists working for purely domestic media – traditionally defenders of their respective regimes – also said it was their job to shake up the status quo.

"The role of the media in shaping public debate and covering politics is one of the most important concerns facing journalists today," according to Samar Fatany, one of Saudi Arabia's leading woman journalists. "[It is] [o]ur mission...to mobilize and move the public debate toward positive attitudes and global thinking – dire needs for the progress and development of our country."[7]

Arab journalists see their own governments as the biggest obstacle to media independence. Seventy percent of respondents chose "government control" as the "most significant challenge" to Arab journalism, statistically tying with "lack of professionalism" when presented with a list of nine possible choices.[8] They put "US threats" against Arab news organizations near the bottom of the list (30%), even though most Arab journalists are convinced that the US military directly targeted Arab reporters in Iraq and Afghanistan [Figure 6].[9] "Any government in the world is *an* enemy of journalists," said Hamdi al-Bokari, a member of the board of the Yemeni Journalists Syndicate. "But in the Arab world, government is the *first* enemy to journalists."

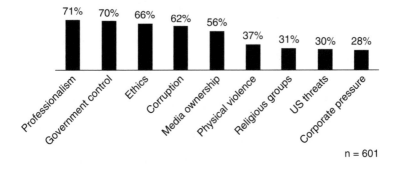

Figure 6 Challenges to Arab journalism

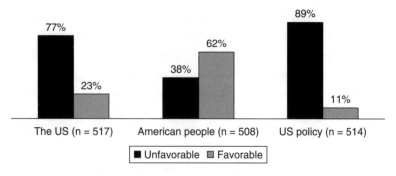

Figure 7 Attitudes toward the US

Attitudes toward the US: Arab journalists drew a clear distinction between US policy and the American people, reporting an overwhelmingly *unfavorable*[10] view of the US (77%) and its polices (89%), and a strongly *favorable* view of the American people (62%) [Figure 7].[11]

Responding at a time when the Bush administration was mid-way through its second term, the reporters and editors indicated that they simply did not believe the US government when it said it supported democratic change in the Arab world or the creation of a Palestinian state, and they were equally cynical about the motives behind US aid to victims of the 2005 Asian tsunami, which killed at least 200,000 people. Roughly two-thirds of respondents indicated that they thought the US policy in each case was primarily aimed at countering anti-Americanism, rather than a sincere desire to help, while just 13 percent expressed any confidence that the Bush administration was genuine in its support for a Palestinian state and about the same number believed the Bush White House was sincere about fostering Arab democracy [Figure 8].

Yet Arab journalists did not rule out American involvement in the region. While they saw America's role in the Middle East as overwhelmingly negative (83%),[12] and indicated that no benefits could justify the US invasion of Iraq (76%), just under half were open to the idea that some Western interference in the Arab world could be justified if it ultimately led to benefits for the Arab people (46%) [Figure 9].

Palestine, Iraq, and terrorism: Despite the perception that Arab journalists are fixated on Palestine, the story fell fifth when respondents

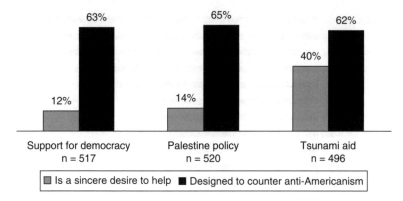

Figure 8   US policy

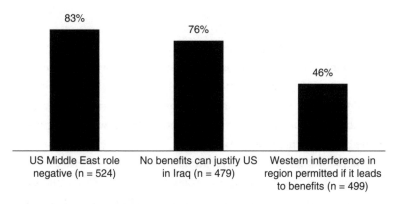

Figure 9   America and the Middle East

were asked to rate the importance of 12 issues facing the region [Figure 10],[13] below political reform, human rights, poverty, and education. Similarly, "support the Palestinian cause" was eighth on the list of most important jobs of an Arab journalist.[14] This is particularly significant given that the survey was conducted from June 2005 to September 2006, a time when fighting between Israel and the Palestinians raged in Gaza and the West Bank, Israel invaded Lebanon, and the US launched an international boycott of the Hamas government.[15] Equally significant, Iraq fell to the sixth position on the journalists' list of important issues facing the Arab world,[16] well below the political and economic challenges noted above, leaving it

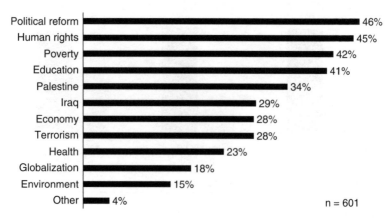

Figure 10   Issues facing the Arab world

statistically tied with the economy and terrorism, which 28 percent of
respondents chose as "the most important."[17] The survey responses, at
a time when Palestine and Iraq dominated the airwaves, were indica-
tive of the fact that the flow of news in any given period is dictated as
much by events as by the journalists' perception of what is important
in the broader scheme of things.

Notably, the influence of perceptions, or journalistic worldview, produced one very interesting set of results. The right of Palestinians displaced in the Arab–Israeli wars since 1948 to return to their homes in
what is now the state of Israel – as opposed to the Occupied Territories
of the West Bank and Gaza – has been one of the most intractable
obstacles to a permanent peace. For many Arabs, it is seen as make-or-
break issue. The journalists were asked whether there were any circumstances under which the right of return might be negotiated away as
part of a settlement. Just 23% of them said yes. However, the response
from Palestinian journalists and journalists in Syria, which has always
maintained a hard-line on negotiations with Israel, was significantly
more positive, with almost 40% in both groups affirming that there
were circumstances in which this could be a bargaining chip. They were
also more than twice as inclined to believe that the Bush administration was genuine about a Palestinian state. The results would seem to
indicate that what is seen as the politically correct stance in most Arab

newsrooms is one least likely to be adopted by those most affected by the conflict.

Much has been written about the Arab media's alleged complicity with terrorism, from use of the word "martyr" to describe those killed by US and Israeli troops to the airing of graphic footage of attacks on Americans and bin Laden tapes. Arab journalists were asked which of four acts of violence they considered to be terrorism. Their responses: The Israeli siege of Ramallah in the spring of 2002 (90%); the 2002 Bali nightclub bombings, carried out by an Indonesian al-Qaeda offshoot (85%); the 2003 US siege of the Iraqi city of Fallujah (82%); and the videotaped beheading of Nicholas Berg, a US contractor in Iraq (73%), a result that appeared to indicate Arab journalists condemn the acts of militants but see certain US government military operations as the moral equivalent of what the American government would consider terrorism [Figure 11].

Mosque and state: Just under 90 percent of the Arab journalists surveyed identified themselves as Muslims. They were about equally divided between those who described themselves as "religious," those who said they were "secular" Muslims, and those who chose not to declare their religiosity. However, overall they generally reflected a largely secular political agenda. Only 25 percent agreed or strongly agreed that politicians who do not believe in God are unfit for office; 78 percent said religious leaders should not influence voting; and 60 percent said

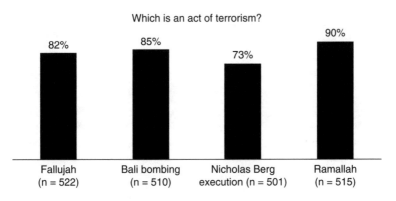

Which is an act of terrorism?

82%	85%	73%	90%
Fallujah (n = 522)	Bali bombing (n = 510)	Nicholas Berg execution (n = 501)	Ramallah (n = 515)

Figure 11   Acts of terrorism

government should be allowed to pass laws even if they contradict *sharia* (religious law). In addition, 49 percent agreed/strongly agreed that it was *not* necessary to believe in God to have good moral values [Figure 12].

They were also skeptical about the role of Muslim clergy. More than half said religious leaders do not give adequate answers to moral problems of the individual (57%), problems of the family (52%), or social problems (67%), and they were evenly split on whether clergy meet the spiritual needs of the people [Figure 13]. That dim view was also seen in responses to another question: About one-third of the journalists

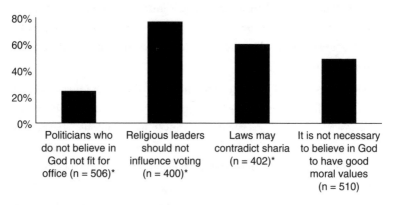

Figure 12   Religion and politics

*Strongly agree/agree.

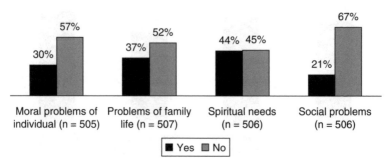

Figure 13   Religious leaders

singled out pressure from religious groups as among the "most significant" challenges to Arab journalism.

A New Journalism Typology

Academics love categorizing things. Throughout the decades, researchers have developed a variety of "typologies" to define media in the Arab world and elsewhere. William Rugh, a former US ambassador in the region, identified the primary trends in the Arab world by country – e.g. "Mobilization" press controlled by revolutionary regimes in Syria, Libya, and Sudan; the "Loyalist" press in Saudi Arabia, the Gulf, and Palestine; the "Diverse" press of Lebanon, Kuwait, Morocco, Yemen and, more recently, Iraq; and the "Transitional" media of Algeria, Egypt, Jordan, and Tunisia.[18] Other researchers working elsewhere have created typologies of the journalists themselves, rather than the media organizations that employ them. For journalism researcher David Weaver and his colleagues, those categories changed slightly over the decades, but by their 2002 survey the team had identified four dominant functional classifications into which they grouped American journalists: "Interpretative," "Disseminator," "Adversarial," and "Popular Mobilizer."[19] In a series of surveys conducted in the developing world by Jyotika Ramaprasad and various partners, the researchers developed an alternative set of functional groupings that took into account the "development journalism" worldview of reporters and editors in Nepal, Tanzania, and Bangladesh. Those groupings were later applied to Egypt.[20] What Ramaprasad called these typologies changed in the various studies, but the broad functions included national development, education, information/analysis, entertainment, culture, and advocacy.

Our survey found that these methods of categorizing the media do not adequately define the new Arab journalist. So, naturally, Dr. Ginges and I created some new ones. From the data emerge two additional typologies that embody the mission of Arab journalism as it is being forged in the post-9/11 era.

The Change Agent

In its "Vision and Mission Statement," Al-Jazeera vows "to support the right of the individual to acquire information and strengthen the values

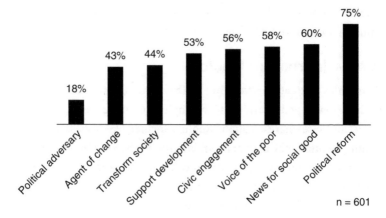

Figure 14 Change agent

of tolerance, democracy, and the respect of liberties and human rights."
The survey data finds that commitment to be a theme running through
the Arab media as a whole. Seven of the top ten roles Arab journalists considered "most significant" together constitute what might be
considered an agenda-setting or Change Agent function [Figure 14],
and two others in the top ten are interpretive or development functions
that, in this context, support change.

The Change Agent functions all involve an overtly activist approach
to journalism aimed at political or societal change on a national and
pan-Arab basis. Hassan Amr, editor of Cairo's *Al-Fajr* newspaper,
summed up this function when he told me the job of a journalist is
"to change everything; from the president, to the government, to the
regime, [to] the rule of the ground." Yemeni journalist Hamdi al-Bokari
said hopefully, "Journalism is a weapon of mass destruction for oppres-
sive governments."

"I think it is in everybody's mind to bring political change," argued
Nakhle el-Hage, director of news and current affairs at Al-Arabiya.
"By having the debate on the television channels about democracy and
about political parties, it gives everybody a platform to say what they ‚
think and this is promotion for democracy." And while the pan-Arab
media concentrated on the big picture, some local journalists aggressively focused on internal reform. "If you do not have a mission to try

to change [the world] around you in a positive way, you might as well work for any of the intelligence agencies," said LBC presenter Tania Mehanna.

Other journalistic tasks in this category can all be seen as playing a supporting role in this mission of change. They include using news for the social good (60%); serving as a voice of the poor (58%); encouraging civic engagement (56%), which is a precursor to political change; supporting national and regional development (53%); transforming Arab society (44%); serving as an agent of change (43%); and acting as a political adversary, which garnered only 18% support, reflecting the general sense, noted above, that change must be gradual.

Closely associated with, and supportive of, this Change Agent function are two other roles that also made the top ten: "Educate the public" (66%) and "analyze complex issues" (51%). A strong argument can be made that, in the context of the other journalistic priorities of Arab journalists, these *are* linked to the mission of change in terms of educating and informing the public about political and social issues that drive change, as in the comments of Samir Khader, a senior producer at Al-Jazeera, who said it is his job to "educate the public to understand the world," his colleague Ahmed Shugi, who believed it was his duty "to give something to the viewers; to educate them, to enlighten them," and Shobokshi who insisted that "create change and educate" are the inseparable missions of Arab journalism, along with communicating "a message of reform, a message of development."

The Change Agent function far outweighs any other self-perceived groupings of roles and provides quantitative evidence that a substantial portion of Arab journalists support the argument of Faisal Kasim, host of one of Al-Jazeera's most popular programs, that, "Our media should be harnessed to liberate the Arab people from their internal gladiators."[21]

The Guardian

There is an encounter in the documentary *Control Room*, a film about the relationship between Al-Jazeera and the US military headquarters in the Gulf during the first weeks of the Iraq war, which epitomizes the sense of defensiveness permeating many Arab newsrooms. In the scene, an American journalism professor counsels a young reporter from Abu Dhabi TV who has been assigned to the US Central Command media center. "Go interview the American spokesman," the professor, himself a former TV correspondent, suggests. "But don't be hostile; smile when you talk to him." "Smile?" the reporter snaps back, physically bristling. "How can I smile when my people are dying?"

That reporter's sense of mission embodies what we have labeled the "Guardian" function. It involves a set of roles associated with the defense of Arab and/or Islamic causes and ideals which are unique to the region, including: "Support the Palestinian cause" (48%), "Foster Arab culture" (37%), "Encourage spiritual values" (33%), "Defend Arab interests" (32%), "Enhance pan-Arab unity" (29%), and "Protect Islamic traditions" (28%) [Figure 15].

The Guardian function demonstrates that the worldview of Arab journalists in the post-9/11 era has a significant defensive aspect, in which they see themselves defending the Arab homeland at a time when an Arab country is being occupied by a foreign army and the Islamic world as a whole is, in the view of many Arabs and other Muslims, under siege. Arab journalists, noted the Saudi writer Fatany, are "not only defending the Arab nation, but also defending the Arab causes. When you are being attacked from everything, and your culture, your

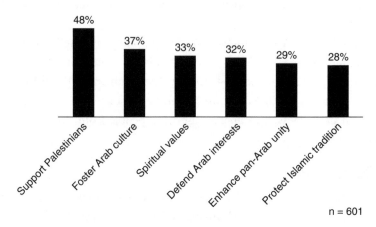

Figure 15   Guardian

principles, your ideas, your thoughts, you have to defend; you have to be on the defensive."[22]

This worldview was not confined to Arab journalists who practice Islam. Most Lebanese Christians have little sympathy for Muslim causes and many do not even consider themselves Arabs, but rather as "Phoenicians" or descendents of the Christian Crusaders. Marwan Matni, a Christian news producer at LBC, said that was true of him as well – until the 2006 war between Israel and the Shi'ite Muslim militia Hezbollah. As the conflict dragged on, he recalled over drinks one evening, "I felt myself changing. Lebanon was under attack. We were all Lebanese. By the end, I, too, felt myself to be Hezbollah."

Industry leaders see the twin issues of identity and responsibility as crucial to the development of the profession. "The culture we are trying to build in this newspaper is one in which people identify themselves as journalists," *Asharq Al-Awsat's* Mirghani had told me back at the beginning of the survey project. "We cannot deny that this is an Arabic daily newspaper but the perception we are trying to build is that this is an international newspaper. If we can build [a] culture [in which reporters] identify themselves as journalists, then to a great degree we free their minds of the bias."

So how do Arab journalists see themselves? Participants knew they were taking part in a survey of journalists; hence, survey researchers would say, they were wearing their journalist "identity hat" when

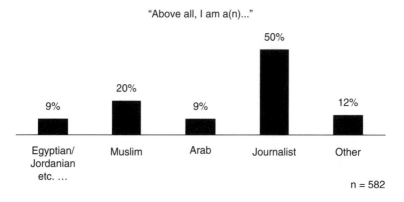

"Above all, I am a(n)..."

Egyptian/Jordanian etc. ...	Muslim	Arab	Journalist	Other
9%	20%	9%	50%	12%

n = 582

Figure 16 Identity

responding. Despite that, it is still worth noting that when asked, "Which one of the following do you think is most accurate, 'Above all, I am...'" and given five prompts, including nationality (e.g. Egyptian, Saudi, Moroccan, etc.), "Muslim," "Arab," "journalist," and "other," fully 50 percent chose, "Above all, I am a journalist," a response Mirghani, for one, was likely to see as a positive sign for the future [Figure 16].[23]

9

Journalistic Roles – Arabs, Americans and the World

[T]o cover international news with a French perspective...
and to carry the values of France throughout the world.
> Mission statement signed by all journalists
> at France 24 television

The heart of the difference between Arab journalists and journalists elsewhere in the world can be found in the set of Arab journalistic approaches that involve political/social change and the defense of Arab/Muslim ideals. These are roles largely absent from the self-perceptions of journalists in the US and other parts of the world.

Proponents of public or civic journalism in the US may seek to mobilize public engagement in the political process but they are not overtly trying to change the political and social landscape. Indeed, the roles at the core of the Arab Change Agent function are anathema to most American civic journalists, much less the mainstream of the profession. Only four of the individual journalistic roles mentioned in Weaver et al.'s surveys of US reporters made it into the top ten roles cited by Arab journalists.

Neither was there a significant overlap in perceived roles with journalists who were studied in an assortment of other surveys in Europe, Latin America, Africa, or Asia. The Change Agent function outlined above forms a subset of a broader set of roles that together reflect an activist or advocacy agenda. However, even when the overtly agenda-setting roles favored by Arab journalists are grouped into a broader category of activist or "Advocacy" roles, which include those that do not overtly seek to change political and social structures, Arab journalists are still far more heavily committed to using their craft as a means to an end than other colleagues elsewhere in the world. "My real job is to cover stuff, but my idealistic job is to make a difference," Roula Mouawad of *An-Nahar* told me, reflecting a common view, "to really motivate people in a good cause."

Far down on the Arab journalists' priority list was the task of straightforward dissemination of news. It is a dominant category for Western journalists but less popular among developing world journalists. While Saudi reporter Samar Fatany agreed that the job of a journalist is "to inform, to be [the audiences'] eyes and ears," she added a caveat: "As a journalist I should be objective as much as I can. Now sometimes you cannot be objective for different reasons. There are limits for everything." The Arabs were in synch with their colleagues around the world on the importance of interpreting news for the viewer, but they strongly rejected the classic development journalism perception of the journalist as a defender of the government and his/her own employer.

As they struggle to define their role in this time of turmoil in Middle East media and politics, Arab journalists come face-to-face with the question of loyalty. "To whom should loyalty be?" Abd el-Latif el-Menawy, the Egypt TV news chief, publicly asked his colleagues at an industry gathering. "Should the loyalty be to the receiver of information, whether it is a reader or a viewer? Or should the loyalty be to the society? Or should the loyalty be to the one who is paying the salary at the end of the month?" The majority of Arab journalists appear to be rejecting the old answers. Two roles that hark back to the classic mouthpiece or "loyalist" function of Arab media barely elicited any backing: "Support government policy" (7%) and "represent interest of the employer" (6%). But neither did they give as high a rating to the "watchdog" function as the US and some other journalists.

Overall, the perspective Arab journalists have of their mission is closer to that of journalists in the developing world, and, to a lesser

extent, Europe, than that of their US colleagues. While they are aban-
doning the loyalist or government mouthpiece role, Arab journalists
do believe they are more than just a conduit for information. As Ziad
Talhouk, a Lebanese journalist working for the Italian news agency
ANSA, put it: "It is [a journalist's] right to use his political opinion to
get feedback, but not to try to impose this point or view." That view
was shared, for example, by Bangladeshi journalists, who endorsed
eight of the top ten roles Arab journalists saw for themselves,[1] and by
Indonesian reporters and editors who, in the years since the overthrow
of longtime dictator Suharto, have seen their primary roles as defending the truth and serving as the public's watchdog,[2] strong parallels to
the overall Arab journalistic mission.

In a 1987 study, Mohamed Kirat of Indiana University surveyed 75
Algerian journalists to assess their professional characteristics and attitudes toward various journalistic norms. He concluded that, "Algerian
journalists conceive of the role and philosophy of the press within the
Algerian context."[3] That included a strong developmental journalism
framework, with priority to the promotion of social change and economic development.[4] Fully one quarter of the journalists defined news
as, "Events that have something to do with the government," indica-
tive of the strong government influence on Algeria's media system.[5] In
another example of the gap between the normative and the empirical,
45 percent of the journalists surveyed said it was extremely important
or very important to criticize the government when needed, which
"contradicts the realities of Algerian journalism in practice."[6] Algeria
is an Arab socialist state shaped by its bloody revolution against the
French. That history was reflected in the fact that more than 73 percent of the journalists said it was extremely important for the media
to "counterattack foreign propaganda," yet they perceived their second
most important function to be one in line with Western journalistic
norms: "Get the information to the public quickly." In many other ways,
the Algerian journalists differed from their Western counterparts, with
large percentages seeing it as their job to "educate and form a modern
Algerian citizen" (69%) and "enhance the objectives of the social revolution" (56%). Religion plays an important role in the self-image of
the Algerian journalist. Almost half saw it as their duty to "enhance the

Islamic values among the population" (48%) and "religious training" came second only to "newsroom learning" as the most important influence in shaping their ethics[7] (notably, newsroom learning also rates at the top of influences cited by US journalists).[8]

The importance of religion was also emphasized in a survey of journalists working on seven Saudi newspapers carried out by Abdulkader Tash in the early 1980s. He found that nearly all of the 149 journalists responding to his survey viewed the enhancement of Islamic principles of the Saudi people as an important function of the media.[9] Propagation of Islamic values was also cited as a top priority by 65 percent of newspaper journalists surveyed in Kuwait at about the same time, with large majorities on two of the five papers holding that view.[10] However, spreading Islamic values still fell ninth on the group's overall list of priorities, after such functions as concentrating on news which is of widest interest, influencing public opinion, investigating government claims, getting information to the public as quickly as possible, and helping achieve the goals of government development plans.[11] As in Algeria, the journalists in Kuwait – the majority of whom were Muslims but not Kuwaitis – listed religion and family upbringing as "extremely influential" in shaping their ethics, but ranked more senior journalist role models as the number one influence.[12] In a separate study, chief news editors at government-run Kuwait Radio and Television denied that their religious beliefs influenced selection of news for broadcasts, but fully one-third said their "personal values and opinions" did shape story choices,[13] raising questions about to what degree religious beliefs and personal values can be separated in a Muslim society, in which Islam is said to provide a "complete system of life for the Muslim community in all its details."[14]

Beyond religious considerations, the Saudi journalists expressed the need for a balance between the needs of the public and the needs of the government and showed little enthusiasm for complete independence. Freedom of the press was rated as the single most important need by only 20 percent of the Saudis, about the same number who said more professionally qualified Saudi journalists were needed, and Tash noted that many of the more sensitive questions on the survey were left unanswered. In contrast, the newspaper journalists in Kuwait said they would be willing to publish confidential government documents without permission and leaned toward a participant press function. They also expressed a much higher regard for their profession than the Saudi journalists. Part of the reason for this difference may lie in the fact that Kuwait has had a relatively free press since its "liberation" from the Iraqis in 1991, and the majority of journalists there are from Egypt, Lebanon, Syria, and other parts of the Arab world, thus under different kinds of constraints from the Saudi nationals operating in a tight-controlled press system where the news media follow the official line.

Not surprisingly, the story for the chief editors at Kuwait TV and Radio was very different. The chief editors avoided news stories that they considered to be against the interests of Kuwait, the Arab world or "friendly countries;" religiously or morally unacceptable; propaganda for Iraq or Israel; lacking news value; or for which they didn't have adequate resources (e.g. video). Only the last two would likely be sufficient reason to kill a story in a Western newsroom. The editors also confirmed what was already obvious to their audiences; 96.6 percent agreed with the statement, "I put news about the emir or the crown prince in the first portion of the newscast."[15] But such strictures were not limited to government-owned news organs. The Kuwait TV and radio findings were in keeping with a 1988 study of newscasts on government-owned stations in four Arab countries, which found that to editors on the government channels, "news had to be ideologically oriented." In the view of the editors on the government-controlled stations, "news is not neutral." They "ideally sought a balance between the good and the bad, the hard and the soft news. In practice, however, domestic news concentrated on the official and the positive."[16]

The role of politics in shaping the self-identity of Arab journalists was evident in a series of surveys of Arab journalists who took part in training sessions organized by the BBC World Service Trust. The 150 media workers surveyed indicated strong agreement with the statement that journalism ethics are "mostly determined by the ideological and political inclinations" of the news organization for which they work (Syrians 74%; Lebanese 44%), while half of the Egyptian journalists said they thought the private media in their country focused "on the commercial aspect even if it comes at the expense of editorial integrity." Tellingly, 70 percent of the Egyptian journalists said they did not depend on the Egyptian media as their primary source of information about local issues. Almost the same number of Lebanese said local reporting was characterized by "political bias of news media organizations," a view with which 41 percent of Syrian journalists agreed. The Syrian regime has been in a constant state of confrontation with Israel for a half-century, and 76 percent of Syrian journalists said it was their job to preserve "a nationalistic momentum through a defined media strategy." Roughly two-thirds of the journalists said the American government's position on Palestine was the issue that most affected media attitudes toward the US and the same percentage of the Syrians also said "constant bias against the American presence no matter what happens on the ground" characterized Syrian coverage of the Iraq conflict. It has been argued that a free press can only exist within a democratic system. The Arab journalists appeared to agree, overwhelmingly endorsing the statement that, "A democratic regime is essential for a free press" (Syrians 61%; Lebanese 60%; Egyptians 61%).[17] However, it is important to remember that many authoritarian regimes in the Arab world portray themselves as "democratic." The code of ethics adopted by Egyptian journalists in 1972 called democracy "the only healthy and sound framework for practicing political liberties"[18] even though the country was effectively a presidential dictatorship.

The primacy of Palestine as a marker of Arab identity was also apparent in Ramaprasad's survey of Egyptian journalists, conducted with Naila Nabil Hamdy of The American University in Cairo.[19] The pair replicated Ramaprasad and Kelly's Nepal study,[20] with the addition of six statements specific to Egypt's Arab and Islamic heritage. "Support the cause of the Palestinians" recorded the highest mean score (4.74 on a five-point scale) and "Defend Islamic societies, traditions and values" drew a 4.53 score. Other top responses included "Preserve Arabic culture" (4.38), "Strengthen spiritual and moral values" (4.26), "Spread a message of pan-Arab unity" (4.16), "Cultivate nationalism/patriotism" (4.24), and "Use the media to advance the social development of the country" (4.22). However, two functions closely associated with Western journalistic mores ranked second and third: "Provide information in a timely manner" (4.72) and "Provide accurate information" (4.68).

An analysis of the 36 questions revealed that those grouped in the category "Support Arabism/values" far outscored the other three categories, drawing a 4.50 on the five-point scale (the other categories were "Sustain democracy" (3.90), "Provide entertainment" (3.78) and "Support government/country" (3.29)). "Egyptian reporters are socialized into considering supporting Arabism/Islam as a basic function of journalism along with providing timely and accurate information," according to Ramaprasad and Hamdy.[21]

When the team examined actual performance of the various functions, "Support Arabism/values," which is not present in a Western journalistic milieu, was the category of functions journalists were most often able to perform and "Sustain democracy," the dominant media function in Western democracies, was rated last. "Support government/country," the group of functions most often associated with the developing world, came in third, after "Provide entertainment," another function associated with Western journalism. The pair concluded:

> Egyptian journalists consider supporting the government, which was the crux of the acrimonious debate over journalism during the UNESCO-situated debate on the New World Information Order, only average in importance. It is support for the Palestinian cause, Islamic values, pan-Arabism and such that takes center stage with these journalists.[22]

Arab and Islamic values also played a large role in the various ethical codes of journalism in the Arab and broader Islamic worlds. In an exhaustive comparison of the codes of Arab and non-Arab Muslim-majority countries and those of European nations, German scholar Kai Hafez found that a "deep divide between the European and some Arab and Islamic codes exists with respect to the role tradition, mores, and religion play in journalism ethics."[23]

> ... sensitivity to personal rights in Oriental codes is accompanied by much lower degree of freedom when it comes to news touching upon interests of the state, the nation, or religion.[24]

The Arab and Islamic codes espoused many of the same normative journalistic values as those of Europe, speaking of the need for "adherence to objective reality and truth" (Federation of Arab Journalists), a "commitment to the requirements of ethics, reliability and truth" (Egyptian Press Syndicate), and the requirement that news reporting be "fair and objective" (General Assembly of the Committee of the Press, Pakistan). There was also much talk of "freedom."[25] But they came with conditions.

> Although ideas of freedom have entered formal media ethics in the Middle East and the Islamic world, only a minority of documents limit the interference into freedom to cases where other fundamental rights (e.g., privacy) are touched, whereas the majority would have journalists accept political, national, religious, or cultural boundaries to their work.[26]

In an article presenting an Islamic perspective on journalism ethics and responsibility, Siddiqi observed that "[T]he meaning and values assigned to concepts such as news, truth, objectivity, freedom, people's right to know, and facts, may change according to particular circumstances or according to the needs and priorities of a particular society at a particular time."[27] Turkey's press charter was unique in that it endorsed censorship in the name of freedom:

> Nothing that restricts freedom of thought, conscience or expression or is damaging or offensive to public morals, religious sentiments or the foundations of the institution of family shall be published.[28]

The Saudi Arabian Media Charter declared that "the mass media oppose destructive trends, atheistic tendencies, materialistic philosophies and attempts to divert Muslims from their faith" and guarantees freedom of expression "within the framework of Islamic and national objectives and values."[29] Its "guidelines" went on to say that the media's job includes "the promotion of the idea of obedience to God, His Messenger, parents and guardians and preservation of the established order" and the protection of "the higher interests of Arabs and Muslims."[30]

Hafez observes that ethics codes in Middle Eastern and Islamic world "often reveal a defensive culture, calling on journalists to protect themselves, their audience, and society from dangerous foreign influences," including that of the foreign media. The 1980 Islamic Mass

Media charter, adopted at the first Islamic Media Conference in Jakarta, Indonesia, represented one of the most conservative approaches to journalism in the Muslim world. It contained an unyielding injunction: "Islamic media-men should censor all materials which are either broadcast or published in order to protect the *Ummah* from influences which are harmful to Islamic character and values." Such a draconian approach to journalism was rejected by the overwhelming majority of Muslim journalists and contradicts other ethical codes of Arab and Islamic countries. In contrast to Saudi Arabia, the most recent code of ethics in Indonesia's Alliance of Independent Journalists was one that most closely resembles Western codes.

With the exception of the Islamic Charter, Hafez found that countries on the "Islamic periphery" imposed fewer conditions than those in the Arab heartland, a fact that appeared to underscore the effect of localized political systems and ethnic or national identity on macro-level mores. Arab codes contained widespread references to the need for journalists to safeguard "national identity," the "Arab nation," or "Arab homeland" and defend "patriotic values." It is the duty of journalism to render "a cultural, social, patriotic, national and humanitarian service" and "mobilize public opinion in defense of the country," said Lebanon's code, adopted before the civil war. Egypt's 1996 code demanded "adherence to the patriotic and moral values of the Egyptian society."[31]

Interestingly, a 10-nation poll carried out in the spring of 2006 found that public trust in media was highest in Indonesia (88%), followed by two other Muslim-majority countries, Nigeria (86%) and Egypt (74%), and in India (82%), which has the second-largest Muslim population in the world. In all those countries (except Egypt, where the question was not asked) trust in media dramatically outranked trust in government. While almost 90 percent of Indonesians said the media strikes the right balance between freedom of speech and respect for cultures, the response in the other three countries was in the 60–70 percent range and only 41–47 percent of those surveyed in Nigeria, Egypt, and India agreed that "journalists are able to report freely."[32]

The Arab region is not a monolith; nor is the broader Islamic world. Each is made up of a wide array of cultures, traditions, belief systems, and ethnicities. So, too, the ethical codes of those regions. Hafez reports that

> they draw upon different secular or religious Islamic lega-
> cies that are clearly shaped by the national or organizational
> interests of those who designed [them]. ... [T]here is, in
> fact, no consensus on the contents of tradition among dif-
> ferent journalistic codes of the Middle East and the Islamic
> world.[33]

Which brings us back to the question of whether Arab journalism fits within a set of "universal" journalistic norms. There is no doubt that the aspirations of journalism – objectivity, fairness, informing the public – are near-universal. They are espoused by journalists of every persuasion on every continent. But as the results of these various surveys vividly demonstrate, the view of the mission of journalism is deeply affected by culture, religion, local/regional politics, and the state of development of any given society. While Arab journalists share with their US counterparts a desire to interpret and analyze information for their audiences, they are closer to developing world journalists in their intention to influence the direction of society. However, on the most important self-described roles, Arab journalists are unique in that their paramount mission is to drive political and social change and to safeguard their region and culture from external threats.

10

Arab Journalists Look at Themselves and the Competition

[J]ournalism can be regarded as an account of "reality," a
cultural narrative or part of the process of political struggle.
John Anderson and Geoff Ward, *The Future of
Journalism in the Advanced Democracies*

"[Western media] has always bragged when comparing itself to the
Russian media but ... it should stop comparing itself with the Soviet
Union and start comparing itself with us," Palestinian author and intellectual Mounir Shafik lectured Arab and Western journalists at a 2006
gathering.

Such comments are more than hyperbole. The traditional respect
with which the US media was long regarded in Arab newsrooms evaporated in the years after 9/11 as Arab journalists watched American
coverage of the Muslim world become gripped by jingoism and stereo-
typing. That shift in view was clearly documented in the survey. Still,
not all agreed with Shafik that the Arab media was a paragon of journalistic virtue. Roughly half those surveyed believed the Arab and US
media were equally unfair in their post-9/11 coverage, but a combined
47 percent of Arab journalists rated the fairness of European journalists
as "good" or "very good" [Figure 17].

While they were not impressed with the independence of the American media – a legacy of the Arab perception that American reporters

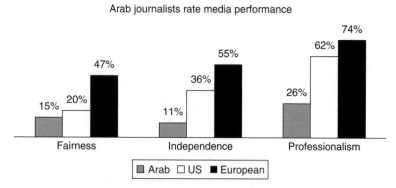

Figure 17 Rating media performance

became mouthpieces for the Bush administration after 9/11 and that US media executives are pro-Israeli – they had an even dimmer view of their own independence; more than half of Arab journalists polled described the independence of Arab news organizations as "poor." The independence of European journalist was seen as "good" or "very good" by 55 percent of their Arab colleagues [Figure 17].

Professionalism was the one area where Arab journalists still had a high regard for American journalists. Close to 40 percent of Arab journalists described the professionalism of the American media as "good" or "very good" while almost as many rated the professionalism of Arab media as "poor." Once again, European journalists scored the highest marks, with more than half the Arabs giving them a "good" or "very good" rating for professionalism [Figure 17]. The elite of Arab journalism could – and did – compete with the best of the West. People like Hisham Melhem, Al-Arabiya's Washington, DC bureau chief who knew the city – and America – better than many of his American counterparts; Yosri Fouda, Al-Jazeera's chief investigative correspondent and host of the documentary series *Top Secret*, who turned out reportage worthy of CBS' *60 Minutes* and PBS' *Frontline*, including his interview with the masterminds of 9/11; Daoud Kuttab, who created Jordan's first private radio station; and print journalists such as Camille Taweel of *Al Hayat* and Khaled Saleh, editor-in-chief of Egypt's *Youm7*. Behind the scenes were world-class news managers like Salah Negm, a BBC Arabic radio service veteran who was part of that original core team who founded

Al-Jazeera, subsequently built Al-Arabiya's news organization, then went on to do the same at BBC Arabic TV. But beyond the elite, as Arab reporters themselves acknowledged, quality quickly plummeted.

A classic example of the generally low quality of journalism that pervaded the region was a sensational series of articles published by Egypt's *Al-Masry Al-Youm* in the spring of 2009, which accused The American University in Cairo of spying on behalf of the Pentagon. "American University in Cairo Signed Contract with the Pentagon to Provide Confidential Information about Egypt," read a banner headline on the paper's front page. "This is the first publicly disclosed evidence recognized by the US Administration that the US military used a US university on Egyptian soil to collect research and information," the article reported. The contract in question actually involved nothing more than research support by AUC for an Egyptian-based US Naval medical research unit studying infectious diseases. "We didn't say that The American University in Cairo is spying on Egypt or has any role in providing intelligence, but we are not responsible about other people's analyses for what we wrote in the article," claimed the paper's editor-in-chief, Magdy el-Galad, when asked about the story. Later articles in the series spoke of "secret" agreements, language el-Galad defended. "What we wrote was clear that there was a secret contract, because no one knew about it from 2006 till now," he explained. In fact, the agreement had been public record and available since it was signed. El-Galad himself admitted that the paper "deliberately" opted not to quote anyone from AUC in the first article in order not to "deprive *Al-Masry Al-Youm* of its scoop."[1]

"There is no comparison, to be honest, between the press in the West and the press in the Arab world," Osman Mirghani, deputy editor-in-chief at the Saudi-owned pan-Arab newspaper *Asharq Al-Awsat,* told me. He saw Western journalists as far more professional than his Arab colleagues. "Having said that, the press in the Arab region is developing, is evolving and I think is moving forward."

Problems Facing Journalism

The harsh view many Arab journalists have of the state of their industry was underlined by the fact that they chose "professionalism" and a lack of ethics as the top challenges facing Arab journalism, along with press freedom issues and business pressure. "We have a childhood stage of media," according to Hassan Satti of *Asharq Al-Awsat*. Samir Khader, a senior editor at Al-Jazeera, agreed. "Do you think Al-Jazeera is like CNN, Fox News or CBS? No, we are not. We are still babies in the world of media. We are still babies." That is particularly true, he says, when it comes to professionalism. He believes part of the blame rests with the conflicting sense of identity among Arab journalists:

> We have three identities, while in the West you may have only one. [For Arabs, they are] the country where you come from; the fact of being a man or a woman; are you Islamist, not Islamist; are you liberal, not liberal; do you agree with this ideology, you do not agree? The ultimate profile is a mix of everything. That is very good of course. But you have to take into consideration that there are others in this news-room that might disagree with you. So you end up with a newsroom that is half professional. Not half the newsroom is professional; no, the *whole* newsroom is *half* professional. Can I tell you now that I am a professional? No I am not.

Many top editors, particularly on the pan-Arab satellite channels, bemoaned the shortage of experienced professionals and the relative trickle of new journalists emerging from the region's universities. In Sudan, 4,000 students graduated from faculties of information in 2008, but only 330 passed the qualifying exam for journalism. Jordan's top journalism school, Yarmuk University, had 20 computers for 1,000 students. "We do not have real institutions with real people with real press people and consequently the newspaper does not have any intention or determination to really work as a professional," Sudanese columnist Mohammed Elhomri complained. "And all the individuals do not have the will to work. It's like they consider training is a waste of money so how are we going to solve this problem?"

"I am really revolted by lots of things that are going on in newspapers," said Algerian editor Omar Belhouchet. As someone frequently interviewed by Arab reporters, I could personally attest to the shoddy quality of journalism. I was rarely quoted accurately and reporting errors abounded. One example: In a 2009 article in the country's leading independent daily, *Al-Masry Al-Youm*, I was identified as an official of the Arab League. "We need to acknowledge our lack of professionalism," said Rana Sabbagh, the director of Jordan-based Arab Reporters for Investigative Journalism. She saw the need for improved professionalism as self-preservation: "The majority of the time a good professional will create problems for a government because if he writes the truth, it will be more difficult for the government to persecute him." Hisham Kassem, a leading Egyptian publisher, blamed the traditional role of the Arab media as government mouthpiece for the shortage of quality journalists who think independently. So soured was he on the prevailing newsroom culture that, as he prepared to start a new newspaper, Kassem vowed not to hire any reporters from the government-owned press. "It is easier to teach journalism to smart young people than to get journalists to unlearn the bad habits they have learned elsewhere," he told me.

Among those "bad habits" was that of taking money from sources. In the Middle East, as in other emerging media markets, an "envelope culture" was pervasive, in which individual journalists or their news organizations frequently benefited financially from the stories they published. The *Cash for Editorial* survey by the International Public Relations Association (IPRA) found that only 40 percent of PR practitioners in Africa and the Middle East agreed with the statement, "Editorial copy appears as a result of the editorial judgment of the journalists and editors involved, not through any influence or payment by a third party." About 80 percent of those polled in the IPRA survey said journalists seldom or never *refused* free travel or products, 60 percent said it was common for favorable stories to be published in return for ad purchases, and 40 percent said journalists commonly accepted payments to print press releases. A study by the Arabic Network for Human Rights found that eight Egyptian newspapers and magazines had run a total of 25 stories about Tunisia during 2006 and 2007 that were paid for by the regime of President Zine el-Abidine Ben Ali.

Kuwaiti journalist Hussain Abdul Rahman went so far as to suggest it was impossible to expect unbiased election coverage in the Arab world due to the frequency with which journalists were bribed by candidates to provide favorable coverage. "They are taking money from the candidates and the parties. This has been happening all over the Arab world," he told a seminar in Qatar. An example on a very different level was Egypt's leading daily, *Al-Ahram*, which gave top editors a percentage of all advertising sold, a situation that left advertisers expecting positive coverage in return for their advertising dollars. Exacerbating the situation were the woefully poor salaries offered by most Arab news organizations. Beginning reporters at *Al-Ahram* were paid in the $80–$90 a month range and the situation was only slightly better at the private papers, while the monthly salary for a newly hired journalist at state-run Egypt television and radio was just $35. The official salary for top editors was often measured in the hundreds, rather than thousands, of dollars.

Those sobering statistics were evident in the survey findings. About 20 percent of respondents earned less than $250 per month and another 8 percent said they made less than $500. It is worth pointing out that the original survey instrument listed $100–$249 as the lowest income range, but some respondents to the paper-and-pencil version of the survey wrote in the margin "under $100." Forty-four percent of respondents earned less than $1,000 per month, with another nine percent earning between $1,500 and $2,499. At the other end of the spectrum, 20 percent reported making between $2,500 and $4,999 per month, with 6 percent in the $5,000–$7,499 range and another 3 percent earning more than $7,500 per month. The responses reflect the vast gulf in income between the majority of working journalists in the Arab world and the elite, primarily employed by the pan-Arab satellite channels: 57 percent of television journalists reported salaries of $2,500 per month or more; in contrast, 90 percent of those earning less than $500 per month said they worked in the print media.

"Sometimes people try to buy your support," said Magdy Salmaan, a young reporter with Egypt's *Al-Masry Al-Youm*. Even in Saudi Arabia, with its high cost-of-living, the average starting salary for a reporter was about $920 a month. Journalists there jokingly called it 'the beggar's job;' "You come up short either way," said *Arab News* Executive Editor Somayya Jabarti. "Low pay and trouble getting serious stories published." One poll found that 40 percent of Arabic-language journalists said they would reprint a press release in return for a gift. "It's the whole structure of the job," Jabarti explained. "If they are well paid and well-trained, they won't need" the gifts or envelopes.

That "envelope culture" extended to media corporations themselves. "We are offered millions from many, many governments," said Abdel Bari Atwan, editor-in-chief of the pan-Arab Palestinian daily *Al-Quds Al-Arabi*, a perennial thorn in the side of the Saudi and Egyptian regimes. "The Saudi government offered. Kuwaiti government offered. Some governments offer because we are outside the Saudi cloak." Atwan claimed he did not accept those offers: "I do not want to compromise my editorial independence." But, he added, "[Until] now we managed to survive, but for how long, I do not know." That aspiration to independence was – in theory, if not in practice – shared by the majority of journalists surveyed. Eighty-one percent of respondents rejected the statement, "It is acceptable to take money to write favorable stories." There was somewhat more ambivalence when asked to respond to the statement, "It is acceptable to take travel money from people or organizations that are the subjects of stories," with 60 percent saying it was never acceptable and 35 percent selecting "sometimes" [Figure 18]. The ambivalence may be traced to the fact that it was common practice for companies holding news conferences to provide "taxi money" to Arab journalists whose news organizations might not otherwise be able to send a reporter. However, three-quarters of respondents opposed the practice of writing favorable stories in return for advertisements.

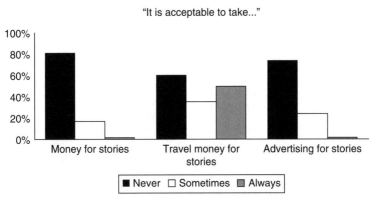

Figure 18   Money and ethics

Al-Jazeera's *Code of Ethics* states that its reporters must "[d]istinguish between news material, opinion and analysis to avoid the pitfalls of speculation and propaganda." In many ways, how to achieve that ideal without the media being reduced to parroting official pronouncements was one of the great conundrums of journalism. Responses to the questions on this topic reflected the degree to which Arab journalists were struggling with the gap between aspiration and reality. "When I'm talking about professionalism, I don't mean *absolute* professionalism," Hassan Satti explained. Part of the reason for that can be directly traced to the environment in which Arab journalists must operate, where psychological, legal, and physical attacks on media workers are commonplace. As the Committee to Protect Journalists reported in 2007, "scores of journalists who challenged the political order were threatened by government agents, hauled before the courts, thrown in prison, or censored in media crackdowns that stretched from Algeria to Yemen."

Still, 84 percent of the journalists completely or partly agreed that the Arab media as a whole was becoming freer and just over half said that they, as individual journalists, were freer to practice their craft [Figure 19].

"It's a matter of degree. The press is free here, but there are influences. We know the best newspapers have restrictions laid on them," said Mirghani of *Asharq Al-Awsat*. In contrast, Weaver found that the percentage of US journalists who said they had almost complete

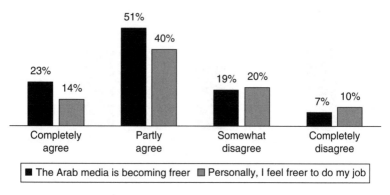

Figure 19 Media freedom

freedom to pursue their stories had dropped by a third over three decades, to about 40 percent. Clearly, the terms "freedom" and "control" must be seen in very different contexts in the Arab and US media environments. American journalists were primarily referring to editorial interference and business pressures, while Arab journalists had more fundamental threats in mind, evident in the fact that their list of perceived challenges to the profession included corruption within the media, the kind of government pressures noted above, physical violence, threats from religious extremists, and, in their eyes, the threat of attacks by the US, such as the American bombing of Al-Jazeera's bureaus in Kabul and Baghdad. But the contrast was nevertheless worth noting, as was the correlation between what Arab journalists ranked as the top five challenges facing Arab journalism – professionalism, government control, ethics, corruption, and media ownership – and the top five problems cited by their US counterparts – quality of coverage, economic/business pressure, credibility/public trust, media environment, and ethics/standards.

The fragmentation of the US media landscape has been accompanied by a shift toward increased politicization of news and information. Arab journalists were particularly critical of – and disappointed by – that, because in their eyes, there was still a quantum difference in the respective stages of development media in the US and the Middle East. By this way of thinking, politicization of news in the West – especially the US – was a step backward, while, in the Arab news media, balance was often still just an aspiration. "Arab journalists, in general, have positions that reflect their societies, on political and other matters. We see religious programs that are politicized with religious flavor. All social issues are being presented from one dimension," according to Diana Moukalled, senior correspondent at Lebanon's Future TV, "I don't think we've reached the stage where we really have high professional standards."

Though Arab journalists were critical of their industry as a whole, when asked about the quality of journalism at the specific news organization for which they worked, they had a far more positive view than did US editors and reporters who were asked the same question about their own outlets. Sixty percent of the Arabs agreed with the statement,

"My news organization is doing an outstanding job," while a Pew survey found that just 15 percent of American reporters gave their organizations an "A" grade.

Post-9/11 Coverage

Since the launch of Al-Jazeera in 1996, there has been enormous qualitative and quantitative change in Arab media. However, as discussed earlier, independent media ventures were dominated by powerful business interests closely linked – sometimes through blood – to the ruling elite. The largest media conglomerate in the Arab world was controlled by the brother-in-law of King Abdullah of Saudi Arabia; the late King Faisal of Saudi Arabia owned 39 percent of the shares in *Asharq Al-Awsat*; Libya's media properties were all in the hands of Muammar Qadaffi's son, Seif; Lebanon's Future TV was owned by – and served as a cheerleader for – the son of the slain former prime minister, Rafiq Hariri; and Egypt's newest family of channels was being built by a powerful tycoon who controlled a construction and telecommunications empire closely linked to the Mubarak regime.

The journalists surveyed acknowledged this situation when they ranked "government control," "media ownership," and "corporate pressure" among the top challenges to Arab journalism. The strictures of ownership meant that even the poster-child for Arab media independence, Al-Jazeera, operated within red lines, evident in a softening of the station's criticisms of Saudi Arabia beginning in late 2007, reportedly on the orders of the Qatar government. "I have restrictions. I am allowed to do this. And I am not allowed to do that," the channel's senior producer, Samir Khader, readily conceded well before that latest incursion of regional realpolitik into the newsroom. "It is a game. It is really a game; a game of survival." Arab editors and reporters gave themselves slightly higher marks than they gave American reporters for post-9/11 coverage of US Middle East policy, with 29 percent partly or completely agreeing that Arab coverage was objective versus 16 percent who said the same of US coverage [Figure 20], but it was still a candid self-assessment.

"There is a crisis for newspapers in the Arab world," Abdulwahab Badrakhan, the former *Al Hayat* opinion editor, told me. "People think

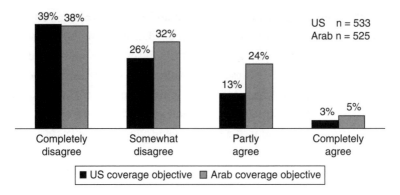

Figure 20   Post-9/11 coverage

that all the papers are from the government and they know very well that there is no freedom." Despite that, the overarching view was that no matter how bad things may have been, they *were* improving. Al-Jazeera's M'Hamed Krichen spoke for an increasing number of Arab journalists when he said he had realized a lifelong dream. "I can look to the whole word with no obstacle, with no instructions [to] 'cover this, do not cover this, it is better to avoid this.' I feel that I am a free journalist and it is a very happy feeling. I can work now as a free journalist; let us say, at least at 90 percent. This 10 percent is OK. We are not always satisfied, not always 100 percent. But it is closer."

While critical of themselves, many Arab journalists resented the holier-than-thou attitude of Western journalists who, as noted in a report about one of the many US–Arab media dialogues, "viewed themselves as more experienced and more knowledgeable about the standards of the profession." As media analyst Khaled Hroub explained at the same dialogue, "Arab media maybe has so many shortcomings and misgivings, but still Western media cannot lecture them and they do not have the moral high ground to give lessons to our media."[2]

No incident better exemplified the differences between Arab and Western journalists in their approach to journalistic norms than the controversy over publication of cartoons depicting the Prophet Muhammad in a way that Muslims considered blasphemous. The row gave new meaning to the phrase, "publish and be damned." Originally appearing in a Danish newspaper, the cartoons were soon republished by other news organizations in Europe and the US, which ostensibly did so to safeguard freedom of the press. "Europe Can Take Pride in Defending Cartoons," proclaimed the headline over an opinion column in *The New York Times*. "These are our values and we will defend them," German Chancellor Angela Merkel declared, seemingly oblivious to the fact that Muslims around the world felt exactly the same way. "Europe joins 'Crusade,'" announced a front-page headline in *The Peninsula* in Qatar, employing a term that resonates with those Muslims who see many Western actions as an extension of the thousand-year-old conflict between Christianity and Islam.

The controversy soon became a more modern clash between free speech and cultural respect. "Imagine a society that added up all the prohibitions of different religions. What would remain of the freedom to think, to speak, even to come and go?" asked *France Soir*, one of several European publications that fueled the uproar by republishing the controversial cartoons. "We would have done exactly the same thing if it had been a pope, rabbi or priest caricature," wrote Editor-in-Chief Serge Faubert. "We had no desire to add oil to the fire as some may think. A fundamental principle of democracy and secularism is being threatened." The editor-in-chief of Egypt's state-owned *Al-Gomhuriya* shot back, "It is not a question of freedom of opinion or belief, it is a conspiracy against Islam and Muslims which has been in the works for years." Yet *France Soir* itself was a microcosm of the clash. Its publisher was Egyptian and wasted no time in firing the managing editor and issuing a statement offering "our regrets to the Muslim community and to all people who have been shocked or made indignant by this publication."

When the controversy broke, I happened to be attending a gathering of Arab and Western journalists in Qatar organized by Al-Jazeera entitled, "Defending Freedom, Defining Responsibility." Several Western news executives found themselves scrambling to manage those very issues in real-time. Between sessions, the head of news for global satellite TV channel BBC World, Richard Porter, fielded a barrage of emails from deputies in London who were doing damage control in the face of complaints from angry Muslim viewers around the world. The complaints came despite the fact that the channel had opted to broadcast pixilated images of the cartoons in its coverage, to give the audience a sense of the cartoons without, the BBC hoped, actually blaspheming the Prophet. Google's news manager, Nathan Stoll, faced a different problem: Computerized algorithms, not human editors, choose what stories appeared on Google News, and the offensive images kept popping up on the site, producing a torrent of protest.

For many in the West, the dramatic response to publication of the cartoons – protest rallies, death threats, economic boycotts, the severing of diplomatic relations – seemed a staggering overreaction. Distance from Western media centers added a degree of perspective for those news managers who happened to be in the region for the conference. "I don't think I would have understood why people were so angry about this if I hadn't been here to talk with them myself," said one British journalist.

Western reporting of the Middle East took a bashing throughout the Al-Jazeera conference. And the cartoon controversy drove home the difference in approaches that define Western and Arab journalism. "When I insult your religion or your feelings it is crossing the limits of freedom of expression," Salama Ahmed Salama, Egypt's most respected columnist, told me over breakfast one morning. "For many Europeans, such things are not so important, but here religion is a daily food and we cannot just accept this." Not all Arab journalists condemned their European counterparts. *Al-Shihan*, a Jordanian gossip tabloid, published the offending cartoons. "Muslims of the world, be reasonable," pleaded Editor-in-Chief Jihad Momani. The parent company quickly pulled the issue and sacked the editor.

Many Arab journalists I spoke with had little doubt that extremist Muslim forces were exploiting the cartoon controversy for their own ends at a time when Islamist parties were flexing their muscles after election victories in Iraq, Egypt, and Palestine. In fact, many months before the controversy broke, Egypt's *Al-Fajr* had displayed some of the cartoons on its front page in an article about their publication in Denmark, with no public outcry. It was only when Danish Muslim leaders traveled to the Middle East to generate support that the public took notice. If people in the West were having a hard time understanding why Muslims were so angry, the public – and journalists – in the

Muslim world saw yet another example of Western double-standards. Europe had laws against anti-Semitism; a writer who denied the existence of the Holocaust had recently been put on trial in France, yet European newspapers were claiming free speech was at stake in the cartoon controversy. "What is allowed for Jews is not allowed for Muslims," Muhammed al-Musfir, the former chief editor of Qatar's *Al Rayah* newspaper, told the Al-Jazeera conference, referring to Western media "anger" over Hamas's election triumph in Palestine and media "celebration" of earlier Likud victories. "It's a double-standard," said another reporter in the audience, referring to the cartoons. "If this is freedom of expression, why can't the same standard be applied to the Holocaust?"

Years later, when many leading US journalists denounced an editorial cartoon in the *New York Post* that appeared to depict President Barack Obama as a monkey, an editor on a Gulf newspaper emailed me a link to the story with this note:

> There is legitimate hue and cry about a cartoon depicting President Obama as a chimpanzee. [The] *New York Post* apologized under pressure. But, when Muslims objected to the Danish cartoons on Prophet Mohammad (PBUH [Peace Be upon Him]), the EU and U.S. media thought we were going out of bound[s] and infringing on what they claim to be the West's most sacred value – freedom of the press. This is hypocrisy at its best.

The comment was a reminder that the debate over the Prophet Muhammad cartoons went far beyond politics or religion, *per se*. "Freedom of expression is only half of the truth," Rashid Khashana, Tunis correspondent for the pan-Arab daily *Al-Hayat*, had told me back at the height of the debate. "The second part is that we must respect things sacred for Christians, Muslims and Jews."

Respect and its corollary, *responsibility*, were terms fundamental to the worldview of Arab journalists, many of whom deeply believed that their hard-earned media freedoms must be used *responsibly*. The idea that individual reporters, or at least the news organizations for which they work, must strive for balanced coverage is a fundamental principle taught in journalism textbooks the world over. However, there is a wide disparity of opinion on just what it is that should be balanced. "In order for newspapers to be beneficial to society," Lebanese newspaper publisher Boutros al-Boustani wrote in the late nineteenth century, they must avoid publishing stories that violated "the right principles."[3] But what was "right" and what constituted "balance?" Arab League Secretary General Amr Moussa unwittingly touched the raw nerve at heart of this philosophical debate in late 2005 when, in his opening comments at an Arab Thought Foundation conference on the media in Dubai, he declared that journalists must strive for a balance between being "respectful and truthful." The comment raised eyebrows among Western and Arab journalists alike and discussion in the hallways quickly turned to definitions of "respect" and "truth" – and where the balance between them lies. As Peter David, foreign editor of *The Economist*, noted during a panel shortly after Moussa's speech, for many reporters, truth must come *before* any consideration of respect.

Prince Bandar bin Khaled al-Faisal, head of the Arab Thought Foundation and publisher of the Saudi daily *Al-Watan*, said the definition of "respectful" or "responsible" journalism is in the eye of the beholder. "I think a government official in Syria would probably mean 'responsible' as the party line," he told me on the sidelines the conference. "But in another society, responsible would mean [adhering to] social values. It means different things to different people, just as the word 'democracy,' I am afraid, in this part of the world means different things to different people." Khaled al-Maenna, the influential editor of *Arab News*, was not convinced. "I think our role is to portray the truth," he explained, as we drank tea on the patio outside. "To *resist* authority, not to respect it in the way Amr Moussa said. If you respect *authority*, you become a part of the government. You become a tool of the government. Our role is to respect the truth." But Al-Maenna, to the degree that he was able to practice what he preached, may be in the minority – or an example of that disconnect between aspirations and reality. The degree to which Arab journalists adhered to Prince Bandar's interpretation was evident in the fact that 80 percent of survey respondents partly or completely agreed with the statement, "Journalists

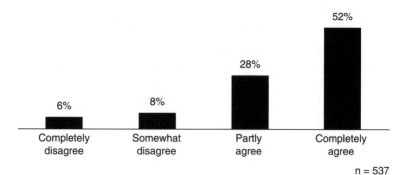

Figure 21   Respect

must balance the need to inform the public with the responsibility to show respect" [Figure 21].The approach held sway even at the region's most aggressive news organization. When Iran put restrictions on Al-Jazeera's correspondents and anti-Jazeera Shi'ite protests broke out in Baghdad after the channel aired comments critical of Iraq's Grand Ayatollah Ali al-Sistani, Al-Jazeera General Director Wadah Khanfar issued a statement declaring, "We affirm that the policy of Al-Jazeera is based on respecting religious and public figures. There was no intention at all to offend his Eminence Sistani."[4]

The cartoon controversy and Sistani incident were reminders that the tumult of modern Middle East politics has a direct impact on how Arab journalists approach their role in society. They also underscored the role of religion in shaping journalistic worldview. Arab journalists identify with religion far more closely than American journalists. Where 88 percent of Arab journalists surveyed identified themselves as Muslims, and one-third of those described themselves as "religious" versus "secular" or undeclared, about one-third of US journalists said they did not practice any religion.[5] Both groups were asked whether it *is* necessary or *is not* necessary to believe in God in order to have good moral values. Almost 40 percent of Arab journalists said it was necessary, versus just 5 percent of US journalists [Figure 22].[6]

A similar divergence could be seen on the question of politics. As noted earlier, some leading Arab media figures wore two hats, that of a

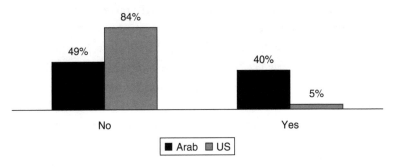

Figure 22 Belief in God/moral values

Source: US data: *State of the News Media* 2007.

journalist and that of a politician. Many others blurred the line between journalist and political activist. US-based Egyptian columnist Mona Eltahawy proudly took part in anti-regime *Kifaya* demonstrations in Cairo's Tahrir Square when she returned to her native land to cover the 2006 elections. "I am no longer just a journalist, I have become the heart of the conflict," Al-Arabiya presenter Giselle Khouri, a Lebanese national, told me in late 2005. Her husband, Samir Kassir, the out-spoken anti-Syrian columnist for Lebanon's largest daily, *An-Nahar*, had been assassinated less than six months before. The Israeli assault on Lebanon left many other Arab journalists sharing her pain. Rami Khouri, the Harvard-educated editor-at-large for Beirut's *Daily Star*, was out of the country when the conflict broke out. In a column enti-tled "Back to Beirut: Ready to Defy Israel," he explained his desire to return home: "I want to return mainly because steadfastness in the face of the Israeli assault is the sincerest – perhaps the only – form of resis-tance available to those of us who do not know how to use a gun, and prefer not to do so in any case, for there is no military solution to this conflict," he told his readers.[7]

The most extreme example of this activism was evident in the shoe seen around the world, when Iraqi journalist Muntadhir al-Zaidi hurled his shoes at President Bush during the latter's last news conference in Baghdad. Most activist Arab journalists preferred to use their pens. They pointed with pride to the role the media played in forcing Syria to withdraw from Lebanon in the so-called "Cedar Revolution" and the media's impact on the broader *Kifaya* (Enough) movement for political change that it inspired in several other Arab countries. "We want independence, and always the Lebanese journalists have a role to play in our independence," journalist Nayla Tueni, heir to the *An-Nahar* dynasty, told me a few months before her father was murdered. Others had a more modest agenda. "Every day you give a new hope. Always there is a bright side, a new day coming. Maybe it is very small, but it is a message you keep in mind and you give it to the people who are watching TV every day," said Ghada Abou Adal Hassoun, host of a morning show on Lebanon's Future TV.

For some Arab journalists, this meant balancing the professional role of a journalist and the obligations of a citizen. "You have a very big responsibility [as a journalist]," said Ibrahim Hamidi, a Syrian who was *Al-Hayat's* Damascus bureau chief, "but this responsibility has two faces. I do not run after scoops because I know a lot of scoops that may harm the country. I might be not objective, but it is the country that you live in that really matters more than your job. The priority is the safety of your country." This conflicting sense of responsibility was reflected in the seeming contradictory way journalists responded on the thorny issue of journalistic objectivity. While 93 percent of respondents said journalists should interpret for their audiences and almost half said they should include their own opinion, 89 percent completely or partly agreed that a journalist must always be objective [Figure 23].

"I think that the problem in the Middle East is that even the correspondents and the journalists are linked in one way or another to a political institution or to a certain political or ideological party and the solution lies in that the journalist is not to join any of these sides," Hussein Jamal of Kuwait TV commented at a journalists' gathering. That linkage could be seen in the media war of words that erupted after the Lebanese Shi'ite group Hezbollah criticized Egypt's stance in 2009 Gaza war. The result was what *Asharq Al-Awsat* columnist Diane Mukkaled called an unprecedented "campaign by state television programs, newspapers, anchors and websites, all replete with disdain and accusations that crossed the media line." That campaign included a move to pull the plug on Hezbollah's TV station Al-Manar, which

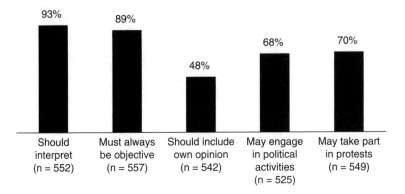

Figure 23 Objectivity and activism

Egypt claimed had broadcast coverage that "constitutes a national humiliation, creates confusion with our neighbors and sectarianism about different groups."[8]

LBC presenter Dolly Ghanem bemoaned the degree to which Lebanese journalists engaged in politics. "Sometimes I see that journalists are working politics more than journalism," she told me. "This is what I do not like to see. We are here not to work politics; we are here to do our job." But the majority of those surveyed disagreed with Ghanem. Where most mainstream US journalists avoid overt involvement in politics, 68 percent of Arab respondents to the survey partly or completely agreed that it was permissible for a journalist to engage in political activities, and 70 percent said they had no objection to a journalist taking part in political demonstrations [Figure 23].

When asked "how should a journalist conceive his task?" 30 percent of Mexican journalists surveyed chose, "politicians with other means."[9] Similarly, a survey of Polish journalists found that "the bulk of them ... did not perceive a danger to impartiality from a journalist's engagement in political and economic activity or the assumption of public functions."[10]

However, such political engagement left some Arab journalists with what, to a Western eye, would seem a dyslexic approach to traditional Western journalistic norms. That was evident in an article written by a Saudi reporter Samar Fatany. To justify the need for a stronger, more professional media, she fell back on that old foreign bogeyman, "the clever – and articulate – Israelis."

> How can Saudi Arabia, as the leader of the Muslim world, confront this smear campaign, waged against Arabs and Muslims or hope to defend the Palestinian and Arab cause when it does not yet have an effective policy to upgrade its media services? We are engaged in a media war, and we are losing the battle because of our inadequate journalistic capabilities.[11]

Arab journalists readily acknowledge their weaknesses. But when asked to rate their overall coverage in the years since 9/11, they believe they have outperformed their American colleagues. The predominant sense among Arab journalists of the state of their industry *vis à vis* news organizations in the West was perhaps best summed up by the motto of the pan-Arab channel Al-Arabiya: "Closer to the Truth."

Not quite the whole truth perhaps, but getting closer every day.

11

Arab Journalists and the Arab People

> There had grown up a new educated class looking at itself
> and the world with eyes sharpened by western teachers, and
> communicating what it saw in new ways.
>
> Albert Hourani, *A History of the Arab Peoples*

The eternal debate among media critics is whether journalists represent the people to whom, and about whom, they report. That question is particularly relevant in regions of the world where there exist wide financial and educational disparities. That is emphatically the case in the modern Middle East.

Religion is fundamental to worldview in the Arab world and Arab journalists are significantly more secular in orientation than the Arab public. Roughly equal percentages of the journalists surveyed identified themselves as "religious" versus "secular" Muslims, while another third did not declare their religiosity. When the public in Saudi Arabia, Jordan, Egypt, and Morocco were asked a similar question, 88 percent chose "religious" and just 12 percent said "not religious."[1] Studies of the Arab public have concluded that religion is not a significant determining factor in political outlook.[2] Much the same is true among Arab journalists. There was no statistically significant difference in the responses of self-declared "religious" and "secular" Muslim journalists, or those declining to declare, on a range of issues involving regional politics, US policy, and the norms of journalism, underlining the merging of agendas of Arab nationalists, nation-state nationalists, and Islamists in the region today.

While, as might be expected, they did disagree on some issues related to religion, a majority of the "religious" journalists (61%) agreed that religious leaders should not influence elections and more than one-third of self-declared "secular" journalists listed the fostering of *spiritual* values as the primary job of an Arab journalist, while more "religious" journalists gave priority to *Arab* causes than did "secular" or undeclared journalists.[3] All this was evidence of the degree to which the distinction was blurring between "Arab" and "Muslim" causes and priorities. And where surveys consistently showed the Arab public strongly identified with the Muslim world and had a much lower identification with the Arab region, 35 percent of Arab journalists identified first with the Arab world, 25 percent with the Islamic world, and just 15 percent with nation [Figure 24].[4]

As noted earlier, Arab journalists saw their main missions as creating political and social change within the Arab world in the face of repressive Arab governments and protecting the Arab people and Muslim values against external threats. Where that primary external threat lay, both the journalists and their publics agreed: Journalists shared with the Arab people a broadly negative view of the US in general, of US Middle East policy overall, and US Iraq policy in particular.

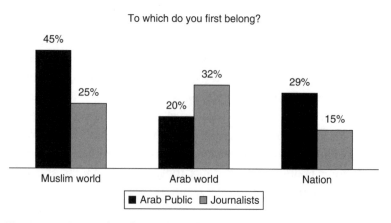

Figure caption: To which do you first belong?

45% — 25% (Muslim world) · 20% — 32% (Arab world) · 29% — 15% (Nation)

■ Arab Public ▨ Journalists

Figure 24 Geographic identity (vs. public)

Source: Arab attitudes data: Telhami/Zogby.

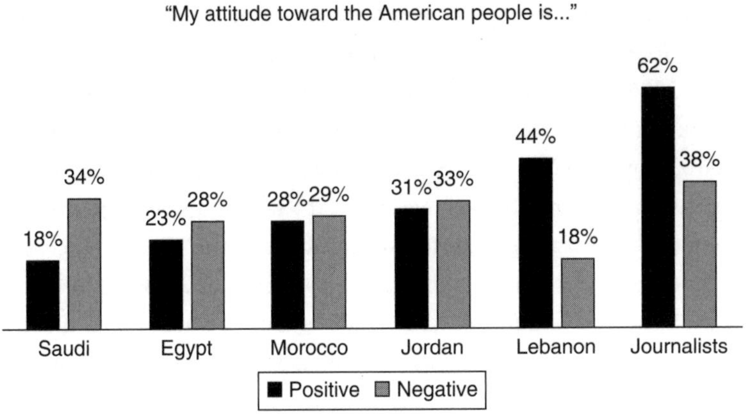

"My attitude toward the American people is..."

Figure 25 Attitude toward American people (vs. public)

Source: Arab attitudes data: *Zogby Five Nation* (2006).

Yet when it came to the American people, the attitude of journalists was light years away from that of the Arab public as a whole, with 62 percent of the journalists expressing a positive view of Americans versus less than one-third of the public in four of five countries surveyed by Zogby [Figure 25].[5]

On the question of the need for representative government, Arab journalists were in synch with their publics. The Arab Barometer and the Moaddel and Latif surveys found that in six of seven Arab countries, more than 80 percent of those surveyed believe democracy is the best form of government. A 2006 Gallup survey found much the same.[6] Journalists were not asked that specific question, but more than half chose "democrat" as their primary political identity and virtually all said the region needs political and social reform.

But that does not mean Arab journalists, or the public, endorsed – or believed – US calls for Arab democracy, which became a voluble element of American Middle East policy in the second Bush administration. A series of surveys conducted by Telhami and Zogby consistently found that "fewer than ten percent of Arabs believe that the spread of democracy was a true U.S. objective, with most believing that oil, Israel, and weakening the Muslim world drive American policy in the region."[7]

The rejection of Hamas's election victory in Palestine and the US refusal to deal with Egypt's Muslim Brotherhood after it won 150 seats in the 2006 Egyptian parliamentary elections only added to that skepticism. On this issue, journalists were in tune with their publics. In the 2006 Zogby/Telhami poll, 65 percent of Arabs said democracy-building was not the real US objective; about the same number of journalists "completely" disagreed with the suggestion that the US was sincere in its desire to foster democratic change, and another 25 percent "somewhat" disagreed [Figure 26]. And a 2007 survey demonstrated that the Egypt public was as skeptical as journalists about the Bush administration's verbal endorsement of a Palestinian state.[8]

Like citizens the world over, Arabs are worried first about their pocketbooks. Based on aggregate responses to various questions in the Arab Barometer survey, Jamal and Tessler concluded that "majorities in the Arab world attach higher priority to solving economic problems than to securing the political rights and freedoms associated with democracy."[9] Asked by the World Values Survey, "How much respect is there for individual human rights nowadays?" 40 percent of Arabs in six countries responded that there is "not much respect" or "no respect at all."[10] Arab journalists were equally concerned about such issues, with the lack of human rights and poverty ranking just below political reform on the list of most important issues facing the Arab world.

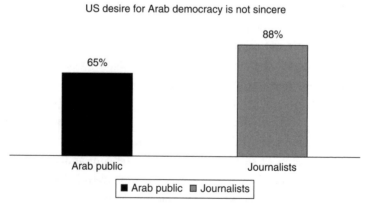

Figure 26 US desire for democracy (vs. public)

Source: Arab attitudes data: Zogby, *Four Years Later* (2007).

In large measure, the difference between Arab journalists and their publics on this subject was a matter of emphasis. Though the average Egyptian or Yemeni may be looking first at putting food on the table, they also long for political change. Ninety-six percent of Arabs questioned for the Arab Barometer agreed that, "Having a democracy system in our country would be good."[11] Exactly the same percentage of journalists favored political reform; the reporters and editors were just more overtly aggressive about it. While 83 percent of the public wants reform to be "gradual,"[12] only about two-thirds of journalists agreed. The rest want "radical" reform.

Religion and Identity

It is on the subject of religion that Arab journalists dramatically depart from their audiences. Where the World Values Survey found that more than two-thirds of the public feel politicians who *do not* believe in God are unfit for office, just 25 percent of Arab journalists agreed; while *less than half* of the public said religious leaders should not influence how people vote, *three-quarters* of Arab journalists want clerics to stay out of politics; and although just 11 percent of the public thinks it is permissible for national laws to contradict *sharia* law, 60 percent of Arab journalists believe *civil* law takes precedence over *religious* law [Figure 27]. The journalists also had far less confidence in religious authorities than the general public. Less than half as many journalists as members of the Arab public responded in the affirmative when asked if religious

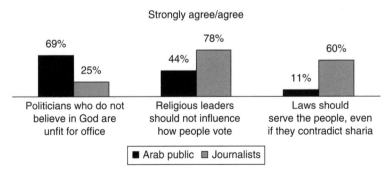

Figure 27   Clergy role (vs. public)

Source: Arab attitudes data: *World Values Survey*.

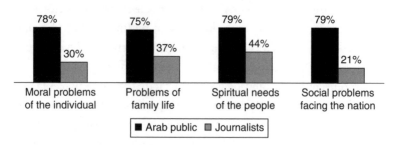

Figure 28 Religious authorities (vs. public)

Source: Arab attitudes data: *World Values Survey.*

authorities give adequate answers to the moral problems of the individual (30% vs. 78%). Substantially fewer journalists than members of the public responded positively when asked whether clerics provide adequate answers to the problems of family life (37% vs. 75%), the spiritual needs of the public (44% vs. 79%, and social problems (21% vs. 79%) [Figure 28].

PART III

Conclusion

12

Border Guards of the New Arab Consciousness

> Satellite patterns are trade routes that have their own agonizing histories and their own differentiated impacts.
>
> Monroe E. Price, *Media and Sovereignty*

"Awake, O Arabs, and turn on your television sets." So might Ibrahim al-Yazjii have begun his famous 1868 ode to Arab nationalism had he written it a century and a half later. By then, he would have noted that pervasive influence of Arab satellite television and the increasingly aggressive ethos of print journalism, bolstered by the Internet and other forms of digital communication, were fueling the rise of a new common Arab consciousness every bit as real as the "imagined communities" that Benedict Anderson, in his classic work on nationalism, tells us are at the core of the concept of nation.[1] This new electronically enhanced "imagined" Arab *watan* (nation) was bound together by many of the classic touchstones of nationalism theory: language, media, and *ethnie*.

Live and incessant coverage of the 2006 Hezbollah–Israel war, which helped vault Hezbollah leader Nasrallah to the status of the most admired Arab leader, was just one example of the degree to which television was helping to craft a new Arab consciousness that formed an overlay on – and in some ways superseded – national borders and religious divisions. It was seen in studies demonstrating a link between television viewing and pan-Arab and pan-Muslim identity, in shifts in public opinion following major regional news events, and in surveys that showed an increased affinity for the Arab world, even among nationalities politically alienated from the mainstream.[2] The result was an increasingly cohesive Arab consciousness that has been given many names: Shibley Telhami's "new Arabism," Marc Lynch's "new Arab public," or Khalil Rinnawi's "McArabism." It all amounted to the same thing: an "imagined" community perceived, in large measure, through the camera lens and pen of the Arab journalist.

Debates over which channels represented the interests of the Islamists and which those of Arab nationalism obscured the reality that in newsrooms from Casablanca to Sana'a the agendas of the two were blurring, producing a synergy of interests reflected on television screens across the region every day. Anthony Smith, another well-known theoretician of nationalism, argued that ideologies such as pan-Arabism and pan-Africanism create "border guards" who provide "a new panoply of symbols and myths, memories and values, that set the included national states apart."[3] In many ways, Arab journalists were the border guards – if not the architects – of this new imagined Arab *watan*. They reflected a worldview that largely transcends borders, a sense of self-identity that sets region above nation and religion above passport, and a commitment to political change that was infecting the body politic of the Arab world through the electronic virus of 24/7 news.

"The genius of Arab Satellite TV," observed Abderrahim Foukara, Washington, DC bureau chief for Al-Jazeera, "is that it [has] captured a deep-seated common existential pain called Arab sensibility and turned it into a picture narrative that speaks to something very deep in the Arab psyche."

Seeking Anderson in the Desert Sands

The role of communication in the formation of national identity was singled out early in the emergence of nationalism theory. In distinguishing between "people," "nationality," and "nation" in his classic postwar work, *Nationalism and Social Communication*, Karl W. Deutsch

(1912–92) focused on the transmission of ideas in the formation of a "people," which he defined as "a larger group of persons linked by…complementary habits and facilities of communication."[4] John A. Armstrong, another leading thinker in the field, argues that different civilizations, whether Western Christendom or the Islamic *umma*, arrive at the point of nation-state from different directions. But at root, he believes, "myth, symbol, communication, and a cluster of associated attitudinal factors" ultimately combine to produce what he calls the "mythomoteur" or "constitutive myth of the polity" in every culture.[5] Hobsbawm points to such disparate examples as the success of Nazi propaganda and the British royal family's Christmas broadcast as evidence of the role of mass media in making post-1918 nationalism an element of everyday life. Through the press, cinema, and radio "popular ideologies could be both standardized, homogenized and transformed." While this facilitated the effectiveness of mass propaganda, that "was almost certainly less significant than the ability of the mass media to make what were in effect national symbols part of the life of every individual, and thus to break down the divisions between the private and the local spheres in which most citizens normally lived, and the public and national one."[6]

This acknowledgment of the import of communications in the formation of national identity most famously finds its expression in Anderson's concept of the "imagined community." The nation, wrote Anderson in his now-classic text, "is an imagined political community:"

> It is imagined because the members of even the smallest nation will never know most of their fellow-members, meet them, or even hear of them, yet in the minds of each lives the image of their communion.

Words are the fundamental unifying force of Anderson's imagined community. "[T]he sacred silent languages were the media through which the great global communities of the past were imagined," he wrote, referring to Christendom, the Islamic *umma*, and the Chinese civilization. The rise of vernacular languages to replace the Latin of the Catholic Church laid the seeds for European ethnic nationalism, which was then fed and nurtured by changing economic structures, social and scientific discoveries. Linking it all was the spread of increasingly rapid means of communication.

> Nothing perhaps more precipitated this search [for iden-
> tity], nor made it more fruitful, than print-capitalism, which
> made it possible for rapidly growing numbers of people to
> think about themselves, and to relate themselves to others,
> in profoundly new ways.[7]

It does not take a major leap of imagination to recognize that what was true in Europe 500 years ago has profound implications for the modern Arab world. Where newspapers and books produced in vernacular languages united European peasants into new collective identities, satellite television has facilitated the spread of Modern Standard Arabic (MSA), often called "news Arabic," which is emerging as a bridge that forms an overlay above the many varieties of colloquial Arabic heard in the region. And where the mobility of the industrial revolution produced a class of workers who broke down barriers of national identity, Arab journalists from North Africa, Lebanon, Syria, Palestine, and Jordan who have migrated to media of the Gulf and London are part of what Anderson called the "countless, ceaseless travels" that contribute to the rise of an imagined community.[8]

Journalistic Agenda-Setting

Media theory tells us that journalists both drive public opinion and reflect it; they influence the agenda and are influenced by it. By comparing how Arab journalists and the Arab public about which, and to whom, they report respond to questions about politics, religion, and society it is clear that the region's journalists stand on the borderlands of Arab identity. They represent a fusing of Muslim and Arab worldviews, leading the body politic in directions that reinforce a sense of shared consciousness.

Nationalism is not a political principle alone. It is also a sentiment. Thus identity is the heart of any discussion of Arab consciousness. "Nationalism is first and foremost a state of mind," wrote Hans Kohn (1891–1971), an early nationalism theorist; it is "an act of consciousness."[9] The "state of mind" of Arab journalists is one in which borders blur and

"Arab" consciousness trumps all others. And it is a worldview that is at once more secular and more "Arab" than that of the public-at-large.

Blood and Treasure

"Nationalist *sentiment*," according to Gellner, is "the feeling of anger aroused by the violation of the principle, or the feeling of satisfaction aroused by its fulfillment. A nationalist *movement* is one actuated by a sentiment of this kind."[10] In the context of the daily bloodshed of the Arab world, this is a critical point. The theme of unity forged in the face of the Other makes frequent appearances in the various theories of nationalism. Anderson insists that popular nationalism is always mobilized "in a language of self-defense."[11] After vernacular literature, Hastings identified a "long struggle against an external threat" as having the most significant effect on formation of national identity. "It arises chiefly where and when a particular ethnicity or nation feels itself threatened in regard to its own proper character, extent or importance."[12]

The Balkanization of the former Yugoslavia, the war between Armenia and Azerbaijan, and the simmering strife between India and Pakistan are all examples of this nationalism in the face of the Other. But confrontation does not only produce feudalization. It can also engender broader associations; especially when facilitated through the media. According to Smith, "the increased power of modern mass communications to amplify and broadcast" cultural and historic differences binds peoples more closely to a shared ethnohistory and heritage when they feel under threat.[13] It is in this defensive role that he believes "pan" nationalisms have their greatest impact. The rapid growth of telecommunications and mass media, according to Smith, creates the possibility that "regional associations based on 'Pan' nationalisms can generate overarching cultures and identities that compete with, or even replace, national state and ethnic identities,"[14] an eventuality left open in Anderson's description of the "finite, if elastic boundaries" of the imagined community.[15]

The journalistic border guards of the Arab media are a critical factor in forging this sense of an overarching Arab/Muslim regional identity in the face of both the domestic and external Other.

The Borderlands of Identity

Writing of two Palestinian notables prominent in the early twentieth century, Rashid Khalidi observed that they embodied a variety of loyalties:

> Among these allegiances were Islamic solidarity, Arabism, Palestinian patriotism, opposition to Zionism, party political affiliation, local Jerusalem loyalties, and family linkages, as well as a commitment to liberal constitutionalism, administrative reform of the state apparatus, and the spread of learning.[16]

That synergy of interests between proponents of Arab nationalism, nation-state nationalism, Arabism and Islamism is echoed in the attitudes of Arab journalists today. Arab journalists are at the forefront of a cyclical convergence of interests between Arab nationalism, nation-state nationalism, and Islamism.

Ernest Gellner's theory of nationalism as a "sentiment" sparked by "the feeling of anger aroused by the violation of principle, or the feeling of satisfaction aroused by its fulfillment" can be seen reflected in the attitudes of both Arab journalists and their publics. Anger at US policy, frustration with the region's totalitarian elites, disillusionment with the clergy, disenchantment with the plight of the poor and disenfranchised – these and other responses provide validity to the argument made by Eickelman and Piscatori that there exists an "implicit consciousness of common notions" among Arabs of all political and religious stripes that "becomes apparent when the shared assumptions are violated or attacked."[17]

Whether the label is Rinnawi's "McArabism" or Telhami's "New Arabism," the data argues for the emergence in the Arab newsroom of a Rawlian "overlapping consensus" among the various streams of political thought in the Arab world today, a "new" Arabism borne of a new electronic regional public sphere. As Marc Lynch explains:

> What makes this new Arab public "new" is the omnipresent political talk shows, which transform the satellite television stations into a genuinely unprecedented carrier of public argument. What makes it "Arab" is a shared collective identity

through which speakers and listeners conceive of themselves as participating in a single, common political project. What makes it a "public sphere" is the existence of contentious debates, carried out by and before this self-defined public, oriented toward defining these shared interests.[18]

In some ways, Arab journalism – like Arabism itself – has come full circle. What modern journalists see as their mission closely tracks the worldview documented among Arab journalists in the early 1950s by diplomat-turned-scholar Tom McFadden. The mission of those early Arab journalists "was defense of their liberty, of independence, of Arab unity and of renaissance," Ghassan Tueni, the grand old man of modern Lebanese journalism, told me as he ruminated about the history of Arab journalism over coffee one day. The 1950s were a time when the confluence of Islamist and Arab nationalist agendas reached a peak with the Free Officers' coup in Egypt. In the following decades, Arab news organizations became mouthpieces of rival nation-states as the remnants of Arab nationalism itself died on the smoking battlefields of the '67 war. Now, in the enervated atmosphere of the post-9/11 Middle East, the political consciousness of Arabs is being reawakened and reconnected in the virtual space between borders, as the conscience of Arab journalists is relit.

Back in the '50s, McFadden identified five priorities of Arab journalists: (1) To fight *against* imperialism; (2) to fight *against* Zionism; (3) to fight *for* Arab nationalism and Arab unity; (4) to fight *against* government corruption and weakness; and, (5) to fight *for* the reform, modernization, and democratization of Arab society.[19] Today, the fight against imperialism, Zionism, and government corruption; the fight for Arab unity, and the effort to drive the reform, modernization, and democratization of Arab society can all be seen in the mission of twenty-first century Arab journalists and the evolving attitudes of the Arab public.

For someone familiar with the revolution in the Arab media, it is hard to read Anderson's descriptions of the role of print media in the rise of eighteenth century nationalism without mentally substituting "Arab television" and considering the equivalent twenty-first-century effect. The 20 million books printed by the year 1500 helped spark "a colossal religious propaganda war ... a titanic 'battle for men's minds,'"[20] while today, some 400 Arabic-language satellite channels reach tens of millions of viewers even as the West and the Islamic world are engaged in a global "war of ideas." In 1535, a worried François I banned the printing of any book in his realm, a move doomed by the fact that books were being published in the states all around him; today, Arab governments fight a losing battle to stem the tide of information pouring into their countries through trans-border television, the Internet, and a host of new media. Print-capitalism created "languages-of-power," just as Arab satellite television is today institutionalizing an evolving and unifying form of spoken Arabic; and where the French and American revolutions were "shaped by millions of printed words into a 'concept' on the printed page, and, in due course, into a model,"[21] satellite television journalists and their counterparts in the region's terrestrial media are today fueling opposition movements and inspiring made-for-television events like Lebanon's "Cedar revolution."

If, as Anderson believes, "[p]rint-language is what invent[ed] nationalism" in eighteenth century Europe, is it any wonder that "Arabic satellite television stations are causing a cataclysmic change in Arabic-language patterns and cultural representation"?[22] And if, as he contends, print-capitalism fed the imagined communities of the nation-state, is it much of a leap to expect that regional broadcast-capitalism would feed some form of regional imagined community in the Arab world? As Anderson put it in 1983, just three years after the launch of CNN and almost a decade before the first Arab satellite channel, "we are simply at the point where communities of the type 'horizontal-secular, traverse-time' become possible."[23]

There is another parallel: This one to the early spread of Arab nationalist thought. As the press became a political force in the late nineteenth century, "all contenders of power tried to befriend, control, or liquidate" offending journalists.[24] With the modern Arab media revolution, history was, unfortunately, repeating itself. An array of pressures shapes the output of Arab news organizations in the twenty-first century. Depending on where they operate and for whom they work, the political economy of the Arab media means that virtually all Arab journalists operate under some degree of overt censorship, psychological pressure, threat of physical violence, and/or corporate strictures. Others face more basic challenges, like poor salaries and a lack of professional training. Make no mistake, the ownership of the pan-Arab television channels – if not the journalists themselves – have a financial/professional stake in fostering a pan-Arab perspective, but the data show that pan-Arab and "domestic" journalists alike share a similar worldview and occupy a common space on the borderlands of Arab identity.

The satellites that transmit pan-Arab television and the Internet cables that carry the content of the region's newspapers do not recognize the lines in the sand imposed by colonial powers, and, in some – but certainly not all – senses, those lines are also being erased in the imagination of the Arab people. Just as Habermas saw "the informal circuit of public communication" serving as a fundamental building block for the emergence of a new European identity,[25] so, too, are changes in the patterns and structures of Arab media having an impact on journalistic self-identity. The array of nationalities in the newsrooms of pan-Arab satellite channels and newspapers and their decided news emphasis on the regional over the local, the emotional over the mundane, the touchstone "Arab" and "Islamic" issues of the day over "domestic" topics like jobs and sewer lines, combine to enhance the trans-border worldview of the journalists working there. And the reporting of those pan-Arab journalists, in turn, influences journalists working on purely domestic news organizations who admire them for the new style of aggressiveness and professionalism that they have introduced.

Underpinning Arab society, according to Islamic Studies professor Ibrahim Abu-Rabi, are "a constellation of competing ideologies." The sum of these forces, he has written, "is different from one Arab country to another and might also be different over time."[26] The same can be said of the political winds within Arab newsrooms from Casablanca to Sana'a. The secular, nation-focused orientation of Arab journalists over the past half-century has given way to a worldview that combines a heightened sense of Muslim identity with a position at the forefront of the "new Arabism" – in which Arab and Muslim goals coincide. This new worldview was summed up by Al-Jazeera anchor Muhammed Krichen. Standing in the channel's newsroom one afternoon as he was about to go on the air, I asked this Algerian national to define himself.

He did not hesitate: "I am an Arab, Muslim journalist," he proudly replied. That multifaceted identity is shared by countless reporters and editors in newsrooms across the Arab world. It is an identity unique to this particular time in the development of Arab journalism and this moment in the political and social evolution of the Arab world.

Meanwhile, after a historic cycle spanning the twentieth century, during which Arab nationalism transitioned through Ba'athism and Arab Socialism, Syrian Nationalism and Nasser's Arabism, Arab nationalism has now returned to a form in which causes and shared ethnic, linguistic, and cultural norms serve as an overlay on a regional map depicting nation-states that few would readily see erased. The realities of modern Arab politics, now as then, mean that the Arab League often cannot even muster a quorum for a ministerial meeting, much less reach agreement on mildly controversial issues of regional and international policy. A "pan-Arab" nation in which Gulf royals, secular autocrats, and Lebanese jointly rule is almost beyond imagination. Yet satellite television and new media means that those disparate nations and groups are also bound together in a new Arab consciousness mediated by the constant mutual exposure to the very external threats that lay at the core of earlier waves of pan-Arab impulses.

"At moments of intense collective crisis, this notion of common membership can expand dramatically, almost overnight, and erase or subordinate differences between members of a single national community," Middle East historian Michael Provence has written. "The Syrian revolt of 1925 was such a moment of crisis."[27] In many ways, this, too, is such a moment.

The "illusion of relative homogeneity against the hegemonic foreigner" that Juan Cole and Deniz Kandiyoti say contributes to "incipient 'national' cohesion" is readily apparent on the TV screens each day.[28] Their use of quotation marks around the word "national" to emphasize it as a relative term underscores its applicability in the pan-Arab context, for the new Arabism of the twenty-first century is not the Arab nationalism of a half-century ago. Like communism, the purist ideas of its early Arab nationalist ideologues were corrupted by opportunistic politicians and bled dry in the prisons of the authoritarian regimes they spawned. Today's new Arabism is an idea shorn of its Socialist Utopian pretensions, representing not a monochromatic political ideology, but a philosophy – a way of seeing the world – that at once lives within and transcends political boundaries, bringing under its wings Arabs from the slums of Beirut and the palaces of the Gulf who "share common sentiments" about Palestine, foreign hegemony, and the plight of the Arabs and Muslims; are part of a common "cultural and linguistic heritage" of which Islam forms an essential base; and, whether secularists or devout Muslims, are united by a sense of despair, frustration, and anger.

Few today seriously speak of regional *political* unity or a realignment of borders, much less suggest that national identifications be shed. What some have called the "dreamy" nationalism of Michel Aflaq has been abandoned. In its place is a new, many-faceted "Arab self;"[29] still uncertain, still taking form, but one which unites Arabs in, if not a common ideology, then a broad shared worldview that can be glimpsed anywhere within the "finite, if elastic boundaries"[30] of the Arab world.

In the early 1980s, describing the rise of nationalism in Latin America, Benedict Anderson wrote, adding his own emphasis, "[N]either economic interest, Liberalism, nor Enlightenment could, or did, create *in themselves* the kind, or shape, of imagined community. ... In accomplishing this specific task, pilgrim creole functionaries and provincial creole printmen played the decisive historic role."[31] Like those provincial creole "printmen," twenty-first century Arab journalists are playing their part in creating the new Arab imagined community; for it is their identity and worldview that is echoed in, and reinforced by, newspapers, radio stations, and television channels across the Arab world every day as they write the narrative of a tumultuous and intensely complex new chapter in the evolution of Arab consciousness.

Postscript

New Media, New Media Models

Adapt or die.

American Journalism Review headline

Hassan Fattah leaned back in his chair, tucked his hands behind his head and told me, "This could be the future of journalism." As frightening as that may have seemed, the former *New York Times* correspondent had hit the nail on the head. The paper he helped run, *The National*, was a high-budget, high-profile effort by the government of Abu Dhabi to demonstrate to the world that it was building the trappings of participatory democracy. The financial structure was similar to that of Al-Jazeera; the façade of an arms-length relationship with the government was maintained by running the budget through an investment fund which supposedly did not interfere in the day-to-day operations of the paper – even though it was controlled by the rulers of Abu Dhabi. The paper was a concrete example of the phenomenon Prince Bandar, the Saudi prince, had described to me a few years earlier: Governments bowing to the fact that change was inevitable, but trying to manage its pace. "We cannot adopt the stance of the exasperated Westerner," Martin Newland, *The National*'s editor-in-chief and former top editor at both *The Daily Telegraph* and Canada's *National Post*, wrote to staff in a prelaunch memo. "We go at the country's cultural pace. Do not pick small fights if there is a bigger one to be won down the road. If in doubt, ask."

How that played out in real terms was evident in the controversy over the son of Abu Dhabi's ruler, who was seen torturing a foreign business associate in a cell phone videotape shot by one of the prince's henchmen. A reporter for *The Columbia Journalism Review* (*CJR*) happened to be in *The National*'s newsroom not long after the tape first surfaced. He was present when Newland was told one of his staff had an interview lined up with a lawyer in the case. "Tell the reporter to back the fuck off. No other people are to work on this story," *CJR* quoted him as saying. The prince was put on trial and eventually acquitted on the grounds that the prescription drugs he was taking meant he couldn't be held accountable, a ruling that raised eyebrows at home and abroad. His henchmen were convicted. Until the formal charges were filed, *The National* barely touched the story.

Still, at some level, that 'slow change' approach was working – particularly in terms of creating an economically viable model of journalism. On the other side of the world, newspapers were closing as fast as dotcoms when the bubble burst. "The Death of Newspapers." "Thinking the unthinkable." Headlines like these were daily fare in the US. But in *The National* newsroom Newland and Fattah reigned over an empire of some 200 reporters with a budget that would fuel a small country. Most staff members were refugees from the troubled world of Western journalism – papers like the *Wall Street Journal* and the *Newark Star-Ledger*. A similar picture of journalistic prosperity could be found just down the road in Doha, where the then-head of Al-Jazeera English, former Canadian Broadcasting Corporation news chief Tony Burman, was struggling to sort through more than 8,000 resumes that had arrived in response to a series of ads for reporters, producers, and camera people. Hassan Fattah wasn't alone in seeing the supposedly benign, arms-length government ownership model as the future of journalism – so did thousands of journalists around the world who wanted to join other refugees from the North American, European, and Australian networks who already worked for the fledgling channel.

As distasteful as "arms-length" government control might have been to Western critics – *CJR* called *The National* "a balancing act" – the fact was that the model provided a framework in which a new kind of Arab journalism was beginning to flourish even as the old business model of Western journalism was dying on the vine. And, in many ways, Arab journalists also were filling the void left by the shrinking ranks of Western – especially American – correspondents covering the world. That was true in terms of audiences in the Middle East and the developing world shifting from Western broadcasters to those based in the

Middle East, but it was also true on the ground, where Arab journalists were increasingly reporting for Western news organizations that could no longer afford to have correspondents in the region. It was all a mixed blessing, but a blessing nonetheless.

A similar mixed blessing could be found on the Internet. As the first decade of the new century drew to a close, Internet journalism held a huge potential for helping to reform Arab journalism as a whole. Online news organizations like *Kalima* in Tunisia and *YemenPortal* were filling an important gap in countries where traditional print media and broadcasting was circumscribed. But the government assault on such outlets was relentless. In early 2010, *Kalima* had its entire online archive deleted by hackers, and around the same time Jordan joined Syria and Tunisia in passing legislation that required websites to register under the Press and Publications Law, which contained vague language prohibiting publication of anything that "denigrates" religion "in any form" or "affronts" individuals.[1] "[W]ithout a voice, without a presence, without a dialog, where does that leave this wonderful, vibrant country of ours?" asked the Jordanian blogger Mommabean. "It leaves us sad, silenced, and lacking critical reasoning." Freedom House apparently agreed, downgrading Jordan from the ranks of "partly free" to "not free." Meanwhile, in Libya, reporters were witnessing a U-turn as a brief liberalization trend was quickly followed by a broad crackdown in early 2010. Journalists inside the country were arrested and independent news sites based abroad were blocked or hacked and YouTube was firewalled after it showed videos of Qadaffi's relatives at parties. "The authorities began to lift the lid on fundamental freedoms, including press freedom and free expression, in 2007, but now they have gone into reverse," Reporters Without Borders observed.[2] Similar stories could be found around the region. Visitors to the leading Bahraini blog aggregator in early 2010 were greeted by this message:

> Note that this URL – http://bahrianblogs.org – has been blocked by the Bahraini Government for perceived violations. We do not believe this is so as the simple service we provide is the aggregation of Bahraini Blogs without any political, sectarian, ethnic or gender prejudice.

Until such time that this block is removed, please go to the alternative URL http://bahrainblogs.net to get your fix of the Bahraini pulse and creativity.

Such web-focused crackdowns prompted US Secretary of State Hillary Clinton to single out close allies Egypt and Saudi Arabia in a 2010 speech criticizing the assault on freedom of information on the Internet.[3] But just as they had expressed doubts about the sincerity of the Bush policy on issues like democracy in their region, Arab journalists were equally skeptical of the Obama administration's stance on behalf of the media. A few days after masked gunmen shot to death Yemeni investigative journalist Mohammed Shu'i al-Rabu'i in his own home, and a week after the Clinton speech, exiled Yemeni journalist Walid al-Saqaf, sent me this email:

Sadly, the US government has been engaging in a partnership with the regime to fight the "war on terror," which is partially defined by Yemeni President Saleh as a war on journalists whom he claims support terrorism and acts that threaten security. Where are the old promises of Obama to promote freedom and human rights? Go figure!

That the Clinton speech followed passage by the US House of Representatives of a bill that would label as "specially designated global terrorists" the satellite distribution companies controlled by Egypt and Saudi Arabia if they didn't pull the plug TV stations run by Hezbollah and Hamas, didn't help that perception of hypocrisy.[4]

Meanwhile, the growing influence of Arab bloggers, led by a group of secular-reformist and Muslim Brotherhood bloggers based in Egypt, was having a mixed impact on the development of Arab journalism. Positive, because they helped shape the public agenda; negative because, too often, bloggers were conflated with journalists, blurring the line between fact and fiction, opinion and reporting. The vast majority of the estimated 35,000 Arabic-language blogs were the electronic equivalent of personal diaries, but in the face of government restrictions on traditional media and other forms of expression, the Internet was emerging as an important public sphere for discussion of culture, social issues and, especially, politics.[5]

From their electronic bully pulpits, activist Arab bl⟨ that the king had no clothes. At times, they even broke stories, as in the case of Egyptian blogger Wael Abba⟨ honored in international journalism and freedom of expi⟨⟨ cles for posting videos about torture by the Egyptian police and othei scandals; Malek Mostafa, who first reported a mass sexual assault on women in downtown Cairo; Jordanian blogger "Who Sane," whose account of his father's poor treatment in an Amman hospital provoked a national outcry and the intervention of the kingdom's health minister; and Bahraini blogs like Chan'ad Bahraini, that regularly carried video images of police raids on political gatherings.

Such postings played in important role in creating safe space for "mainstream" journalists to cover stories that would otherwise have been off limits – and goading them into more aggressive reporting of their own. By 2010, the Committee to Protect Journalists noted an overall increase in reporting on human rights issues in the Arab world, in large measure because of the impact of the Internet. "Reports [about torture] that used to collect dust on shelves are now being read by thousands of people," journalist Noha Atef of TortureinEgypt.net told Committee to Protect Journalists. "You couldn't get people to read this type of material years ago, not even if you printed it and distributed it free of charge. But, online, people encounter it on their favorite blog or news Web site and they read it. It has become mainstream."[6] Wael Abbas put it this way when he received a Knight journalism award:

> We are not inverting the roles. Bloggers are not journalists.
> We are about promoting freedom of speech. We are the ones
> who will defend free journalism. But... we are also becoming
> more and more a "reliable source" for traditional journalists.
> I think we offer journalists good topics, controversial ones,
> dangerous ones.[7]

Most achieved that by shedding any pretense of balance. "Yes, I'm biased and I like it this way," blogger Mahmoud Saber proudly told *Egypt Today*. Indeed, the Arab blogosphere made even the agenda-laden writings of politicized American bloggers look downright tame. Bloggers took pride in shock value; societies long locked in fear need to be jolted

ake. The explicative-laced personal attacks on, and unproven allega-
tions about, politicians, journalists, and other figures in "official" circles – what Americans in another era would have called "the man" – by
many bloggers were meant as an electronic slap in the face for regimes
that had long kept the media in chains to keep themselves in power.

"[P]athetic, paranoid mother fuckers!!!" Abbas wrote in one Twitter
post, describing Egyptian state security (which would later – somewhat
ironically – charge him with breaking an Internet cable, a trumped up
conviction that carried a six month prison sentence, later overturned);
The Religious Policeman, an exiled Saudi, wrote of "the institutionalized insanity that the House of Saud and their friends with long beards
have created;" a Jordanian blogger sent a message to Iraqi refugees
in his country: "If you don't like the way Jordan treats you then get
the hell out of it!" and Egyptian bloggers held a "wedding party" on
the streets of Cairo to mark the marriage of Gamal Mubarak, son and
heir-apparent to Egyptian President Hosni Mubarak, under the title,
"Heyya ah! Baladna La!" which roughly translates as, "Go and marry
her, but don't marry our country!"

Those sorts of comments and activities were a reminder that Western-
style news values did not necessarily apply in the blogosphere. "Young
activists use the Internet to announce their presence, to protest and tell
their own stories," Egyptian journalist Olfa Tantawi commented on my
Facebook page. "It is no longer about the need to know but rather the
need to tell." Muslim Brotherhood activist Abdel Moneim Mahmoud,
whose blog was called *Ana Ikwan* (I am a Brother) and who claims he
was tortured during a 2007 detention, listed his interests as "being more
than willing to sacrifice for the freedom of this nation."

Some bloggers *were* journalists for whom the Internet was a tool
to avoid circumvent censorship. For Libyan anti-corruption journalist
Dhaif Al-Ghazaly, the Internet was the only way to avoid his country's
draconian media controls. He paid the ultimate price in 2006; the first
Arab online writer to be killed. Before stabbing him to death, his mur-
derers cut off his fingers as a chilling message to the rest. Other bloggers
had what might be called journalistic proclivities. "I am not a journalist by training, nor do I have any serious journalistic aspirations," the
Egyptian blogger "Zeinab" wrote on the EgyptBlogsAmerica.blogspot.

com site. She was among those bloggers who fell somewhere in the no man's land between journalist and activist. "I will not always necessarily be objective" and "I don't believe in detachment... or making sure that I am balanced." But she added, "I do try to be fair. I do try to check my facts and make sure that I am not citing make-believe figures. I try not to accuse anyone of anything too outlandish without proof and I generally attempt to stay away from unfounded hypotheses or offensive content."

It may well be that the next generation of Arab journalists will emerge, in part, from the bloggers' ranks. In the meantime, the struggle of those striving to practice fair, factual, and balanced journalism needed to be bolstered, not undermined by blurring the distinction between journalist and web activist, as some Western journalist rights organizations were in danger of doing. "This is a country where barbers used to do the job of doctors," said Abdelmonem Said, head of Egypt's al-Ahram Center for Political and Strategic Studies, who wrote a newspaper column but did not consider himself a journalist. "We should not refer to [bloggers] as journalists unless they are qualified to perform the job of a journalist. Defending an activist in the name of journalism further complicates an already complicated situation."

Online journalists across the region were already under siege. With Arab governments using such arbitrary terms as "immoral" and "irresponsible" to shut down satellite TV channels, the danger was that by failing to distinguish between online journalists and online activists who used blogging to further their political agendas, the journalists were being left vulnerable. Professionalism was the Arab journalist's best defense. If everything on the web was the same, governments had an excuse to crack down on it all.

Professionalism. It all kept coming back to that. Arab journalists themselves had made clear how important they felt that issue of professionalism was; it was the common denominator to which both Arab and Western journalists aspired, even if the Arab view of the mission of journalism – to create political and social change – diverged from that of many Western journalists.

But in that commitment to driving change, were Arab journalists really all that different from their cousins in the West? The precedent for their hybrid role could be found in the journalistic change agents of American and European history, such as America's revolutionary-era pamphleteer and patriot Thomas Paine, British journalist and social reformer Charles Dickens, and American muckraker Upton Sinclair, who used their craft to drive political and social change. The difference between Western and Arab journalists of the modern era was that the latter continued to toil in societies where political rights were few, tyrants continued to cling to power, and journalism was seen by governments as a subversive force.

Still, one needed only turn on a television in the Arab world to see reason for hope; to hear a panoply of "opinion and the other opinion;" to come face-to-face with the forces of change. As the assassinated Lebanese columnist Samir Kassir put it shortly before his murder, "Thanks to a handful of journalists, we have indeed re-conquered our freedom of opinion and expression – if not yet fully our freedom of information."

Notes

Introduction A Matter of Perspective

1. Unless otherwise credited in footnotes or text, all quotations in this book are from conversations or formal interviews with the author or from his contemporaneous notes of public comments made at events he attended.
2. George H.W. Bush, "President's Remarks at US University Presidents Summit on International Education," ed. The White House (The White House, 2006).
3. Dan Schiller, *Objectivity and the News: The Public and the Rise of Commercial Journalism* (Philadelphia: University of Pennsylvania Press, 1981).
4. "Vision and Mission." (Doha: Al-Jazeera, Jan. 2006).
5. *Al-Arabiya News Channel.* (Al-Arabiya), 2005 [accessed Dec. 31, 2006] available from http://www.alarabiya.net/english.htm/.
6. Myles Breen, "Introduction," in *Journalism: Theory & Practice*, ed. Myles Breen (Paddington NSW: Macleay Press, 1998).
7. Brian Stelter, *After Appearing in Anti-Bush Ad, Batiste Asked to Step Down as CBS Consultant.* (Media Bistro), May 11, 2007 [accessed May 12, 2007] available from http://www.mediabistro.com/tvnewser/.

1 Red Lines – The Boundaries of Journalistic Freedom

1. Gadi Dechter, *President Kerry on Israel.* (United Press International), 2004 [accessed Jul. 9, 2004] available from http://www.upi.com/view.cfm?StoryID=20040709–042549-2017r.
2. "Attacks on the Press 2003." (New York: Committee to Protect Journalists, 2004).
3. "In Memory of Martyred Arab Journalists and Writers." (Amman, Jordan: Arab Archives Institute, May, 2007).
4. *Media Forum Examines Widespread Press Freedom Abuses.* (World Association of Newspapers), Dec. 11, 2006 [accessed Dec. 11, 2006] available from http://www.wan-press.org/article12549.html.

5. "Baathist Regime Has Dissident Journalist Sentenced to Three Years in Jail." (Paris: Reporters Sans Frontières, May 13, 2007).

6. "Letter to President Saleh About Threats to Press Freedom." (Paris: Reporters Sans Frontières, Sep. 4, 2007).

7. "The Middle East Needs Media Freedoms Even More Than Other Parts of the World," *Daily Star* 2008.

8. Freedom of the Press 2007.

9. AFP, "Jordan Parliament Approves Jail for Journalist Law." *The Daily Star Egypt*, Mar. 6, 2007.

10. Nidal Mansour, "Media Freedom Status in Jordan 2006." (Amman: Center for Defending Freedom of Journalists, May, 2007), pp. 1, 4.

11. "Government Censors Al-Jazeera, Seizes Tapes of Interview with Prince." (Paris: Reporters Sans Frontières, Apr. 24, 2007).

12. *Worldwide Press Freedom Index 2006: Middle East Index.* (Reporters Sans Frontières), Oct. 23, 2006 [accessed Feb. 3, 2007] available from http://www.rsf.org/IMG/pdf/cm2006_mo-2.pdf.

13. *Predators of Press Freedom.* (Reporters Sans Frontières), 2007 [accessed May 6, 2007] available from http://www.rsf.org/article.php3?id_article=13580.

14. "No Censorship except Self Censorship." Arab Press Network (Aug. 3, 2007). [accessed Aug. 4, 2007] available from http://www.arabpressnetwork.org/articlesv2.php?id=1349.

15. Fawaz Turki, *How to Lose Your Job at a Saudi Newspaper.* (The Washington Post), Apr. 21, 2006 [accessed Jun. 7, 2006] available from http://ijnet.org/Director.aspx?P=Article&ID=304879&LID=1.

16. *Censorship: What You Didn't See.* Arab Media & Society (Cairo: Kamal Adham Center for Journalism Training and Research) Issue 1, Spring 2007 [accessed Apr. 5, 2007] http://www.arabmediasociety.org/?article=53.

17. Mona Eltahawy, "A Perilous Dance with the Arab Press." *International Herald Tribune*, Jun. 19, 2006.

18. Abdul Hamid Ahmad, "Self-Censorship Virus Plagues Media." *Gulf News*, May 5, 2006.

19. Wahid Sha'ban, "Strong Denunciation of the Azhar Shaykh's Fatwa on Flogging Journalists," *Al Wafd*, Oct. 12, 2007.

20. "Saudi Clerics Launch New Attack on TV Bosses over Immoral Content," *BBC Monitoring* (2009).

21. "Role of the Media Must Be Acknowledged," *Gulf News*, Jan. 20, 2009.

22. "Journalist Lamees Dhaif Summoned to Public Prosecutor's Office." (Bahrain: Bahrain Center for Human Rights/IFEX, 2009).

23. No Rules, No Limits: Sexual Assaults and Fabrication of Cases against Journalists and Activists – "Tunisia, Egypt, and Bahrain". (Cairo: Arab Network for Human Rights Information, 2006). [accessed Sep. 8, 2006] available from http://www.hrinfo.net/en/reports/re2006/.

24. *The Time Has Come: A Call for Freedom and Good Governance in the Arab World.* (United Nations Development Program), Apr. 5, 2005 [accessed Apr. 8, 2006] available from www.undp.org/rbas/ahdr.

25. *Worldwide Press Freedom Index 2005.* (Reporters sans Frontières), 2005 [accessed May 5, 2006] available from http://www.rsf.org/rubrique.php3?id_rubrique=554.

26. *Freedom of the Press: Middle East and North Africa.* (Freedom House), 2006 [accessed Sep. 30, 2006] available from http://www.freedomhouse.org/template.cfm?page=251&year=2006.

27. *Backsliders: 10 Countries Where Press Freedoms Have Most Deteriorated.* (Committee to Protect Journalists – CPJ), May 2, 2007 [accessed Jun. 3, 2007] available from http://www.cpj.org/backsliders/index.html.

28. Figures cited by the two main press freedom organizations differ. As of Feb. 23, 2008, CPJ, which does not include accidents "unless caused by aggressive human actions" or health-related deaths, counted 126 journalists and 50 media workers dead, while the RSF tally was 209.

29. "Government Orders Al-Arabiya's Baghdad Bureau Closed for One Month." (Paris, via email: Reporters Sans Frontières, Sep. 8, 2006).

30. Ibrahim Nawar, "Introduction," in *The State of the Arab Media 2004: Freeing the Arab Media from State Control*, ed. Youssef Fadel (London: Arab Press Freedom Watch, 2004), p. 8.

31. Moataz El Fegiery, *Arab Media and Elections: The Triumph of Politics over Professionalism* (Arab Reform Bulletin, Carnegie Endowment for International Peace), Sep. 14, 2006 [accessed Sep. 14, 2006] available from http://www.carnegieendowment.org/publications/index.cfm?fa=view&id=18706&prog=zgp&proj=zted#media.

32. Arab Press Network, *Latest Press Freedom News from the Region.* (World Association of Newspapers), Jul. 17, 2007 [accessed Jul. 17, 2007] available from http://www.arabpressnetwork.org/articlesv2.php?id=1280.

33. *Private Media Hurdle Bureaucracy to Break New Ground.* (UN Office for the Coordination of Humanitarian Affairs), Nov. 16, 2006 [accessed

Jan. 6, 2007] available from http://www.irinnews.org/Report.aspx?Report Id=61944.

34. Natasha Tynes, "Launch of Jordan's First Independent TV Station Delayed." (Aug. 14, 2007).

35. "Doha Centre Journalist Banned from Leaving Qatar." *Mediame.com*, no. March 24 (2009).

36. Those countries were, in order, Qatar, Kuwait, Jordan, Lebanon, Palestinian Territories, Morocco, and Saudi Arabia. *Media Sustainability Index – Middle East and North Africa* ed. Theo Dolan and Mark Whitehouse (Washington, DC: IREX, 2006), p. viii.

37. "Press Freedom Findings in Middle East and North Africa Disappointing after Earlier Hopeful Years." (New York: Freedom House, May 2, 2007).

38. Hajar Smouni, "Freedom of the Press Worldwide in 2008 – Middle East." (Paris: Reporters Sans Frontières, 2008).

39. Samar Fatany, "Media Reforms, Welcome Steps." *Arab News*, Mar. 8, 2009.

40. Ami Ayalon, *The Press in the Arab Middle East: A History.* (New York: Oxford University Press, 1995), p. 111.

41. Ayalon, *The Press in the Arab Middle East*, p. 244

42. William A. Rugh, *Arab Mass Media: Newspapers, Radio, and Television in Arab Politics.* (Westport, CT: Praeger, 2004).

43. Lawrence Pintak, *Seeds of Hate: How America's Flawed Middle East Policy Ignited the Jihad.* (Sterling, VA: Pluto Press, 2003).

44. Rugh, *Arab Mass Media*, p. 171.

45. Jon Alterman, *New Media, New Politics: From Satellite Television to the Internet in the Arab World.* (Washington, DC: The Washington Institute for Near East Policy, 1998).

46. "Editor of Pan-Arab Newspaper Sentenced to Jail in Absentia." *Dar al-Hayat*, Apr. 23, 2004.

47. Ibid.

48. M.I. Ayish, "Political Communication on Arab World Television: Evolving Patterns." *Political Communication*, 19, no. 2 (2002), p. 138.

49. US Senate Foreign Relations Committee, Subcommittee on International Relations and Terrorism, *Comments on Radio Sawa and Al Hurra Television*, Apr. 29, 2004.

50. Rugh, *Arab Mass Media*, p. 7.

51. William A. Rugh, "Arab Media and Politics During the October War." *Middle East Journal*, 29, no. 3 (1975), p. 311.

52. H. Amin, "Freedom as a Value in Arab Media: Perceptions and Attitudes among Journalists." *Political Communication*, 19, 2 (2002), p. 128.

53. Amin, "Arab Media."

54. Dabbous, Sonia, "A Study of the Egyptian Press." In *Media Ethics & Journalism in the Arab World*. Institute for Professional Journalists, Magda abu-Fadl (ed.). (Beirut 2004). p. 95.

55. Tom Johnston McFadden, *Daily Journalism in the Arab States* (Columbus: Ohio State University Press, 1953), p. 18.

56. Ibid., p. 46.

57. Ibid., pp. 14–15.

58. Ibid., p. 37.

59. Ibrahim Nawar, *Freedom of Expression in the Arab World*. (Arab Press Freedom Watch), 2000 [accessed May 25, 2004] available from http://www.apfw.org/indexenglish.asp?fname=report\english\spe1001.htm.

60. *State of the Arab Media 2001*. (Arab Press Freedom Watch), 2001 [accessed Nov. 5, 2003] available from http://www.apfw.org/data/annualreports/2001/english/2001annualreport.pdf.

61. Ibid.

62. Amin, "Arab Media," p. 128.

63. *Freeing the Arab Media from State Control*. [Final communiqué] (Arab Press Freedom Watch), May 6, 2004 [accessed Dec. 4, 2005] available from http://www.apfw.org/indexenglish.asp?fname=annualconference\2004\english\0004.htm.

64. Nayla Assaf, "Facing Local Restrictions, Mideast Media Finds an International Voice." *The Daily Star*, Jun. 15, 2004.

65. Naomi Sakr, *Satellite Realms: Transnational Television, Globalization and the Middle East*. (London: I.B.Tauris, 2001), p. 4.

66. Abdelwahab el-Affendi, "Eclipse of Reason: The Media in the Muslim World." *Journal of International Affairs*, 47, no. 1.

67. El-Affendi, "Eclipse of Reason: The Media in the Muslim World."

68. Amin, "Arab Media," p. 129.

69. "Heikal's Enduring Word." *Al-Ahram Weekly*, Feb. 8–14, 2007.

70. Fatemah Farag, "Media Development in a Context of Political Transition: Focus Egypt." (Cairo: British Council, May 29, 2006).

71. Nakhle el-Hage,"Author's Contemporaneous Notes, M100 Sancoussi Dialogue." (Potsdam: Sept. 6, 2007).

72. Ibn Khaldun, *An Arab Philosophy of History: Selections from the Prolegomena of Ibn Khaldun of Tunis (1332–1406)*. trans. Charles Issawi,

second ed. (Princeton, NJ: The American University in Cairo Press, 1992), p. 147.

73. Mark Steyn, "Muslim Paranoia: Enemies Made Us Impotent!" *Chicago Sun-Times*, Oct. 26, 2003.

74. George Packer, "Caught in the Crossfire; Letter from Baghdad." *The New Yorker*, 80, no. 12.

75. Ibid.

76. Quoted in el-Affendi, "Eclipse of Reason: The Media in the Muslim World."

77. Mark Tessler, "Arab and Muslim Political Attitudes." *International Studies Perspectives*, 4 (2003).

78. Yvonne Yazbeck Haddad, "Islamist Perceptions of US Policy in the near East," in *The Middle East and the United States: A Historical and Political Reassessment*, ed. David W. Lesch (Boulder, CO: Westview Press, 1996).

79. Adel Darwish, "Anti-Americanism in the Arabic Language Media." *Middle East Review of International Affairs*, 7, no. 4 (2003).

80. Rugh, "October War Media."

81. M. Diamond, "No Laughing Matter: Post-September 11 Political Cartoons in Arab/Muslim Newspapers." *Political Communication*, 19 (2002).

82. *The World through Their Eyes.* (The Economist), Feb. 24, 2005 [accessed Feb. 26, 2005] available from http://www.economist.com/displaystory.cfm?story_id=3690442.

83. Dan Williams, "A Real News Maker." *Jerusalem Post*, Jul. 13, 2001.

84. John Kifner, "At Arab All-News Channel, Western Values Prevail." *New York Times*, Oct. 12, 2001.

85. Mohammed el-Nawawy and Adel Iskandar, *Al-Jazeera: How the Free Arab News Network Scooped the World and Changed the Middle East.* (Cambridge, MA: Westview Press, 2002), p. 23.

86. Quoted in el-Nawawy and Iskandar, *Al-Jazeera: How the Free Arab News Network Scooped the World and Changed the Middle East*, p. 116.

87. *Kuwait Shuts Down Al-Jazeera Bureau.* (Reuters), Nov. 3, 2002 [accessed Jul. 3, 2003] available from http://news.bbc.co.uk/2/hi/south_asia/2395085.stm.

88. Nadia al-Saqqaf, *Impressions from Beirut.* (Arab Press Network), Jun. 22, 2007 [accessed Jul. 8, 2007] available from http://www.arabpressnetwork.org/articlesv2.php?id=1199.

2   Satellite TV and Arab Democracy

1. Paula Dobriansky, undersecretary of state for global affairs, told reporters, "As the president noted in Bratislava just last week, there was a rose revolution in Georgia, an orange revolution in Ukraine, and, most recently, a purple revolution in Iraq. In Lebanon, we see growing momentum for a cedar revolution." See *On-the-Record Briefing on the Release of the 2004 Annual Report on Human Rights*. vol. 2007 (Washington, DC: US Dept. of State, 2005).

2. Claude Jean Bertrand, *An Arsenal for Democracy: Media Accountability Systems*. (Creskill, NJ: Hampton Press, 2003).

3. J. Herbert Altschull, *Agents of Power: The Media and Public Policy*. 2nd ed. (White Plains, NY: Longman Pub. USA, 1995), p. 5. Italics in original publication.

4. Fredrick Seaton Siebert, Theodore Peterson, and Wilbur Schramm, *Four Theories of the Press: The Authoritarian, Libertarian, Social Responsibility, and Soviet Communist Concepts of What the Press Should Be and Do*. (Urbana: University of Illinois Press, 1956).

5. Naomi Sakr, *Arab Media and Political Renewal: Community, Legitimacy and Public Life* (London: I.B.Tauris, 2007), p. 11.

6. Abdul Rahman al-Habib, "Out of Ideas? Then Curse the West." *Arab News*, Apr. 5, 2006.

7. "The Role of Media in Activating Good Governance." In *Final Report*. Amman, Jordan: Center for Defending the Freedom of Journalists (CDFJ), 2005.

8. Richard Gunther and Anthony Mughan, *Democracy and the Media: A Comparative Perspective. Communication, Society, and Politics* (Cambridge; New York: Cambridge University Press, 2000), p. 403.

9. Shanto Iyengar, *Is Anyone Responsible? How Television Frames Political Issues*. (Chicago: University of Chicago Press, 1991).

10. Peter Gross, *Entangled Evolutions: Media and Democratization in Eastern Europe*. (Washington, DC, Baltimore: Woodrow Wilson Center Press; Johns Hopkins University Press, 2002), p. 167.

11. Monroe Edwin Price, Beata Rozumilowicz, and Stefaan Verhulst, *Media Reform: Democratizing the Media, Democratizing the State*. Routledge Research in Cultural and Media Studies (London, New York: Routledge, 2002).

12. Catharin E. Dalpino, "Does Globalization Promote Democracy? An Early Assessment." *Brookings Review*, 19, no. 4 (2001).

13. Marc Lynch, *Assessing the Democratizing Power of Satellite TV.* (Center for Electronic Journalism, The American University in Cairo), Spring/Summer, 2005 [accessed Oct. 7, 2006] available from http://www.tbs journal.com/Archives/Spring05/lynch.html.

14. Pecquerie, Bertrand, "Al-Jazeera Has Replaced Political Parties, Editor's Weblog (World Editors' Forum.) Jun. 2, 2004 [accessed Jul. 15, 2007] available from http://www.editorsweblog.org/editors_forum/2004/06/al_jazeera_has_replaced_political_partie.php.

15. Guy Taylor, "Middle East: Beyond the Bombs, an Exploding Pop Culture." *World Politics Review* (Aug. 16, 2006). [accessed Jul. 15, 2007] available from http://www.worldpoliticsreview.com/article.aspx?id=122.

16. Adel Iskandar, "Is Al-Jazeera the Alternative? Mainstreaming Alterity and Assimilating Discourses of Dissent." *Journal of Transnational Broadcasting Studies*, 1, no. 2 (2005), p. 250.

17. Philip Meyer, "Creating and Keeping Journalism's Identity." *Journal of Mass Media Ethics*, 15, no. 1 (2000).

18. Fawaz Turki, "How to Lose Your Job at a Saudi Newspaper." *The Washington Post*, Apr. 15, 2006.

19. *Twenty-One Years of Achievements.* Egypt State Information Service, Dec. 2005 [accessed Apr. 25, 2006] available from http://www.sis.gov.eg/En/Pub/achievements/tweentyoneyears/110301000000000008.htm.

20. "Election Offers Public Debate, Not Free Choice." *Human Rights Watch* (Washington, DC: Sep. 2, 2005).

21. "Freedom of Opinion & Expression in Egypt 2007." Cairo: Arabic Network for Human Rights Information (HRInfo), 2008.

22. Gamal Mkrumah, "No Time to Sit Back," *Al-Ahram Weekly*, May 29–June 4, 2008.

23. "On World Press Freedom Day: A Report by a Regional Group Calls for Reforming the Media in Bahrain." *Bahrain Center for Human Rights.* Manama: Bahrain Center for Human Rights, 2008.

24. Gross, *Entangled Evolutions*, p. 171.

25. Marc Lynch, "Reality Is Not Enough: The Politics of Arab Reality TV." *Journal of Transnational Broadcasting Studies*, 1, no. 2 (2005), p. 37.

26. "Egypt's Torture Epidemic." In *Briefing papers*. New York: Human Rights Watch, 2004.

27. *Amnesty International Report 2007 – Egypt*. London: Amnesty International, 2007.

28. "Egypt 2007." In *Country Reports on Human Rights Practices*. Washington, DC: Bureau of Democracy, Human Rights and Labor, US State Department, 2008.

29. Jehl, Douglas and David Johnston, "Rule Change Lets C.I.A. Freely Send Suspects Abroad to Jails." In *The New York Times*. New York. Mar. 6, 2005.

30. "Qatar Emir Hails First Arab Victory." *The Peninsula*, Aug. 22, 2006 [accessed Sep. 3, 2006] available from http://www.gulfinthemedia.com/index.php?m=search&id=237173&lang=en.

31. Suzan Zawawi, "The Agony of the 'Qatif Girl.'" *Saudi Gazette*. Jeddah. Nov. 20, 2007.

32. Ahmed al-Omran, "The Qatif Girl again." In *Saudi Jeans* (blog). Riyadh, 2007.

33. Abdullah el-Areefg, "The Judge in El Riyad: Ulterior Motives of How the Foreign Media Dealt with the Kotaif Girl Incidence." *Okaz*. Riyadh. Nov. 26, 2007.

34. Ebtihal Mubarak, "'Qatif Girl' Subjected to Brutal Crime: King." *Arab News*. Jeddah. Dec. 19, 2007.

35. "Predators of Press Freedom" (Paris: Reporters sans Frontières, 2007).

36. Nabil H. Dajani, "Re-Feudalization of the Public Sphere." *Journal of Transnational Broadcasting Studies*, 2, no. 1 (2006).

37. Dajani, "Re-Feudalization."

38. Ziadeh, Hanna, "In Defence of National Television: A personal account of eclectic Lebanese media affinities." *Journal of Transnational Broadcasting Studies*. Vol. 1, Issue 2. (Cairo: Kamal Adham Center for Journalism Training and Research, 2005). pp. 321–322.

39. Samar Fatany, "Media Reforms, Welcome Steps." *Arab News*, Mar. 8, 2009.

40. Jihad N.Fakhreddine, "Imbalanced Economics of the Pan Arab Satellite Television Sector." *Maktoob Business*, http://business.maktoob.com/reportdetails-20060329092602-Imbalanced_Economics_Of_The_Pan_Arab_Satellite_Television_Sector.htm.

41. "Arab League Satellite Broadcasting Charter." In *Arab Media & Society*. (Cairo: Kamal Adham Center for Journalism Training and Research, 2008). http://www.arabmediasociety.org/?article=684.

42. Amy Glass, "Du CEO Plays down Net Censorship." In Arabianbusiness. com. Dubai, 2008. http://www.arabianbusiness.com/516483-du-exec-plays-down-restriction-fears.

43. "Government Cancels License of Independent Weekly." In *Alert*. (Toronto: IFEX: International Freedom of Expression Exchange, 2008).

44. Alaa al-Ghatrifi, "Al-Masry Al-Youm Exclusively Publishes the Draft Law of Audio-Visual Transmission and Monitoring the Internet." Cairo, Al-Masry Al-Youm. Jul. 9, 2008. http://www.almasry-alyoum.com/default. aspx?l=en&IssueID=1096.

45. Yasime Saleh, "Lawyer Expects 'Facebook Girl' to Become Mahalla Scapegoat, Receive Prison Sentence." *Daily News*. Cairo, Apr. 12–13, 2008. It later turned out that she was acting at the behest of her boss, a political activist and blogger, who was then himself arrested and, according to his account, stripped, hung by his arms, and tortured.

46. Safaa Abdoun, "Nazif's Heckler at Cairo University Says He Was Provoked by PM's Speech." *Egypt Daily News*, Cairo, Apr. 22, 2008.

47. Lisa Schnellinger and Mohannad Khatib, *Fighting Words: How Arab and American Journalists Can Break through to Better Coverage*. (Washington, DC: International Center for Journalists, 2006), p. 99.

48. "Bahraini Press Complains About Islamic Distortion [of Their Image]." (Beirut: Mideastwire.com, 2006).

49. "Saudi Arabia Al-Qa'ida Critic Arrested for 'Destructive Thoughts'." Human Rights Watch, Apr. 12, 2006 [accessed Apr. 12, 2006] available from http://hrw.org/english/docs/2006/04/12/saudia13161.htm.

50. Human Rights Watch, "Saudi Arabia Al-Qa'ida Critic."

51. "No Rules, No Limits: Sexual Assaults and Fabrication of Cases against Journalists and Activists – Tunisia, Egypt, and Bahrain." (Cairo: Arab Network for Human Rights information, Apr. 9, 2006).

52. "Yemen: Women Journalists Subjected to Censorship and Slanderous Attack," (London: Article 19, 2009).

53. For example, see Matthew A. Baum, "Sex, Lies, and War: How Soft News Brings Foreign Policy to the Inattentive Public." *American Political Science Review*, 96, no. 1 (2002).

54. Robert Greenwald et al., *Outfoxed Rupert Murdoch's War on Journalism*. (New York, NY: www.outfoxed.org; Distributed by The Disinformation Company, 2004), videorecording.

55. Lynch, *Assessing*.

3 Media Politics and Corporate Feudalism

1. "Five Journalists Given Three-Month Prison Sentences over Critical Articles." *IFEX: International Freedom of Expression* Exchange. Amman: AAI/IFEX, Mar. 18, 2008. http://www.ifex.org/en/content/view/full/91766/.

2. "Khanfar's Removal from Al-Jazeera Board of Directors Preliminary Step Towards Removal as Director General." (Jul. 29, 2007). The move followed the publication of a series of articles attacking Khanfar's management style, which were published in a leading Qatari newspaper. Recognizing that such an assault would not be published with official sanction, Khanfar submitted his resignation from the company, according to Al-Jazeera sources. That was rejected, but his ability to act independently was severely, if temporarily, curtailed.

3. George Galloway, "The Threat to Al-Jazeera," *Guardian*, http://www.guardian.co.uk/commentisfree/story/0,2103785,00.html.

4. "National Media Council Clarifies Closure of GEO, ARY TV stations." Emirates News Agency (WAM). Dubai, Nov. 17, 2007. http://www.wam.org.ae/servlet/Satellite?c=WamLocEnews&cid=1193028279857&pagename=WAM%2FWamLocEnews%2FW-T-LEN-FullNews.

5. "Two French Magazines Censored," IFEX: International Freedom of Expression Exchange. (2009), http://www.ifex.org/en/content/view/full/102732/.

6. Lisa Schnellinger and Mohannad Khatib, *Fighting Words: How Arab and American Journalists Can Break through to Better Coverage* (Washington, DC: International Center for Journalists, 2006), p. 15.

7. Jihad Fakhreddine, "Imbalanced Economics of the Pan Arab Satellite Television Sector." Maktoob Business. http://business.maktoob.com/reportdetails-20060329092602-Imbalanced_Economics_Of_The_Pan_Arab_Satellite_Television_Sector.htm.

8. Bill Kovach and Tom Rosenstiel, *The Elements of Journalism* (London: Atlantic Books on behalf of Guardian Newspapers Ltd. 2003), p. 13.

9. Elizabeth Fox and Silvio R. Waisbord, *Latin Politics, Global Media*. 1st ed. (Austin: University of Texas Press, 2002), p. xxii.

10. *Media Sustainability Index – Middle East and North Africa* ed. Theo Dolan and Mark Whitehouse (Washington, DC: IREX, 2006), pp. ix–x.

11. Both quotations from Sabah Hamamou, "Local Print Media Going against the Grain," *Daily News Egypt*, Apr. 17, 2009.

12. Khalaf al-Harb, "The Bombardment of the Arab Mind," *Okaz*, Jan. 5, 2009.

13. Khaled al-Ghanami, "To All Arab Media: Unite!," *Al-Watan*, Jan. 8, 2009.

14. Charles Levinson, "Plus Ça Change." *Journal of Transnational Broadcasting Studies*, 1, no. 2 (2005), p. 223.

15. Verma, Sonia, "New Abu Dhabi Newspaper Aims to Create Fully Free Press." *The Globe and Mail*. Toronto, Apr. 19, 2008.

16. Rami Khouri, "Arab Reform, a Boxer in between Rounds." *The Daily Star*, Apr. 12, 2006 [accessed Apr. 28, 2006] available from http://www.dailystar.com.lb/article.asp?edition_ID=10&article_ID=23663&categ_id=5.

17. Michael Young, "Kicking off a New Era of Bad Feelings." *The Daily Star*, Apr. 20, 2006 [accessed Apr. 28, 2006] available from http://www.dailystar.com.lb/article.asp?edition_ID=10&article_ID=23833&categ_id=5.

4   Islam, Nationalism and the Media

1. David D. Laitin, *Hegemony and Culture: Politics and Religious Change among the Yoruba*. (Chicago: University of Chicago Press, 1986), p. 11.

2. John L. Esposito, *Unholy War: Terror in the Name of Islam*. (Oxford and New York: Oxford University Press, 2002), p. 55.

3. Graham E. Fuller, *The Future of Political Islam*, 1st ed. (New York: Palgrave Macmillan, 2003), p. xi.

4. Hussein Fadlallah, *Friday Speeches 12 Zu Elqi'da 1425*. (Bayynat), Dec. 24, 2004 [accessed Aug. 30, 2006] available from http://english.bayynat.org.lb/se_002/standthisweek/stand28122004.htm.

5. Muhammad Shahin Hamza, al-'Abqariyya, p. 124 quoted in Raz Ronen, "Interpretations of Kawakibi's Thought, 1950–1980s." *Middle Eastern Studies*, 32, no. 1 (1996).

6. Ibid. p. 171.

7. A.I. Dawisha, *Arab Nationalism in the Twentieth Century: From Triumph to Despair*. (Princeton, NJ: Princeton University Press, 2003), pp. 23–24.

8. Gary S. Gregg, *The Middle East: A Cultural Psychology*. (Oxford; New York: Oxford University Press, 2005).

9. Keith David Watenpaugh, *Being Modern in the Middle East: Revolution, Nationalism, Colonialism, and the Arab Middle Class*. (Princeton, NJ: Princeton University Press, 2006), p. 143.

10. Majid Khadduri, *Political Trends in the Arab World; the Role of Ideas and Ideals in Politics*. (Baltimore: Johns Hopkins Press, 1970), p. 256.

11. Talal Asad, *The Idea of an Anthropology of Islam*. (Washington, DC: Center for Contemporary Arab Studies Georgetown University, 1986).

12. Maxime Rodinson, *Marxism and the Muslim World*. (New York: Monthly Review Press, 1981).

13. Geert H. Hofstede, *Culture's Consequences: Comparing Values, Behaviors, Institutions, and Organizations across Nations*. 2nd ed. (Thousand Oaks, CA: Sage Publications, 2001), p. 454.

14. See for example the writings of Shibley Telhami, Walid Khalidi, Rashid Khalidi, Bernard Lewis, Fouad Ajami, Ghassan Salame, R. Stephen Humphreys, and others.

15. Shibley Telhami, "Power, Legitimacy, and Peace-Making in Arab Countries: The New Arabism," in *Ethnic Conflict and International Politics in the Middle East*, ed. Leonard Binder (Gainesville: University Press of Florida, 1999).

16. Watenpaugh, p. 140.

17. Elie Kedourie, *Islam in the Modern World and Other Studies*. 1st American ed. (New York: Holt Rinehart and Winston, 1981), pp. 53–66.

18. Peter G. Mandaville. *Global Political Islam*. (New York: Routledge, 2007), p. 341.

19. P. Shaista, Ali-Karamali, and Fiona Dunne, "The Ijtihad Controversy." *Arab Law Quarterly*, 9, no. 3 (1994), p. 238. See also Ghazz'al'i and Michael E. Marmura, *The Incoherence of the Philosophers: Tah'afut al-Fal'asifah: A Parallel English–Arabic Text*. 1st ed. (Provo, UT: Brigham Young University Press, 1997), George Fadlo Hourani and Michael E. Marmura, *Islamic Theology and Philosophy: Studies in Honor of George F. Hourani*. (Albany: State University of New York Press, 1984).

20. Cited in Rachel Anne Codd. "A Critical Analysis of the Role of Ijtihad in Legal Reforms in the Muslim World." *Arab Law Quarterly,* 14, no. 2 (1999), pp. 112–131.

21. Miriam cooke and Bruce B. Lawrence, *Muslim Networks from Hajj to Hip Hop*. (Chapel Hill: University of North Carolina Press, 2005), p. 23. cooke stylizes her name with all lower-case letters.

22. This is the dominant transliteration of *iqra*, the first word of the Revelation, as found in Mohammad Marmaduke Pickthall. *Holy Qur'an*. (Islamic Computing Centre, 1997) [cited Apr. 2] available from http://www.usc.edu/ dept/MSA/quran/. and M.H. Shakir, *Holy Qur'an, Al-Qur'an Al-Hak'im*. 10 vols. (London: Muhammadi Trust, 1985); while Yusuf Ali includes both "proclaim" and "read" as alternate translations [Abdullah Yusuf Ali, *The Holy Quran: Text, Translation & Commentary*. New ed. (Lahore:

Sh. M. Ashraf, 1983)], Bloom favors "recite," arguing that the dominant culture of the Arabian peninsula at the time was oral. See Jonathan Bloom, *Paper before Print: The History and Impact of Paper in the Islamic World.* (New Haven: Yale University Press, 2001), pp. 94–95.

23. Syed H. Pasha, "Toward a Cultural Theory of Political Ideology and Mass Media in the Muslim World." *Media, Culture & Society*, 15, no. 1 (1993).

24. Abdelhadi Boutaleb, "Information Policy in Islam." *Islam Today*, 4 (1986), p. 8.

25. Ziauddin Sardar, "Paper, Printing and Compact Disks: The Making and Unmaking of Islamic Culture." *Media, Culture & Society*, 15, no. 1 (1993), p. 43.

26. Dagmar Glass, "The Global Information Flow: A Critical Appraisal from the Perspective of Arabi-Islamic Information Sciences," in *Mass Media, Politics, and Society in the Middle East*, ed. Kai Hafez (Cresskill, NJ: Hampton Press, 2001), p. 218.

27. Glass, "The Global Information Flow," pp. 219, 223.

28. Hamid Mowlana, "The New Global Order and Cultural Ecology." *Media, Culture & Society*, 15, no. 1 (1993), p. 11.

29. Muhyi al-Din Abd al-Halim, *Islamic Information and Its Scientific Implications*, 2nd ed. (Cairo: Maktabat Al-Khanji, 1984), p. 147. Cited in Glass, "The Global Information Flow," p. 224.

30. M.A. Salahi, *Muhammad: Man and Prophet: A Complete Study of the Life of the Prophet of Islam.* (Shaftesbury, Dorset; Rockport, MA: Element, 1995), p. 217.

31. Asghar Fathi, "Communication and Tradition in Revolution: The Role of the Islamic Pulpit." *Journal of Communication*, 2 (1979).

32. Ahmed Rateb Armoush, *The Political and Military Leadership of the Prophet Muhammad.* trans. Muhammad Badawi (Beirut: Dar An-Nafaes, 1997), pp. 220–221.

33. Abul Hasan Ali Nadwi and Mohiuddin Ahmad, *Muhammad Rasulullah: The Apostle of Mercy.* 3rd English ed. (Lucknow: Academy of Islamic Research and Publications, 2001), pp. 274–294.

34. Afzal Iqbal, *The Prophet's Diplomacy: The Art of Negotiation as Conceived and Developed by the Prophet of Islam.* (Cape Cod, MA: C. Stark, 1975), p. 56.

35. Quoted in Ami Ayalon. "*Sihafa*: The Arab Experiment in Journalism." *Middle Eastern Studies*, 28, no. 2 (1992), pp. 258–280; p. 259.

36. Ibn Warraq, *The Origins of the Koran: Classic Essays on Islam's Holy Book*. (Amherst, NY: Prometheus Books, 1998), p. 10.

37. As distinct from the chain of transmitters through which the authenticity of *hadith* is traced.

38. Robert Killebrew, "Dying to Belong." *The Washington Post*, Jun. 4, 2000.

39. Sardar, "Paper, Printing," p. 45.

40. *Fath al-Bari*, Vol. 9, p. 9, quoted in John Burton, *The Collection of the Qur'an*. (Cambridge; New York: Cambridge University Press, 1977), p. 119.

41. Bloom, *Paper before Print: The History and Impact of Paper in the Islamic World*, p. 101.

42. Warraq, *The Origins of the Koran*, p. 15.

43. Suhaib Hassan, *An Introduction to the Science of Hadith*. Electronic Edition: USC-MSA Compendium of Muslim Texts: http://www.usc.edu/dept/ MSA/fundamentals/hadithsunnah/scienceofhadith/acov.html (London: Al-Quran Society, 1994).

44. Bloom, *Paper before Print: The History and Impact of Paper in the Islamic World*, p. 122.

45. Sardar, "Paper, Printing," p. 48.

46. Miriam Cooke and Bruce B. Lawrence, *Muslim Networks from Hajj to Hip Hop*. (Chapel Hill: University of North Carolina Press, 2005), p. 6.

47. For a complete history of the evolution of Islamic and Arab media, see George N. Atiyeh, *The Book in the Islamic World: The Written Word and Communication in the Middle East*. (Albany, Washington, DC: State University of New York Press, 1995); Ami Ayalon, *The Press in the Arab Middle East: A History*. (New York: Oxford University Press, 1995); William A. Rugh, *Arab Mass Media: Newspapers, Radio, and Television in Arab Politics*. (Westport, CT: Praeger, 2004).

48. Glass, "The Global Information Flow," p. 219.

49. Cited in Ibid., pp. 223–224.

50. Sayeed al-Seini, "An Islamic Concept of News." *American Journal of Islamic Social Sciences*, 3, no. 32 (1986), p. 288.

51. Mohammad A. Siddiqi, "Ethics and Responsibility in Journalism: An Islamic Perspective." *Media Development*, 46, no. 1 (1999), p. 5.

52. Glass, "The Global Information Flow," p. 226.

53. Sayyid Qutb and William E. Shepard, *Sayyid Qutb and Islamic Activism: A Translation and Critical Analysis of Social Justice in Islam. Social, Economic,*

and *Political Studies of the Middle East and Asia*, V. 54 (Leiden; New York: E.J. Brill, 1996).

54. *JMCC Public Opinion Poll No. 32: On Palestinian Attitudes Towards Politics.* (Jerusalem Media & Communication Centre), Aug. 1999, available from http://www.jmcc.org/publicpoll/results/1999/no32.htm/.

55. Hamid Mowlana, "The New Global Order and Cultural Ecology." *Media, Culture & Society*, 15, no. 1 (1993).

56. Quoted in Majid Tehranian, "Communication Theory and Islamic Perspectives," in *Communication Theory: The Asian Perspective*, ed. W. Dissanayake (Singapore: Asian Mass Communication Research and Information Centre. 1998). p. 191.

57. Pasha, "Toward a Cultural Theory," p. 65.

58. Al-Seini, "An Islamic Concept of News," p. 287.

59. Ibid., p. 288.

60. http://www.islamonline.net/English/AboutUs.shtml.

61. http://www.almanar.com.lb/newssite/AboutUs.aspx?language=en.

62. Ibn Khaldun, *An Arab Philosophy of History: Selections from the Prolegomena of Ibn Khaldun of Tunis (1332–1406).* trans. Charles Issawi, Second ed. (Princeton, NJ: The American University in Cairo Press, 1992), pp. 27–29.

63. Pasha, "Towards a Cultural Theory," pp. 73–77.

64. Ibid., pp. 76, 61.

65. Mowlana, "The New Global Order and Cultural Ecology," pp. 13, 17.

66. Amal Jamal, *Media Politics and Democracy in Palestine: Political Culture, Pluralism, and the Palestinian Authority.* (Brighton: Sussex Academic Press, 2005), p. 161.

67. S. Abdullah Schleifer, "Islam and Information: Need, Feasibility, and Limitations of an Independent News Agency." *American Journal of Islamic Social Sciences*, 3, no. 1 (1986), pp. 122–123, 113.

68. Glass, "The Global Information Flow."

69. Walter J. Ong, St. Louis University. Committee on the Sesquicentennial, and St. Louis University, *Knowledge and the Future of Man – An International Symposium.* 1st ed. (New York: Holt Rinehart and Winston, 1968), p. 13. See also Walter J. Ong, *Hopkins, the Self and God.* (Toronto; Buffalo: University of Toronto Press, 1986).

70. Quoted in Fauzi Najjar, "The Arabs, Islam and Globalization." *Middle East Policy*, 12, no. 3 (2005), p. 96.

71. Fred Halliday, *The Middle East in International Relations: Power, Politics and Ideology*. (Cambridge, UK; New York: Cambridge, 2005), p. 210.

72. Samir Kassir, *Being Arab*. trans. Will Hobson, 2006 ed. (London; New York: Verso, 2006), pp. 34, xiii.

73. Anthony D. Smith, *Nations and Nationalism in a Global Era*. (Cambridge, UK; Cambridge, MA: Polity Press; Blackwell, 1995), p. 159.

74. Halliday, *The Middle East*, p. 244.

75. Mansoor Moaddel, "The Saudi Public Speaks: Religion, Gender and Politics." *International Journal of Middle East Studies*, 38 (2006), pp. 82–84. Interestingly, a separate 2006 survey in Iraq found that 60 percent of Baghdad residents identified themselves as "Iraqis, above all," compared to 12 percent in the Jordanian capital Amman (2001), 17 percent in Riyadh (2003), and 11 percent in Cairo (2001). The Baghdad figure literally doubled since it was asked in a 2004 survey. Source: Moaddel, "Iraq: Growing Support for Secular Politics and Nationalism in the Midst of Insecurity and Violence," Unpublished Paper provided to the author.

76. Quoted in Dawisha, *Arab Nationalism*, p. 21.

77. Abou Rijaili Khalil, "Boutros al-Boustani (1819–1883)." *Prospects: Quarterly Review of Education*, 23, no. 1 (1994).

78. Weldon C. Matthews, "Pan-Islam or Arab Nationalism? The Meaning of the 1931 Jerusalem Islamic Congress Reconsidered," *International Journal of Middle East Studies*, 35 (2003), p. 5.

79. Ghada Hashem Talhami, "Syria: Islam, Arab Nationalism and the Military." *Middle East Policy*, 8, no. 4 (2001), pp. 111–115.

80. Joshua Landis, *Is Ba'thism Secular?* [Blog] (SyriaComment.com), Jul. 14, 2004 [accessed Aug. 17, 2006] available from http://faculty-staff.ou.edu/L/Joshua.M.Landis-1/syriablog/2004/07/is-bathism-secular.htm.

81. Sayed Khatab, "Arabism and Islamism in Sayyid Qutb's Thought on Nationalism." *The Muslim World*, 94, no. 2 (2004), p. 232.

82. Dawisha, *Arab Nationalism*, pp. 136–137.

83. Martin Kramer, "Arab Nationalism: Mistaken Identity." *Daedalus*, 122, no. 3 (1993).

84. Fouad Ajami, "The Arab Inheritance." *Foreign Affairs*, 76, no. 5 (1997). For his earlier critique, see Fouad Ajami, "The End of Pan-Arabism." *Foreign Affairs*, Winter (1978–1979).

85. As'ad AbuKhalil, As'ad. "A New Arab Ideology? The Rejuvenation of Arab Nationalism." *The Middle East Journal*, 46, no. 1 (1992). pp. 22, 26.

86. James Zogby, *What a Difference a Year Makes*. (Arab American Institute), Dec. 1, 2006 [accessed Dec. 4, 2006] available from http://www.aaiusa.org/washington-watch/2635/w120106.

87. Kassir, *Being Arab*, p. 12.

88. Michael Slackman, "And Now, Islamism Trumps Arabism." *New York Times*, Aug. 20, 2006.

89. Dale F. Eickelman and James P. Piscatori, *Muslim Politics*. (Princeton, NJ: Princeton University Press, 1996), p. 16.

90. Khalil Rinnawi, *Instant Nationalism: McArabism, Al-Jazeera, and Transnational Media in the Arab World*. (Lanham, MD: University Press of America, 2006), p. 20.

91. Barry Rubin, "Dealing with the Challenge of a 'National Islamism.'" *The Daily Star*, Jan. 11, 2007.

92. Najjar, "The Arabs, Islam and Globalization," p. 102.

93. Emmanuel Sivan, "Arab Nationalism in the Age of the Islamic Resurgence," in *Rethinking Nationalism in the Arab Middle East*, eds James P. Jankowski and I. Gershoni (New York: Columbia University Press, 1997), p. 209.

94. Elias Khouri, "Sociology Cafe, Author's Contemporaneous Notes." (Beirut: May 23, 2007).

95. Najjar, "The Arabs, Islam and Globalization," p. 104.

96. Khatab, "Arabism and Islamism," p. 220.

97. Kedourie, *Islam in the Modern World*, p. 56.

98. *Nasrallah Updates Followers on Lebanon's Situation*. [email] (MideastWire.com), Jul. 29, 2006 [accessed Sept. 6, 2006] available from http://www.mideastwire.com.

99. *Hezbollah Secretary General Hassan Nasrallah on Al-Manar*. [email] (Mideastwire.com), Jul. 14, 2006 [accessed Sept. 7, 2006] available from http://www.mideastwire.com.

100. Quoted in Nadia Abou el-Magd. *For the Majority of Arabs, Hezbollah Won, and Israel Is No Longer the Undefeatable Army*. [Internet] (Associated Press), Aug. 15, 2006 [accessed Aug. 18, 2006] available from http://www.dailystaregypt.com/article.aspx?ArticleID=2663.

101. Joshua Mitnick, *Palestinian Hit Song Taps into Nationalism*. (The Washington Times), Aug. 25, 2006 [accessed Sep. 1, 2006] available from http://www.washingtontimes.com/world/20060824-115150-5073r.htm.

102. Fadlallah, *Friday Speeches 12 Zu Elqi'da 1425*. [accessed Aug. 30, 2006].

103. Kedourie, *Islam in the Modern World*, p. 56.

104. *Qatar Emir Hails First Arab Victory.* (The Peninsula), Aug. 22, 2006 [accessed Sep. 3, 2006] available from http://www.gulfinthemedia.com/ index.php?m=search&id=237173&lang=en.

105. Abdul Rahman Rashad, *The Courage of Nasrallah*. (Asharq Al-Awsat), Aug. 30, 2006 [accessed Sep. 3, 2006] available from http://www.aawsat. com/english/news.asp?section=2&id=6196.

106. Rami Khouri, "A New Man for the Mideast?" *Newsweek*, Aug. 21, 2006.

107. Michael Slackman and Mona el-Naggar, "Mubarak's Son Proposes Nuclear Program." *The New York Times*, Sep. 20, 2006.

5 Covering Darfur – A Question of Identity

1. Pamela J. Shoemaker and Stephen D. Reese, *Mediating the Message: Theories of Influences on Mass Media Content*, 2nd ed. (New York: Longman, 1996), p. 265.

6 Arab Journalism in Context

1. Michael Schudson, *Origins of the Ideal of Objectivity in the Professions: Studies in the History of American Journalism and American Law, 1830–1940*. (New York: Garland Pub., 1990), p. 3.

2. Hamid Mowlana, "The New Global Order and Cultural Ecology." *Media, Culture & Society*, 15, no. 1 (1993), pp. 9–27.

3. Michael Schudson and Susan E. Tifft, "American Journalism in Historical Perspective," in *The Press*, ed. Geneva Overholser and Kathleen Hall Jamieson, Institutions of American Democracy Series. (New York: Oxford University Press, 2005), pp. 27–28.

4. Daniel C. Hallin and Robert Giles, "Presses and Democracies," in *The Press*, ed. Geneva Overholser and Kathleen Hall Jamieson, Institutions of American Democracy Series. (New York: Oxford University Press, 2005), p. 7.

5. Bill Kovach and Tom Rosenstiel, *The Elements of Journalism*. (London: Published by Atlantic Books on behalf of Guardian Newspapers Ltd., 2003), p. 37.

6. Vin Ray, *The Television News Handbook: An Insider's Guide to Being a Great Broadcast Journalist*. (London: Pan Books, 2003), p. 20.

7. Jack Fuller, *News Values: Ideas for an Information Age.* (Chicago: University of Chicago Press, 1996), pp. 86–87.

8. Hillel Nossek and Dan Berkowitz, "Telling 'Our' Story through News of Terrorism." *Journalism Studies*, 7, no. 5 (2006), p. 691.

9. Max Weber and S.M. Miller, *Max Weber; Selections from His Work.* Major Contributors to Social Science Series (New York: Crowell, 1963).

10. Schudson, *Origins*, p. 10.

11. Ibid., pp. 3–4.

12. Ibid., p. 265.

13. Ibid., p. 7.

14. Fuller, *News Values*, pp. 18–19.

15. David Brinkley, "Interview." *TV Guide*, Apr. 11, 1964. Italics added by the author.

16. James Fenimore Cooper, *The American Democrat; a Treatise on Jacksonian Democracy.* (New York: Funk & Wagnalls, 1969).

17. Lt. Commander Arthur A. Humphries, "Two Routes to the Wrong Destination: Public Affairs in the South Atlantic War," *Naval War College Review,* XXXVI, no. 3 (1983), p. 57.

18. Edward Rothstein, "Yellow or Otherwise, American Newspapers as Media That Molded the Masses." *The New York Times*, Sept. 20, 2006.

19. Isaac Clark Pray, *A Journalist: Memoirs of James Gordon Bennett.* (New York: Stringer and Townsend, 1855), p. 34.

20. Horace Greeley, *Recollections of a Bush Life.* (New York: J.B. Ford, 1869), p. 39.

21. Schudson, *Origins*, pp. 174–176.

22. Ibid., p. 174.

23. Ibid., p. 184.

24. Ibid., p. 219.

25. Dan Schiller, *Objectivity and the News: The Public and the Rise of Commercial Journalism.* (Philadelphia: University of Pennsylvania Press, 1981), p. 2.

26. Gaye Tuchman, *Making News: A Study in the Construction of Reality.* (New York: Free Press, 1978).

27. Ibid.

28. James S. Ettema and Theodore L. Glasser, "The Irony in – and of – Journalism: A Case Study in the Moral Language of Liberal Democracy." *Journal of Communication*, 44, no. 2 (1994).

29. John L. Hess, *My Times: A Memoir of Dissent*. A Seven Stories Press 1st ed. (New York: Seven Stories Press, 2003), p. 17.

30. Kovach and Rosenstiel, *The Elements of Journalism*, p. 42.

31. Ibid., p. 42.

32. Herbert J. Altschull. *Agents of Power: The Media and Public Policy*. 2nd ed. (White Plains, NY: Longman Pub. USA 1995), p. 52.

33. Schudson, *Origins*, p. 267.

34. Tom Fenton, *Bad News: The Decline of Reporting, the Business of News, and the Danger to Us All*. 1st ed. (New York, NY: Regan Books, 2005), pp. 193–194.

35. Nicholas Boles, "The DIY Test That Proves BBC Bias," *The Spectator*, Oct. 4, 2003.

36. Schudson, *Origins*, pp. 229–230.

37. Schudson and Tifft, "American Journalism in Historical Perspective," p. 23.

38. Phillip Knightley, *The First Casualty: The War Correspondent as Hero and Myth-Maker from the Crimea to Kosovo*. (Baltimore, MD: Johns Hopkins University Press, 2002), p. 207.

39. Jean K. Chalaby, *The Invention of Journalism* (Houndmills, Basingstoke, Hampshire; New York: Macmillan Press; St. Martin's Press, 1998).

40. See, for example, Marc Weingarten, *The Gang That Wouldn't Write Straight : Wolfe, Thompson, Didion, and the New Journalism Revolution*. 1st ed. (New York: Crown Publishers, 2006). Tom Wolfe and Edward Warren Johnson, *The New Journalism*. 1st ed. (New York: Harper & Row, 1973).

41. Norman Finklestein, *With Heroic Truth: The Life of Edward R. Murrow*. (New York: Clarion Books, 1997).

42. Schudson and Tifft, "American Journalism in Historical Perspective," p. 30.

43. See John Lloyd, *Martin Bell Interview*. (Prospect), issue 95, Feb. 20, 2004 [accessed Aug. 17, 2007] available from http://www.prospectmagazine. co.uk/2004/02/martinbell/; Sherry Ricchiardi, "Giving Great War." *Columbia Journalism Review*, 18, no. 7 (September 1996).

44. Joseph B. Atkins, *The Mission: Journalism, Ethics and the World*. 1st ed. International Topics in Media (Ames, IA: Iowa State University Press, 2002), p. 220.

45. For more on this movement, see Clifford G. Christians, John P. Ferré, and Mark Fackler, *Good News: Social Ethics and the Press*. (New York: Oxford University Press, 1993).

46. Davis Merritt, *Public Journalism and Public Life: Why Telling the News Is Not Enough*. (Hillsdale, NJ: Erlbaum, 1995), p. 42.

47. Don H. Corrigan, *The Public Journalism Movement in America: Evangelists in the Newsroom*. (Westport, CT: Praeger, 1999), p. 14.

48. Cited in ibid., pp. 13–14.

49. Ibid., p. 19.

50. Email correspondence with the author, Aug. 5, 2006.

51. Corrigan, *Public Journalism Movement*, p. 187.

52. Merritt, *Public Journalism and Public Life*, p. 14.

53. Corrigan, *Public Journalism Movement*, p. 177.

54. Altschull, *Agents of Power: The Media and Public Policy*, p. 128.

55. Bill Moyers, "Buying the War," (PBS, 2007). [accessed May 12, 2008] available from http://www.pbs.org/moyers/journal/btw/transcript1.html.

56. Christians, Ferré, and Fackler, *Good News: Social Ethics and the Press*, p. 110.

57. Jack Lule, "News Values and Social Justice: US News and the Brazilian Street Children." *Howard Journal of Communications*, 9, no. 3 (1998), p. 183.

58. See, for example, Majid Tehranian, "Peace Journalism: Negotiating Global Media Ethics." *The Harvard International Journal of Press/Politics*, 7, no. 2 (2002); Seow Ting Lee and Crispin C. Maslog, "War or Peace Journalism? Asian Newspaper Coverage of Conflicts." *Journal of Communication*, 55, no. 2; Gadi Wolfsfeld, *Media and the Path to Peace. Communication, Society, and Politics* (Cambridge; New York: Cambridge University Press, 2004).

59. Edmund B. Lambeth. *Committed Journalism: An Ethic for the Profession*. 2nd ed. (Bloomington: Indiana University Press 1992), p. 8.

60. Margaret A. Blanchard, *The Hutchins Commission, the Press and the Responsibility Concept*. (Minneapolis: Association for Education in Journalism, 1977).

61. "The Playboy Interview," *Playboy*, June 1973, p. 26.

62. S. Robert Lichter, Stanley Rothman, and Linda S. Lichter, *The Media Elite*. 1st ed. (Bethesda, MD: Adler & Adler, 1986), p. 54.

63. Often attributed to H.L. Mencken, author Ralph Keyes says this line was coined by Chicago journalist Finley Peter Dunne at the turn of the twentieth century in his column "Mr. Dooley's Opinions." Quoting his fictitious Irish bartender character, he wrote: "Th newspaper does ivrything f'r us.

It runs th' polis foorce an' th' banks, commands th' milishy, controls th' ligislachure, baptizes th' young, marries th' foolish, comforts th' afflicted, afflicts th' comfortable, buries th' dead an' roasts thim aftherward." See Dave Astor, "Press-Quote Primer." *Editor & Publisher*, 139, no. 5 (2006).

64. Lambeth, *Committed Journalism*, p. 1.
65. W.A. Swanberg, *Luce and His Empire*. (New York: Scribner, 1972), pp. 142–143.
66. Schudson, *Origins*, p. 53.
67. Phillip Knightley, *The First Casualty: The War Correspondent as Hero and Myth-Maker from the Crimea to Kosovo* (Baltimore, MD: Johns Hopkins University Press, 2002), p. 58.
68. Helen Thomas, *Watchdogs of Democracy? The Waning Washington Press Corps and How It Has Failed the Public*. (New York: Scribner, 2006), pp. xiii–xiv.
69. Ray, *TV News Handbook*, p. x.
70. Quoted in Ibid., p. 198.
71. David Ignatius, *A Firing Offense*, first ed. (New York: Random House, 1997), p. 300.
72. B.S. Brennan, "What the Hacks Say: The Ideological Prism of Us Journalism Texts." *Journalism*, 1, no. 1 (2000).
73. Mark Feldstein, "A Muckraking Model: Investigative Reporting Cycles in American History." *The Harvard International Journal of Press/Politics*, 11, no. 2 (2006), p. 116.
74. Kovach and Rosenstiel, *The Elements of Journalism*, p. 17.
75. John Wallace Claire Johnstone, Edward J. Slawski, and William W. Bowman, *The News People: A Sociological Portrait of American Journalists and Their Work*. (Urbana: University of Illinois Press, 1976).
76. David H. Weaver and G. Cleveland Wilhoit, *The American Journalist in the 1990s: US News People at the End of an Era*. (Mahwah, NJ: L. Erlbaum, 1996), p. xv.
77. Ray, *TV News Handbook*, p. xi.
78. See John Wallace Claire Johnstone, Edward J. Slawski, and William W. Bowman, *The News People: A Sociological Portrait of American Journalist and Their Work*. (Urbana: University of Illinois Press, 1976); David H. Weaver and G. Cleveland Wilhoit, *The American Journalist: A Portrait of US News People and Their Work*. (Bloomington: Indiana University Press, 1986).

79. Weaver and Wilhoit, *The American Journalist in the 1990s*, p. 127.

80. Ibid., p. 135.

81. Quoted in Michael J. Robinson and Margaret A. Sheehan, *Over the Wire and on TV: CBS and UPI in Campaign '80*. (New York: Russell Sage Foundation, 1983).

82. "Immigration Debate Sparks PR Push to Boycott and Censure Lou Dobbs." *PR News*, 28, no. 63 (2006).

83. John Nerone and Kevin G. Barnhurst, "News Form and the Media Environment: A Network of Represented Relationships." *Media, Culture & Society*, 25, no. 1 (2003), p. 122.

84. Andrew Kohut and Carol Doherty, *State of the News Media*. (Pew Research Center for the People and the Press), May 23, 2006 [accessed Aug. 22] available from http://www.stateofthemedia.org/2006/prc. pdf. 16.

7   Western Ethics, Western Arrogance

1. Daniel C. Hallin and Robert Giles, "Presses and Democracies," in *The Press*, ed. Geneva Overholser and Kathleen Hall Jamieson (New York: Oxford University Press, 2005), pp. 10–11.

2. Owais Aslam Ali, "Values: Idle Concept or Realistic Goal?" in *Asian Values in Journalism*, ed. M. Masterton (Singapore: Asia Media, Information, and Communication Centre, 1996), p. 147.

3. Quoted in Herbert J. Altschull, *Agents of Power: The Media and Public Policy*. 2nd ed. (White Plains, NY: Longman Pub. USA 1995), p. 233.

4. Jiafei Yin and Gregg Payne, "Asia and the Pacific," in *Global Journalism: Topical Issues and Media Systems*, eds. A.S. de Beer and John Calhoun Merrill (Boston: Pearson/Allyn and Bacon, 2004), pp. 387–388.

5. Altschull, *Agents of Power: The Media and Public Policy*, p. 236.

6. John V. Vilanilam, *Reporting a Revolution: The Iranian Revolution and the Niico Debate*. (New Delhi; Newbury Park, CA: Sage Publications, 1989).

7. Source: InterMedia national surveys of adults (15+) in Bangladesh (2004), Cambodia, India, Indonesia, Pakistan, and Thailand (Greater Bangkok only) (2005).

8. Janet Steele, *Wars Within: The Story of Tempo, an Independent Magazine in Soeharto's Indonesia* (Jakarta, Singapore: Equinox Pub.; Institute of Southeast Asian Studies, 2005), p. 94.

9. Quoted in Angela Rose Romano, *Politics and the Press in Indonesia: Understanding an Evolving Political Culture.* (London; New York: Routledge Curzon, 2003), p. 45.

10. Ibid., p. 44.

11. Ibid., pp. 57–58 and 61.

12. Thomas Hanitzsch, "Journalists in Indonesia: Educated but Timid Watchdogs." *Journalism Studies*, 6, no. 4 (2005).

13. Thomas Hanitzsch, "Mapping Journalism Culture: A Theoretical Taxonomy and Case Studies from Indonesia." *Asian Journal of Communication*, 16, no. 2 (2006), p. 179.

14. Hanitzsch, "Journalists in Indonesia," p. 504.

15. Bettina Peters, "The Media's Role: Covering or Covering up Corruption?" in *Transparency International Global Corruption Report 2003*, ed. Robin Hodess (London: Profile Books, 2003). A 1999 survey of Indonesian journalists found some making as little as US$25 per month. That had been raised to about $70 by 2004. Sri Muninggar Saraswati, *Low Paid Journalists Produce Poor News.* (The Jakarta Post), Oct. 1, 2004 [accessed Apr. 17, 2006] available from http://www.asiamedia.ucle.edu/article.asp?parentid=15348.

16. Zassoursky writes of the "rat theory" of journalism, in which the initial explosion of media outlets following media liberalization produces an overabundance of outlets that is not economically sustainable. Already-low wages fall, ethics are abandoned, and journalists begin "devouring each other" and seek new sources of income, including bribes. See Ivan Zassoursky, *Media and Power in Post-Soviet Russia.* (Armonk, NY; London: M.E. Sharpe, 2004), p. 93.

17. Thomas Hanitzsch, "Journalists in Indonesia."

18. Simon Ingram, *Malaysia's Much-Maligned Media.* (BBC News Online), Nov. 16, 1999 [accessed May 5, 2004] available from http://news.bbc.co.uk/1/hi/world/asia-pacific/522848.stm.

19. Email correspondence with the author, Feb. 28, 2006.

20. R. Massey and P. Chang, "Locating Asian Values in Asian Journalism: A Content Analysis of Web Newspapers." *Journal of Communication*, 52, no. 4 (2002).

21. Myles Breen, *Journalism: Theory and Practice.* (Paddington, NSW, Australia: Macleay Press, 1998), p. 5.

22. David H. Weaver, "Journalists: International Profiles," in *Global Journalism: Topical Issues and Media Systems*, eds. A.S. de Beer and John Calhoun Merrill (Boston: Pearson/Allyn and Bacon, 2004), pp. 145–146.

23. Ibid., pp. 144–146.

24. Maria Jose Canel and Antoni M. Pique, "Journalists in Emerging Democracies: The Case of Spain," in *The Global Journalist: News People around the World*, ed. David H. Weaver and Wei Wu (Cresskill, NJ: Hampton Press, 1998), pp. 316–317.

25. Jerzy Oledzki, "Polish Journalists: Professionals or Not?" in *The Global Journalist: News People around the World*, eds. David H. Weaver and Wei Wu (Cresskill, NJ: Hampton Press, 1998), p. 291.

26. Heloiza G. Herscovitz and Adalberto M. Cardoso, "The Brazilian Journalist," in *The Global Journalist: News People around the World*, eds. D.H. Weaver and W. Wu (Cresskill, NJ: Hampton Press, 1998), p. 153.

27. Maria-Elena Gronemeyer, "Chilean Journalists: Autonomy and Independence Blocked by Conformism and Insecurity." (University of North Carolina, 2002), pp. 194–195, 122, 195.

28. Jurgen Wilke, "Journalists in Chile, Ecuador and Mexico," in *The Global Journalist: News People around the World*, eds. David H. Weaver and Wei Wu (Cresskill, NJ: Hampton Press, 1998), pp. 440–441.

29. Maria Cristina Caballero, "A Journalist's Mission in Colombia: Reporting Atrocities Is Not Enough." *Columbia Journalism Review*, 39, no. 1.

30. Jyotika Ramaprasad, "A Profile of Journalists in Post-Independence Tanzania." *Gazette*, 63, no. 6 (2001).

31. Jyotika Ramaprasad and James D Kelly, "Reporting the News from the World's Rooftop." *Gazette*, 65, no. 3 (2003).

32. Jyotika Ramaprasad and Shafiqur Rahman, "Tradition with a Twist: A Survey of Bangladeshi Journalists." *International Communication Gazette*, 68, no. 2 (2006), p. 150.

33. Ibid., p. 148.

34. Ibid., pp. 160–162.

35. Xiaoming Hao, *In Search of the Ideal Press: A Cross-Cultural Study of Journalistic Values.* (The University of Missouri, 1993), p. 228.

36. Elanie Steyn and Arnold de Beer, "The Level of Journalism Skills in South African Media: A Reason for Concern within a Developing Democracy?" *Journalism Studies*, 5, no. 3 (2004), p. 391.

37. Nelson Mandela. *Address to the International Press Institute Congress.* [Internet] (African National Congress), Feb. 14, 1994 [accessed Aug. 31] available from http://www.anc.org.za/ancdocs/history/mandela/1994/sp940214.html.

38. Peter Gross, *Entangled Evolutions: Media and Democratization in Eastern Europe.* (Washington, DC; Baltimore, MD: Woodrow Wilson Center Press; Johns Hopkins University Press, 2002), pp. 91–93.

39. Karol Jakubowski, "From Party Propaganda to Corporate Speech? Polish Journalism in Search of a New Identity." *Journal of Communication*, 42, no. 3 (1991), p. 60.

40. Ildiko Kaposi and Eva Vajda, "Between State Control and the Bottom Line," in *The Mission: Journalism, Ethics and the World*, ed. Joseph B. Atkins (Ames, IA: Iowa State University Press, 2002).

41. Gross, *Entangled Evolutions*, pp. 106–116.

42. Peter Golding, "Media Professionalism in the Third World: The Transfer of an Ideology," in *Mass Communication and Society*, eds. James Curran, Michael Gurevitch, and Janet Woollacott (Beverly Hills, CA: Sage Publications, 1979), p. 304.

43. Kenneth Starck and Anantha Sudhaker, "Reconceptualizating the Notion of Journalistic Professionalism across Differing Press Systems." *The Journal of Communication Inquiry*, 4, no. 2 (1979), p. 36.

44. Alex S. Edelstein, *Comparative Communication Research. Sage Commtext Series. V. 9* (Beverly Hills, CA: Sage Publications, 1982), p. 104.

45. Olivia Boyd-Barrett, "Journalism Recruitment and Training: Problems in Professionalism," in *Media Sociology; a Reader*, ed. Jeremy Tunstall (Urbana: University of Illinois Press, 1970), p. 181.

46. Francis B. Nyamnjoh, *Africa's Media, Democracy, and the Politics of Belonging.* (London; New York: Zed Books: Distributed in the USA. exclusively by Palgrave Macmillan, 2005), p. 27.

47. Gross, *Entangled Evolutions*, pp. 117–118.

48. David H. Weaver and Wei Wu, *The Global Journalist: News People around the World.* (Cresskill, NJ: Hampton Press, 1998), p. 468.

49. Romano, *Politics and the Press.*

50. Mohamed Kirat, *The Algerian News People: A Study of Their Backgrounds, Professional Orientation and Working Conditions.* Unpublished dissertation (School of Journalism, Indiana University, Bloomfield, IN, 1987), p. vii.

51. See, for example R. Herrscher, "A Universal Code of Journalism Ethics: Problems, Limitations, and Proposals." *Journal of Mass Media Ethics*, 17, no. 4 (2002) and Reese, "Understanding the Global Journalist: A Hierarchy-of-Influences Approach."

52. Sidney Callahan, "New Challenges of Globalization for Journalism." *Journal of Mass Media Ethics*, 18, no. 1 (2003), pp. 3–15.

53. Stephen J.A. Ward, "Philosophical Foundations for Global Journalism Ethics." *Journal of Mass Media Ethics*, 20, no. 1 (2005), p. 3.

54. Ibid., p. 5.

55. Herrscher, "Universal Code."

56. The Bangladesh journalist code of ethics, for example, dictates that it is "the moral responsibility of a journalist to maintain extra precaution in publishing any news involving man–woman relationships or any report relating to women," while the Saudi code states that "the media will observe in their programs the nature of women and the role she is called to play in society without that role conflicting with such nature." Source: Gunaratna, "Child Combatants." http://www.journalism-islam.de/konferenzen/codes.html

57. The 1982 Egyptian code says it is the "sacred duty" of a journalist to protect "public opinion and public taste," while the Pakistani code bans articles about "immorality."

58. Ward, "Philosophical Foundations," p. 5.

59. Shakuntala Rao and Seow Ting Lee, "Globalizing Media Ethics?" pp. 106–108.

60. Merrill, John C., "Chaos and Order: Sacrificing the Individual for the Sake of Social Harmony," in *The Mission: Journalism, Ethics and the World*, ed. Joseph B. Atkins (Ames, IA: Iowa State University Press, 2002). pp. 18–19.

61. Kai Hafez, "Journalism Ethics Revisited: A Comparison of Ethics Codes in Europe, North Africa, the Middle East, and Muslim Asia." *Political Communication*, 19, no. 2 (2002). p. 237.

62. "Journalists' Opinion Poll." (Amman: Center for Defending Freedom of Journalists, 2008).

63. Akbar S. Ahmed, *Living Islam: From Samarkand to Stornoway* (New York: Facts on File, 1994).

64. Rao and Lee, "Globalizing Media Ethics?", p. 21.

65. Geert H. Hofstede, *Culture's Consequences: Comparing Values, Behaviors, Institutions, and Organizations across Nations*. 2nd ed. (Thousand Oaks, CA: Sage Publications, 2001), p. xix.

66. De Beer and Merrill, *Global Journalism*, p. xvi.

8   The Mission of Arab Journalism

1. From 13 Arab countries in North Africa, the Levant, and the Arabian peninsula, 601 journalists responded. For details on methodology, see Lawrence Pintak and Jeremy Ginges, "The Mission of Arab Journalism: Creating Change in a Time of Turmoil," *The International Journal of Press/ Politics*, 13, no. 3 (2008).

2. "Complete the following sentence: "It is the job of a journalist to ..."" Respondents were given a list of 21 possible roles, adapted from surveys of journalists elsewhere in the world, and asked to evaluate them on a five-point Likert scale, from "completely insignificant" to "most significant" and "don't know."

3. The goal was to ascertain perceived importance of threats beyond that of Israel, which dominates Arab discourse. Respondents were asked, "What is the greatest threat facing the Arab world today?" and given a list of eight choices, based on responses to previous surveys of the Arab public. Israel was specifically excluded.

4. Twice as many Syrians saw lack of political change as a threat (44%) than US policy (19%), and the proportion was almost as dramatic among Moroccans (53% vs. 30%).

5. "Democrat" was the self-identification among 83 percent of Syrians and 75 percent of Moroccans and cited least frequently by Palestinians (32%), Egyptians (36%), and journalists based in the UAE (38%).

6. Where the majority of the other journalists identified first with the Arab world, the primary geographic identity of Moroccans (61%) was to the Muslim world, with just 8 percent of them identifying first with the Arab world. In contrast, just 4 percent of journalists in Syria, which is a largely secular society, identified first with the Muslim world, with the largest portion (34%) citing "locality" first, followed by Arab world (34%), and nation (20%).

7. Samar Fatany, "Journalists Face Challenges Preserving Watchdog Role" Arab News, Feb. 12, 2007 [accessed Mar. 5, 2007] available from http:// www.arabnews.com/?page=7&section=0&article=92074&d=12&m=2&y =2007.

8. These options were drawn from surveys of journalists elsewhere in the world. Journalists in Syria and Lebanon gave higher priority to threats from religious extremists (55% and 45% respectively), presumably a reflection

of the secular character of Syrian society and the fact that about half the Lebanese sample were Christians.

9. The percentage that saw the USA as a threat was highest in the Emirates (42%) and Syria (40%) and lowest in Morocco (16%).

10. Based on a four-point scale, with percentages combining very unfavorable/somewhat unfavorable and somewhat favorable/very favorable respectively.

11. The Moroccans had the most *unfavorable* view of US policy (97% somewhat/very unfavorable), while the Syrians had the most *positive* view of the American people (85% somewhat/very favorable).

12. Just 34 percent of the Lebanese, and 40 percent of the Syrians, agreed.

13. Respondents were given a list of 12 issues, drawn largely from surveys of the Arab public, and asked to "Rate the importance of the following issues to the Arab world today," using a five-point scale from "not important" to "the most important." It was possible to choose more than one as "the most important."

14. It was ranked fifth by journalists working for pan-Arab media and, not surprisingly, third by Palestinian journalists.

15. The Palestine-related questions produced some of the more interesting country-specific results. Almost 40 percent of Palestinian journalist based in the West Bank said the right of Palestinians to return to their preoccupation lands could be negotiated as part of a final settlement, a percentage more than double that of the overall sample (22%). Other responses: Lebanon (17%), Egypt (18%), Morocco (16%), and UAE (16%). Only journalists in Syria, traditionally seen as taking the most aggressive stand toward Israel, had a response proportionate to that of the Palestinians, with 37 percent expressing willingness to negotiate this benchmark issue. Likewise, more than twice as many Palestinians and Syrians (29% each) than the overall sample (13%) partly or completely agreed that the Bush administration was genuine in its stated support for a Palestinian state. The Syrians also ranked Palestine well down (9th) on their list of the most important issues in the Arab world. Also notable, the Palestinians themselves put the economy in a statistical tie with "Palestine" at the top of their issue ranking. The findings are based on relatively small samples, with the Palestinian data coming from the Fatah-controlled West Bank and not the Hamas-controlled Gaza, but the degree to which the data challenges conventional wisdom about the stance of Palestinian and Syrian journalists argues for further study.

16. The Syrians put it tenth.

17. The Syrians and Palestinians each put it tenth, with 14 percent each.

18. William A. Rugh, *Arab Mass Media: Newspapers, Radio, and Television in Arab Politics.* (Westport, CT: Praeger, 2004).

19. David H. Weaver et al., *The American Journalist in the 21st Century: U.S. News People at the Dawn of a New Millennium*, Lea's Communication Series (Mahwah, NJ: L. Erlbaum Associates, 2007).

20. Jyotika Ramaprasad, "A Profile of Journalists in Post-Independence Tanzania." *Gazette* 63, no. 6 (2001); Jyotika Ramaprasad and Naila Nabil Hamdy, "Functions of Egyptian Journalists: Perceived Importance and Actual Performance." *International Communication Gazette* 68, no. 2 (2006); Jyotika Ramaprasad and James D Kelly, "Reporting the News from the World's Rooftop." *Gazette* 65, no. 3 (2003); Jyotika Ramaprasad and Shafiqur Rahman, "Tradition with a Twist: A Survey of Bangladeshi Journalists." *International Communication Gazette* 68, no. 2 (2006).

21. Faisal Kasim, "Humanizing the Arab Media." *Middle East Broadcasters Journal*, no. Nov/Dec (2005).

22. The sense of "guardianship" is lowest in Morocco. As the outlier of the Arab world, its journalists demonstrate a very low sense of connection with Arab causes, evident in percentages endorsing journalistic roles of enhancing Arab unity (8%), defending Arab interests (14%), and fostering Arab culture (14%). And despite their identification with the broader Muslim world (above), just 21 percent say it is their job to protect Islam or encourage spiritual values. Support for the Guardian functions is highest in Egypt, the UAE, and the West Bank; lowest in Morocco, Syria, and Lebanon. More surprising in light of the fact that it is one of the fonts of Arab nationalism, only 14 percent of Syrian journalists said it was their job to enhance Arab unity, and, while their other responses evince a largely secular worldview, 51 percent of Syrian journalists saw fostering spiritual values as a very important role.

23. The choice "journalist" was highest among Moroccans (79%) and lowest among Egyptians (30%).

9 Journalistic Roles – Arabs, Americans and the World

1. Jyotika Ramaprasad and Shafiqur Rahman, "Tradition with a Twist: A Survey of Bangladeshi Journalists." *International Communication Gazette*, 68, no. 2 (2006), p. 150.

2. Thomas Hanitzsch, "Journalists in Indonesia: Educated but Timid Watchdogs." *Journalism Studies*, 6, no. 4 (2005); Angela Rose Romano, *Politics and the Press in Indonesia: Understanding an Evolving Political Culture* (London, New York: RoutledgeCurzon, 2003).

3. Kirat, Mohamed, "The Algerian News People: A Study of Their Backgrounds, Professional Orientation and Working Conditions." Unpublished dissertation (Indiana University, 1987), p. vii.

4. Ibid., p. 166.

5. Ibid., p. 168.

6. Ibid.

7. Ibid., pp. 169–177.

8. David H. Weaver and G. Cleveland Wilhoit, *The American Journalist in the 1990s: US News People at the End of an Era.* (Mahwah, NJ: L. Erlbaum, 1996), p. 144.

9. T. Abdulkader Tash, "A Profile of Professional Journalists Working in the Saudi Arabian Daily Press." Unpublished dissertation (Carbondale, IL: Southern Illinois University, 1983).

10. Anas al-Rasheed, "Professional Values: A Survey of Working Journalists in the Kuwaiti Daily Press." Unpublished dissertation (Carbondale, IL: Southern Illinois University, 1998), p. 66.

11. Ibid., p. 67.

12. Ibid., p. 74.

13. Khaled al-Anezi, "Factors Influencing Chief Editors' News Selection in Kuwait Television and Kuwait Radio." Unpublished dissertation (Carbondale, IL: Southern Illinois University, 2000), p. 122.

14. Sayyi/d Qutb, *Milestones*. Rev. translation ed. (Indianapolis: American Trust, 1993), p. 194.

15. Ibid., p. 125.

16. Ahmad S. Turkistani, "News Exchange Via Arabsat and News Values of Arab Television." Unpublished dissertation (Bloomington, IN: Indiana University, 1988), p. 288.

17. BBC World Service Trust Symposia. Lebanon, Apr. 14–16, 2004; Syria, Apr. 18–20, 2004; Egypt, Jun 23–25, 2004. A total of approximately 150 journalists took part. Data provided to the author by the BBC World Service Trust, 2005.

18. "Arab Journalism Codes," *Al-Bab.com*, [accessed Apr. 3, 2007] available from http://www.al-bab.com/media/docs/arabcodes.htm.

19. Jyotika Ramaprasad and Naila Nabil Hamdy, "Functions of Egyptian Journalists: Perceived Importance and Actual Performance." *International Communication Gazette*, 68, no. 2 (2006).

20. Jyotika Ramaprasad and James D Kelly, "Reporting the News from the World's Rooftop." *Gazette*, 65, no. 3 (2003).

21. Ramaprasad and Hamdy, "Functions of Egyptian Journalists," p. 176.

22. Ibid., p. 180.

23. Kai Hafez, "Journalism Ethics Revisited: A Comparison of Ethics Codes in Europe, North Africa, the Middle East, and Muslim Asia." *Political Communication*, 19, no. 2 (2002), p. 241.

24. Ibid., 244.

25. Rohan Gunaratna, "LTTE Child Combatants." *Janes' Intelligence Review* (July 1998).

26. Hafez, "Journalism Ethics Revisited," p. 225.

27. Mohammad A. Siddiqi, "Ethics and Responsibility in Journalism: An Islamic Perspective." *Media Development*, 46, no. 1 (1999): p. 42.

28. Source: Gunaratna, "Child Combatants."

29. Ibid.

30. Ibid.

31. Ibid., p. 236.

32. *BBC/Reuters/Media Center Poll: Trust in the Media.* (GlobeScan), May 3, 2006 [accessed May 15] available from http://www.globescan.com/news_ archives/bbcreut.html.

33. Hafez, "Journalism Ethics Revisited," p. 243.

10   Arab Journalists Look at Themselves and the Competition

1. Doha Al Zohairy, "Unpublished Interview," (Cairo, April 15, 2009). Details of interview were shared with the author.

2. Lisa Schnellinger and Mohannad Khatib, *Fighting Words: How Arab and American Journalists Can Break through to Better Coverage* (Washington, DC: International Center for Journalists, 2006).

3. Quoted in Ami Ayalon, "*Sihafa*: The Arab Experiment in Journalism." *Middle Eastern Studies*, 28, no. 2 (1992), p. 268.

4. *Al-Jazeera Emphasizes Respect for Iraq's Sistani.* (Fars News Agency), May 26, 2007 [accessed Jun. 19, 2007] available from http://english. farsnews.com/newstext.php?nn=8602200162.

5. Ibid., p. 15.

6. *State of the News Media.* (Project on Excellence in Journalism), 2007 [accessed Feb. 20, 2007] available from http://www.stateofthenewsmedia. com/2007/.

7. Rami Khouri, *Back to Beirut: Ready to Defy Israel.* (The Daily Star), Jul. 19, 2006 [accessed Jul. 19, 2006] available from http://www.dailystar.com.lb/ article.asp?edition_id=10&categ_id=5&article_id=74059#.

8. "Egypt Turns Off Hezbollah TV," *The Laylina Review of Public Diplomacy and Arab Media*, no. 9 (2009), http://www.layalina.tv/Publications/Review/ PR_V.9/PR_V.9.html.

9. Jurgen Wilke, "Journalists in Chile, Equador and Mexico," in *The Global Journalist: News People around the World*, eds. David H. Weaver and Wei Wu (Cresskill, NJ: Hampton Press, 1998).

10. Jerzy Oledzki, "Polish Journalists: Professionals or Not?," in *The Global Journalist: News People around the World*, eds. David H. Weaver and Wei Wu (Cresskill, NJ: Hampton Press, 1998), p. 291.

11. Samar Fatany, "Media Reforms, Welcome Steps." *Arab News*, Mar. 8, 2009.

11   Arab Journalists and the Arab People

1. Data provided directly to the author by survey researchers Mansoor Moaddel of Eastern Michigan University and Hamid Latif of The American University in Cairo. Portions of the data appeared in various forms in Mansoor Moaddel, "The Saudi Public Speaks: Religion, Gender and Politics." *International Journal of Middle East Studies*, 38 (2006), Mansoor Moaddel and Hamid Latif, "Events and Value Change: The Impact of September 11, 2001, on the Worldviews of Egyptians and Moroccans." *Interdisciplinary Journal of Research on Religion*, 2 (2006). The specific question asked by Moaddel and Latif was, "Independently of whether you go to religious services, which of these describe you? Religious person; Not a religious person; A convinced atheist."

2. Amaney Jamal and Mark Tessler, "Attitudes in the Arab World," *Journal of Democracy*, 19, no. 1 (2008),p. 105. See also Mark Tessler, "Islam and Democracy in the Middle East: The Impact of Religious Orientations on Attitudes toward Democracy in Four Arab Countries," *Comparative Politics*, 34, no. 3 (2002).

3. Even among the subgroup of Muslim journalists who described them- selves as "religious" (as opposed to "secular" or "undeclared"), the clergy

received relatively low marks on the question of whether they were providing adequate answers to problems of the individual (55%) and family life (56%), and social problems (42%). Most significantly, even on the question of whether clergy was meeting spiritual needs, just 53 percent of the "religious" journalists believed the clergy wss doing an adequate job. Otherwise, as expected, "religious" journalists gave the clergy much higher marks than their self-described "secular" and "undeclared" colleagues. More than twice as many self-described "religious" Muslim journalists as "secular" or "undeclared" said politicians who did not believe in God were unfit for office; half as many "religious" Muslim journalists as "secular" or "undeclared" agreed that laws that contradict *sharia* should be allowed; and, about twice as many of those in the "religious" subgroup said it is necessary to believe in God to have good moral values. Other points of difference involved specific issues of self-identity and the role of journalists. Almost half the self-declared "religious" Muslims answered, "Above all, I am a Muslim," but just 9 percent of the "secular" journalists and the same percentage of "undeclared" chose "Muslim" first and 30 percent of the "religious" Muslims joined the "secular" (52%) and undeclared participants (58%) in selecting, "Above all, I am a journalist." The number in all three groups stating their primary identity as Arab (9%, 14%, and 7% respectively) or identifying most closely with their individual nation (7%, 10%, and 10%) was negligible. On the question of geographic identity, almost half of the "religious" Muslim journalists identified first with the Muslim world, in itself, not a surprising result. However, about one-third of the "religious" journalists chose the Arab world as their primary geographic identity; only 10 percent of the "secular" journalists identified first with the broader Muslim world; the Arab and Muslim worlds were each selected by about a quarter of the undeclared journalist; and, a small percentage of all three groups put national identity paramount. When it came to political philosophy, "religious" Muslims differed dramatically from their "secular" and "undeclared" colleagues, but even then, the proportion of each group identifying with political Islam was low: More "religious" Muslims identified their primarily political identity as "democrat" (34%) than those who chose "Islamist" (28%), and a substantial majority of both "secular" journalists and the "undeclared" chose "democrat" (63% and 57%), with a statistically insignificant number of both of those groups identifying themselves as Islamists. Equally interesting, more self-declared "religious" journalists identified themselves as Arab Nationalists (21%) than did "secular" (16%) and "undeclared" (11%).

4. Shibley Telhami and John Zogby, "Anwar Sadat Chair for Peace and Development University of Maryland/ Zogby International 2006 Annual Arab Public Opinion Survey," (College Park: University of Maryland, 2007). Mansoor Moaddel, "The Saudi Public Speaks." "Arab Barometer," 2006, [accessed July 9, 2007] available from http://arabbarometer.org/reports/countryreports/comparisonresutls06.html.

5. James Zogby, "Five Nation Survey of the Middle East," Arab American Institute, http://www.aaiusa.org/washington-watch/2635/w120106.

6. Dalia Mogahed, "Islam and Democracy." Special Report: Muslim World (New York: Gallup, March 6, 2006).[accessed May 5, 2006] available from http://www.gallup.com/se/127907/Gallup-Center-Muslim-Studies.aspx.

7. Shibley Telhami, "Symposium," *Dissent*, no. Spring (2007).

8. Unpublished data from 2007 Egypt survey provided to the author by Hamid Latif of The American University in Cairo. Actual statement on the Latif survey: "The U.S. goal is to see the existence of an independent and viable Palestinian State."

9. Jamal and Tessler, "Attitudes," p. 99.

10. "World Values Survey," World Values Survey Association, [accessed Oct. 12, 2007] available from http://www.worldvaluessurvey.org/.

11. Jamal and Tessler, "Attitudes," p. 98.

12. Ibid., p. 98. The authors based the distinction on frequency of Qur'an reading.

12   Border Guards of the New Arab Consciousness

1. Benedict R. O'G Anderson, *Imagined Communities: Reflections on the Origin and Spread of Nationalism*, Rev. ed. (London; New York: Verso, 2006).

2. Katherine Meyer, Helen Rizzo, and Yousef Ali, "Changed Political Attitudes in the Middle East," *International Sociology*, 22, no. 3 (2007).

3. Anthony D. Smith, *Nations and Nationalism in a Global Era* (Cambridge, UK; Cambridge, MA: Polity Press; Blackwell, 1995), p. 120.

4. Karl Wolfgang Deutsch, *Nationalism and Social Communication: An Inquiry into the Foundations of Nationality* ([Cambridge, MA]: Published jointly

by the Technology Press of the Massachusetts Institute of Technology, and Wiley, 1953), pp. 70–71.

5. John Alexander Armstrong, *Nations before Nationalism* (Chapel Hill: University of North Carolina Press, 1982), pp. 9, xii.

6. E.J. Hobsbawm, *Nations and Nationalism since 1780: Programme, Myth, Reality* (Cambridge [UK]; New York: Cambridge University Press, 1990), pp. 141–142.

7. Anderson, *Imagined Communities*, pp. 6, 14, 36.

8. Anderson, *Imagined Communities*, p. 54.

9. Hans Kohn, *The Idea of Nationalism: A Study in Its Origins and Background* (New York: Macmillan Company, 1944), pp. 10–11.

10. Ernest Gellner, *Nations and Nationalism* (Ithaca: Cornell University Press, 1983), p. 1. Italics in the original.

11. Anderson, *Imagined Communities*, p. 161.

12. Adrian Hastings, *The Construction of Nationhood: Ethnicity, Religion, and Nationalism* (Cambridge [UK]; New York: Cambridge University Press, 1997), p. 5.

13. Smith, *Nations and Nationalism in a Global Era*, p. 145.

14. Ibid., p. 121.

15. Anderson, *Imagined Communities*, p. 7.

16. Rashid Khalidi, "Ottoman Notables in Jerusalem: Nationalism and Other Options." *Muslim World*, LXXXIV, no. 1–2 (1994).

17. Dale F. Eickelman and James P. Piscatori, *Muslim Politics*. (Princeton, NJ: Princeton University Press, 1996), p. 16.

18. Marc Lynch, *Voices of the New Arab Public: Iraq, Al-Jazeera, and Middle East Politics Today*. (New York: Columbia University Press, 2006), p. 32.

19. Tom Johnston McFadden, *Daily Journalism in the Arab States*. (Columbus: Ohio State University Press, 1953), pp. 14–15.

20. Anderson, *Imagined Communities*, p. 40.

21. Ibid., pp. 80–81.

22. Ali Darwish, *Language, Translation and Identity in the Age of the Internet, Satellite Television and Directed Media*. (Melbourne: Writescope Pty Ltd, 2005), p. 442.

23. Anderson, *Imagined Communities*, p. 37.

24. Kemal H. Karpat, *The Politicization of Islam: Reconstructing Identity, State, Faith, and Community in the Late Ottoman State*. (New York: Oxford University Press, 2001), p. 119.

25. Jurgen Habermas, "Citizenship and National Identity: Some Reflections on the Future of Europe," in *The Nationalism Reader*, eds. Omar Dahbour and Micheline Ishay (Atlantic Highlands, NJ: Humanities Press, 1995), p. 338.

26. Ibrahim M. Abu-Rabi, *Contemporary Arab Thought: Studies in Post-1967 Arab Intellectual History.* (London; Sterling, VA: Pluto Press, 2004), p. xvi.

27. Michael Provence, *The Great Syrian Revolt and the Rise of Arab Nationalism*, 1st ed. (Austin: University of Texas Press, 2005), p. 21.

28. Juan Cole and Deniz Kandiyoti, "Nationalism and the Colonial Legacy in the Middle East and Central Asia: Introduction." *International Journal of Middle East Studies*, 34 (2002), p. 198.

29. Fauzi Najjar, "The Arabs, Islam and Globalization." *Middle East Policy*, 12, no. 3 (2005), p. 102.

30. Anderson, *Imagined Communities*, p. 7.

31. Ibid., p. 64.

Postscript   New Media, New Media Models

1. Mohamed Abdel Dayem, "Jordan May Extend Repressive Law to Electronic Media." Committee to Protect Journalists, Feb. 2, 2010 [accessed Feb. 10, 2010] available from http://cpj.org/blog/2010/02/jordan-may-extend-repressive-press-law-to-electron.php.

2. "After Crackdown, Regime Goes into Reverse and Cracks Down on Media, Journalists." Reporters without Borders, Feb. 17, 2010 [accessed Mar. 10, 2010] available from http://www.rsf.org/After-progress-regime-goes-into.html.

3. Hillary Rodham Clinton, "Remarks on Press Freedom," US State Department, Jan. 21, 2010 [accessed Mar. 15, 2010] available from http://www.state.gov/secretary/rm/2010/01/135519.htm.

4. "Anti-American Incitement to Violence in the Middle East," in *H.R. 2278* (U.S. House of Representatives, 2009).

5. Bruce Etling et al., "Mapping the Arabic Blogosphere: Politics, Culture, and Dissent," (Cambridge, MA: Berkman Center Research Publication, 2009).

6. Mohamed Abdel Dayem and Robert Mahoney, "Human Rights Coverage Spreads, Despite Government Pushback," in *Attacks on the Press 2009* (New York: Committee to Protect Journalists, 2010).

7. Rita Barotta, "Wael Abbas: The Arab Internet's Unlikely Superhero." *Menassat.com*, Nov. 9, 2007 [accessed Dec. 15, 2008] available from http://www.menassat.com/?q=en/news-articles/2097-wael-abbas-arab-internets-unlikely-superhero.

Bibliography

Abu-Rabi, Ibrahim M. *Contemporary Arab Thought: Studies in Post-1967 Arab Intellectual History*. London; Sterling, VA: Pluto Press, 2004.

"After Crackdown, Regime Goes into Reverse and Cracks Down on Media, Journalists." Reporters without Borders, http://www.rsf.org/After-progress-regime-goes-into.html.

Ahmed, Akbar S. *Living Islam: From Samarkand to Stornoway*. New York: Facts on File, 1994.

Al-Ghanami, Khaled. "To All Arab Media: Unite!" *Al-Watan*, Jan. 8, 2009.

Al-Harb, Khalaf. "The Bombardment of the Arab Mind." *Okaz*, Jan. 5, 2009.

Anderson, Benedict R. O'G. *Imagined Communities: Reflections on the Origin and Spread of Nationalism*. Rev. ed. London; New York: Verso, 2006.

"Anti-American Incitement to Violence in the Middle East." In H.R. 2278. USA: US House of Representatives, 2009.

"Arab Barometer." http://arabbarometer.org/reports/countryreports/comparisonresutls06.html.

"Arab Journalism Codes." Al-Bab.com, http://www.al-bab.com/media/docs/arabcodes.htm.

Armstrong, John Alexander. *Nations before Nationalism*. Chapel Hill: University of North Carolina Press, 1982.

Barotta, Rita. "Wael Abbas: The Arab Internet's Unlikely Superhero." Menassat.com (2007), http://www.menassat.com/?q=en/news-articles/2097-wael-abbas-arab-internets-unlikely-superhero.

Bloom, Jonathan. *Paper before Print: The History and Impact of Paper in the Islamic World*. New Haven, CT: Yale University Press, 2001.

Bush, George H.W. "President's Remarks at U.S. University Presidents Summit on International Education," edited by The White House. The White House, 2006.

Clinton, Hillary Rodham. "Remarks on Press Freedom," US State Department. Washington, DC: 2010.

Cole, Juan and Deniz Kandiyoti. "Nationalism and the Colonial Legacy in the Middle East and Central Asia: Introduction." *International Journal of Middle East Studies* 34 (2002): 189–203.

Darwish, Ali. *Language, Translation and Identity in the Age of the Internet, Satellite Television and Directed Media.* Melbourne: Writescope Pty Ltd, 2005.

Dayem, Mohamed Abdel. "Jordan May Extend Repressive Law to Electronic Media." Committee to Protect Journalists, http://cpj.org/blog/2010/02/jordan-may-extend-repressive-press-law-to-electron.php.

Deutsch, Karl Wolfgang. *Nationalism and Social Communication; an Inquiry into the Foundations of Nationality.* [Cambridge]: Published jointly by the Technology Press of the Massachusetts Institute of Technology and Wiley, 1953.

"Doha Centre Journalist Banned from Leaving Qatar." Mediame.com, no. March 24 (2009).

"Egypt Turns Off Hezbollah TV." *The Laylina Review of Public Diplomacy and Arab Media*, no. 9 (2009), http://www.layalina.tv/Publications/Review/PR_V.9/PR_V.9.html.

Esposito, John L. *Unholy War: Terror in the Name of Islam.* Oxford and New York: Oxford University Press, 2002.

Etling, Bruce, John Kelly, Robert Faris, and John Palfrey. "Mapping the Arabic Blogosphere: Politics, Culture, and Dissent." Cambridge, MA: Berkman Center Research Publication, 2009.

Fakhreddine, Jihad. "Imbalanced Economics of the Pan-Arab Satellite Television Sector" *Maktoob Business*, http://business.maktoob.com/reportdetails-20060329092602-Imbalanced_Economics_Of_The_Pan_Arab_Satellite_Television_Sector.htm.

Fatany, Samar. "Journalists Face Challenges Preserving Watchdog Role" *Arab News*, http://www.arabnews.com/?page=7&section=0&article=92074&d=12&m=2&y=2007.

——. "Media Reforms, Welcome Steps." *Arab News*, March 8, 2009.

Fuller, Graham E. *The Future of Political Islam.* First ed. New York: Palgrave Macmillan, 2003.

Gellner, Ernest. *Nations and Nationalism.* Ithaca: Cornell University Press, 1983.

Habermas, Jurgen. "Citizenship and National Identity: Some Reflections on the Future of Europe." In *The Nationalism Reader*, edited by Omar Dahbour and Micheline Ishay, 333–343. Atlantic Highlands, NJ: Humanities Press, 1995.

Hallin, Daniel C. and Robert Giles. "Presses and Democracies." In *The Press*, edited by Geneva Overholser and Kathleen Hall Jamieson, pp. xxvi, 473. New York: Oxford University Press, 2005.

Hamamou, Sabah. "Local Print Media Going against the Grain." *Daily News Egypt*, April 17, 2009, 2.

Hanitzsch, Thomas. "Journalists in Indonesia: Educated but Timid Watchdogs." *Journalism Studies* 6, no. 4 (2005): 493–508.

Hastings, Adrian. *The Construction of Nationhood: Ethnicity, Religion, and Nationalism. Cambridge.* New York: Cambridge University Press, 1997.

Hobsbawm, E.J. *Nations and Nationalism since 1780: Programme, Myth, Reality.* Cambridge, UK; New York: Cambridge University Press, 1990.

Jamal, Amaney and Mark Tessler. "Attitudes in the Arab World." *Journal of Democracy* 19, no. 1 (2008): 97–110.

"Journalist Lamees Dhaif Summoned to Public Prosecutor's Office." Bahrain: Bahrain Center for Human Rights/IFEX, 2009.

"Journalists' Opinion Poll." Amman: Center for Defending Freedom of Journalists, 2008.

Karpat, Kemal H. *The Politicization of Islam: Reconstructing Identity, State, Faith, and Community in the Late Ottoman State.* New York: Oxford University Press, 2001.

Kasim, Faisal. "Humanizing the Arab Media." *Middle East Broadcasters Journal*, no. Nov./Dec. (2005): 42.

Khalidi, Rashid. "Ottoman Notables in Jerusalem: Nationalism and Other Options." *Muslim World* LXXXIV, no. 1–2 (1994): 1–18.

Knightley, Phillip. *The First Casualty: The War Correspondent as Hero and Myth-Maker from the Crimea to Kosovo.* Baltimore, MD: Johns Hopkins University Press, 2002.

Kohn, Hans. *The Idea of Nationalism: A Study in Its Origins and Background.* New York: Macmillan Company, 1944.

Lynch, Marc. *Voices of the New Arab Public: Iraq, Al-Jazeera, and Middle East Politics Today.* New York: Columbia University Press, 2006.

Mahoney, Mohamed Abdel Dayem and Robert Mahoney. "Human Rights Coverage Spreads, Despite Government Pushback." In *Attacks on the Press 2009.* New York: Committee to Protect Journalists, 2010.

Matthews, Weldon C. "Pan-Islam or Arab Nationalism? The Meaning of the 1931 Jerusalem Islamic Congress Reconsidered." *International Journal of Middle East Studies* 35 (2003): 1–22.

McFadden, Tom Johnston. *Daily Journalism in the Arab States*. Columbus, OH: Ohio State University Press, 1953.

Meyer, Katherine, Helen Rizzo, and Yousef Ali. "Changed Political Attitudes in the Middle East." *International Sociology* 22, no. 3 (2007): 289–324.

"The Middle East Needs Media Freedoms Even More Than Other Parts of the World." *Daily Star*, Dec. 13, 2008.

Mkrumah, Gamal. "No Time to Sit Back." *Al-Ahram Weekly*, May 29–June 4 (2008): 3.

Moaddel, Mansoor. "The Saudi Public Speaks: Religion, Gender and Politics." *International Journal of Middle East Studies* 38 (2006): 79–109.

Mogahed, Dalia. "Islam and Democracy." New York: Gallup, 2006.

Moyers, Bill. "Buying the War." 60: PBS, first aired April 6, 2007. Television broadcast. Transcript available at http://www.pbs.org/moyers/journal/btw/transcript1.html.

Packer, George. "Caught in the Crossfire; Letter from Baghdad." *The New Yorker* 80, no. 12 (May 17, 2004): 063.

Pintak, Lawrence and Jeremy Ginges. "The Mission of Arab Journalism: Creating Change in a Time of Turmoil." *The International Journal of Press/Politics* 13, no. 3 (2008): 193–227.

Price, Monroe Edwin. *Media and Sovereignty: The Global Information Revolution and Its Challenge to State Power*. Cambridge, Mass.: MIT Press, 2002.

Provence, Michael. *The Great Syrian Revolt and the Rise of Arab Nationalism*. First ed. Austin: University of Texas Press, 2005.

Ramaprasad, Jyotika. "A Profile of Journalists in Post-Independence Tanzania." *Gazette* 63, no. 6 (2001): 539–555.

—— and James D. Kelly. "Reporting the News from the World's Rooftop." *Gazette* 65, no. 3 (2003): 291.

—— and Naila Nabil Hamdy. "Functions of Egyptian Journalists: Perceived Importance and Actual Performance." *International Communication Gazette* 68, no. 2 (2006): 167–185.

—— and Shafiqur Rahman. "Tradition with a Twist: A Survey of Bangladeshi Journalists." *International Communication Gazette* 68, no. 2 (2006): 148–165.

Rao, Shakuntala and Seow Ting Lee. "Globalizing Media Ethics? An Assessment of Universal Ethics among International Political Journalists." *Journal of Mass Media Ethics* 20, nos. 2&3 (2005): 99–120.

"Role of the Media Must Be Acknowledged." *Gulf News*, Jan. 20, 2009.

Rugh, William A. *Arab Mass Media: Newspapers, Radio, and Television in Arab Politics.* Westport, CT: Praeger, 2004.

"Saudi Clerics Launch New Attack on Tv Bosses over Immoral Content." *BBC Monitoring* (2009).

Schiller, Dan. *Objectivity and the News : The Public and the Rise of Commercial Journalism.* Philadelphia: University of Pennsylvania Press, 1981.

Schnellinger, Lisa and Mohannad Khatib. *Fighting Words: How Arab and American Journalists Can Break through to Better Coverage.* Washington, DC: International Center for Journalists, 2006.

Sha'ban, Wahid. "Strong Denunciation of the Azhar Shaykh's Fatwa on Flogging Journalists." *Al Wafd*, Oct. 12, 2007.

Shoemaker, Pamela J. and Stephen D. Reese. *Mediating the Message: Theories of Influences on Mass Media Content.* Second ed. New York: Longman, 1996.

Sivan, Emmanuel. "Arab Nationalism in the Age of the Islamic Resurgence." In *Rethinking Nationalism in the Arab Middle East*, edited by James P. Jankowski and I. Gershoni, pp. xxvi, 372. New York: Columbia University Press, 1997.

Smith, Anthony D. *Nations and Nationalism in a Global Era.* Cambridge, UK; Cambridge, MA: Polity Press; Blackwell, 1995.

Smouni, Hajar. *Freedom of the Press Worldwide in 2008 – Middle East.* Paris: Reporters without Borders, 2008.

Steele, Janet. *Wars Within: The Story of Tempo, an Independent Magazine in Soeharto's Indonesia.* Jakarta, Singapore: Equinox Pub.; Institute of Southeast Asian Studies, 2005.

Telhami, Shibley. "Symposium." *Dissent*, no. Spring (2007): 57–58.

Telhami, Shibley and John Zogby. "Anwar Sadat Chair for Peace and Development University of Maryland/Zogby International 2006 Annual Arab Public Opinion Survey." College Park: University of Maryland, 2007.

Tessler, Mark. "Islam and Democracy in the Middle East: The Impact of Religious Orientations on Attitudes toward Democracy in Four Arab Countries." *Comparative Politics* 34, no. 3 (2002): 337.

"Two French Magazines Censored." IFEX (2009), http://www.ifex.org/en/content/view/full/102732/.

Weaver, David H., Randall A. Beam, Bonnie J. Brownlee, Paul S. Voakes, and G. Cleveland Wilhoit. *The American Journalist in the 21st Century: U.S. News People at the Dawn of a New Millennium*, Lea's Communication Series. Mahwah, NJ: L. Erlbaum Associates, 2007.

"World Values Survey." World Values Survey Association, http://www. worldvaluessurvey.org/.

"Yemen: Women Journalists Subjected to Censorship and Slanderous Attack." London: Article 19, March 8, 2009. http://www.article19.org/pdfs/publications/yemen-an-analysis-of-women-in-the-media.pdf.

Zogby, James. "Five Nation Survey of the Middle East." Arab American Institute, http://www.aaiusa.org/washington-watch/2635/w120106.

Zohairy, Doha Al. "Unpublished Interview." Cairo, Apr. 15, 2009.

Index

2601650586